Scandinavian Historic Inns

Scandinavian
Historic Inns

By Elisa M. Hansen

PELICAN PUBLISHING COMPANY

Gretna 1999

*The word "Pelican" and the depiction of a pelican are trademarks
of Pelican Publishing Company, Inc., and are registered
in the U.S. Patent and Trademark Office.*

Library of Congress Cataloging-in-Publication Data

Hansen, Elisa M.
    Scandinavian historic inns / by Elisa M. Hansen.
       p. cm.
    Includes index.
    ISBN 1-56554-134-0 (pbk. : alk. paper)
    1. Hotels—Scandinavia—Guidebooks. 2. Historic buildings—
Scandinavia—Guidebooks. 3. Scandinavia—Guidebooks. I.
Title.TX907.5.S34H36 1998
647.9448'01—dc21   98-34065
                                                 CIP

Maps by Flemming Søgaard.
Front cover illustration: Bregnerød Kro, Copenhagen, Denmark
Back cover illustration: Solstrand Fjord Hotel, Bergen, Norway

*Information in this guidebook is based on authoritative data available at
the time of printing. Prices are subject to change without notice. Readers are
asked to take this into account when consulting this guide.*

Manufactured in the United States of America
Published by Pelican Publishing Company, Inc.
1000 Burmaster Street, Gretna, Louisiana 70053

To my two daughters,
Inga and Anna Sofia,
who accompanied me on many of my trips
and contributed their helpful
thoughts and impressions

Contents

Acknowledgments

I am especially indebted to my husband, Flemming Søgaard, who not only showed great patience during the writing of this book, but who also contributed a substantial number of the illustrations. I would also like to thank Paul Eller at the Danish Hotel and Restaurant Association who was extremely helpful in beginning this project; Einar Vaardal-Lunde, Director of the Kultur Hotell in Norway; Hans Henrik Tøsdal, General Manager of De Historiske Hotel and De Norske Gjestehus; Ulrika Petersson of De Historiske Hotel in Sweden; Håkan Hising, Manager of Countryside Hotels in Sweden; and Hanne Simony of Danske Slotte & Herregårde. All of these kind people went out of their way to put me in contact with the historic hotels and inns that interested me. Without them I could not have completed this book.

Scandinavian
Historic Inns

Introduction

Scandinavia is one of the truly splendid places to visit in Europe. It holds a place very near to my heart and has been a part of my life since my early childhood. My father emigrated from Denmark and introduced its many treasures and wonders to me during our family's many travels. The countries of Denmark, Norway, and Sweden continue to hold a fascination for me and I am still finding delight in their beauty and history. Geographically, Scandinavia has everything from high mountains to flat fields and forests, from still inland fjords to crashing seas on sand-duned beaches, from large, cosmopolitan cities to provincial country villages, and from wilderness to cultivated farmlands. Reminders of its long and intriguing history are everywhere. There is no shortage of fairy-tale castles and manor houses and superb collections of art; every small town seems to have its own local history museum. The people of all three countries are friendly, helpful, and welcoming, and virtually everyone speaks English so well that if you try to speak one of the Scandinavian languages to a native, he or she is likely to answer in English. There are no slums, no poverty, and the traveler is constantly amazed by the consistent level of cleanliness encountered in restaurants, hotels, and public buildings.

Perhaps one of the greatest advantages to the foreign traveler is how safe the Scandinavian countries are. There are, of course, certain areas of the large cities that should be avoided at night, but one need not be afraid to explore any city, town, or rural area alone or on foot during the daylight hours. Scandinavia is the perfect destination for women traveling alone because that is totally accepted, and there is no reason to be nervous about being out and about without an escort. For families traveling with children, it is a great feeling to know that you are in child-friendly countries where you are safe and where children are catered to and accepted in all inns, hotels, and restaurants. In fact, most inns and hotels will add an extra bed to make up a family room and many will allow younger children to stay free in the room with their parents. Most restaurants have a special menu for children.

As an American who has always sought out historic inns and hotels while traveling in the U.S., I felt that it would be helpful to the English-speaking traveler to have a resource book for the special places in Scandinavia that have a documented history as well as buildings and locations that are unique. I have always found it boring to stay in hotels that look the same no matter where they are in the world. To stay in an old inn or hotel is to experience the history and culture of that place. Sometimes it is a matter of just being in a building that has a more interesting atmosphere compared with the modern hotel. At other times, it is to feel as though one is actually walking back in history to a time and place different from our own, where one can perhaps find an old-fashioned hospitality that is sometimes missing in our contemporary era. In my travels, I have met some of the nicest people, who truly seem to care about their guests and their well being. I have also met interesting people with great stories to tell who can relate the history of their part of the country. I have found that the owners of the inns around the Scandinavian countries are delighted to take the time to talk with their guests and truly make them feel at home.

It has been my goal for this book to provide the reader with a wide selection of types of accommodations. I have also endeavored to include inns and hotels from all price ranges, from extravagant to extremely economical. The places that are less expensive, however, are included not only because of their low price but, rather, because they have special historic interest and are great places to stay. You will find accommodations that have everything the visitor could possibly want from tennis courts and spas to the fanciest restaurants, but you will also see listed small inns or old castles where you will have to share the bathroom down the hall. When a hotel does not have the more modern amenities, such as private baths, I have mentioned it in the description so that the reader can make a more informed decision about where to stay. Included are the larger, well-established hotels in the major cities about which everyone has heard, but also listed are the out-of-the-way country inns that have never been included in a travel guide before.

I must say that although I have at times been a bit disappointed by some of the rooms in which I have stayed, the overall experience of being at that inn—perhaps because of the location or the friendly, comfortable atmosphere—has compensated for the lack of modern-day luxury. I can think of one of the older inns from the sixteenth century that I visited that required using a rope to get up the steep staircase. Had I not given in to the centuries-old idiosyncrasies of the building, I would never have experienced the special pleasure of the view of the cathedral outside my window and the inspiring sounds of its bells waking me in the morning. It has been a thrill for me when I have by serendipity discovered an old inn, one that I had not seen listed anywhere else. I have also found that it has been helpful to talk with natives of a particular area and ask for their own recommendations. I believe that one finds the most interesting places and the best values by word of mouth, and these leads have resulted in some of my most rewarding finds.

Most of the hotels and inns selected for this book are at least one hundred years old—although there are quite a few from the turn of the century—and many of them are centuries older. The two exceptions to this rule were chosen because they were reproductions of the older style of inn, and the owners have gone out of their way to recreate a historic and cultural atmosphere for the guest. In the case of several of the old inns, the reader will discover that the original inn no longer exists and has been replaced at some point in history by another building, although the newer version is also historic. Fires were a major problem for these old buildings—especially if they had a thatched roof—and it is rare to find one that has not experienced some degree of fire damage along the way. The property on which many of these inns are located also has an even longer history that precedes the present inn building. For each listing, I have tried to give as much of the history of the area as possible.

HISTORY OF SCANDINAVIAN INNS

The concept of a place for travelers to spend the night actually goes back to the sixth century B.C. in Persia. The history of inns in northern Europe, however, can be traced to the Middle Ages, when it was possible for weary travelers to find a safe place to stay in a convent, a priest's home, or with a friendly farm family willing to take in guests.

The history of Danish inns is a long one and provides an interesting insight into the origin of places designated for the care and feeding of overnight guests. The very first inn in Denmark was Bromølle Kro (see the listing under Zealand), which is said to have been built in 1198 during the time of King Knud IV. King Erik Klipping, in 1283, was the first to come up with the novel idea of actually providing an authorized place with overnight accommodations. These inns, of course, should be located along the royal roads traveled by the king and his companions, as well as the sites of various ferryboat landings. Ironically enough, King Erik was later killed in a barn where he was forced to spend the night because he could not find an inn nearby. In 1396 Queen Margrethe I, the powerful queen who united the three

Scandinavian countries, actually set up the program by which there should be an inn every four miles. This was later changed by King Christian II to two miles, because this was considered a comfortable distance for a traveler to cover in one day. The inns were still placed along the royal roads and, in order to receive a "royal privilege," the inn had to always have rooms available for the monarch and his or her servants, even if it meant others had to be turned away.

In 1422 King Erik of Pommerania made the decision that innkeepers could sell beer, food, and feed for the horses, but that they could not sell these things to anyone else. Permission to brew beer and distill liquor often went with the royal inn privilege granted by the king. Interestingly enough, local citizens, especially farmers, were not allowed to buy a drink in the inn, only those "from out of town" or others considered more refined or distinguished. Perhaps one of the biggest advantages to the privilege was being released from the responsibility of housing soldiers! These rowdy men were apparently not a responsibility the innkeepers wanted.

By the time of the Reformation during the first half of the sixteenth century, the idea of the royal privileged inn was commonly accepted and the number had grown to 113 in little Denmark. They were evenly spaced throughout the country, including the far-off island of Bornholm. There were approximately 450 inns in the country, but only the privileged ones were issued licenses by the king. The last privilege was awarded in 1912 and, although many have experienced fires and other devastating events, most of these inns can be visited today. Many have been included in this book.

Inns in Norway have a different history because of the natural terrain and geography of the country. Travel on the mountainous and often snow-bound roads was difficult, if not impossible, during many months of the year. Norway's isolation made it a difficult place for other European travelers to reach and therefore placed it a bit off the beaten track. The *fjellstue* (mountain cabins), however, were an old traveling tradition. They were small cabins in the country that, like the Danish inn, were placed a comfortable day's walking distance apart from each other and provided the traveler on foot with a warm, dry place to spend the night. Walking or skiing was the most practical method for travel since even horse-drawn wagons could not be used during much of the colder seasons. The *fjellstue* actually began to be built during the time of the Vikings, and one of the Norse sagas tells us that King Øystein (1103-1123) had them built on the road that crosses Dovrefjell in eastern Norway. The Gulating Law from A.D. 950 lists the rules that must be followed at the mountain shelters. For example, all travelers have an equal right to use them but one must give up one's place after three nights if it is needed by someone else. If a traveler is turned out and he or she comes to harm and dies, then the victim's family has the right to claim blood money from those who committed the crime. Later on in the eighteenth century, the managers of these government-owned mountain inns were exempted from taxes and given the right to hunt and fish as much as they desired. The innkeepers' only responsibilities were to provide accommodations and food to the traveler and make a number of horses available for hire. Some of these charming wooden buildings have now been restored and it is again possible for the traveler to stay in them (I have included several in this book).

In both Norway and Sweden, the advent of the train system, steam-operated boats, and newer and more dependable roads meant that travelers in the nineteenth century could reach places previously cut off from the outside. In Sweden, for example, the word *hotel* meant a large building. It was not until the end of the nineteenth century that it began to be defined as a place where one could rent a room for the night. It was a whole new industry and the hotel business began to experience a boom. From England, many of the noble and wealthy families traveled to Norway for the fresh air and excellent salmon fishing. From Germany and other European countries, royalty headed north to out-of-the-way places, frequently returning to the same hotels. Today, with the completion of the tunnel under the Storebælt, the body of water dividing Zealand from Funen in Denmark, and the soon-to-be-opened tunnel under the sound between Denmark and Sweden, all of Scandinavia will become more accessible to the Continent. Thus, tourism in the north will once again change.

PRACTICAL TRAVEL INFORMATION
Getting Around

Public transportation in Scandinavia is excellent. It is efficient, clean, safe, and accessible. If you are planning on spending several weeks traveling in Scandinavia and Finland, it may be most economical to buy a *ScanRail Pass*, which will allow you to use all three train systems as often as you wish from five days to one month. The ScanRail Pass also entitles the traveler to hotel and ferryboat discounts. The pass can be purchased in the United States through your travel agent or through one of the railroad offices in Scandinavia. Inter-Scandinavian air travel is extremely expensive as a rule. Trains in Scandinavia are a great alternative and they allow the traveler the opportunity to see so much more. They must be among the most comfortable and reliable in the world, with the friendliest, most helpful staffs imaginable. If you are traveling with children, you can even reserve seats in the special children's car, where there is a padded play area for the little ones. Our family has always found that this is the perfect way to travel.

In the three capital cities, buses and trains take you everywhere you could possibly want to go. With a route map, it may never be necessary to take taxis, which are rather expensive in Scandinavia. In Copenhagen, for example, there are special sightseeing buses during the summer that cost the same as a ticket on a regular city bus. They follow a route designed to take the tourist to the sites most visited in the city and it is possible to get off and on at any of the locations.

Remember that none of the three capitals are very big—Copenhagen is the largest with a population of one and a half million—and distances are relatively short. If you are an American who is accustomed to major cities, you will be surprised at how little time it takes to get around in these cities. In Oslo, for example, you take a rather short train trip from the center of the city at the station on Karl Johans Gate and you suddenly find yourself in open fields and forests. While attending the University of Oslo as an undergraduate, I often marveled at how students could step out the door of the dormitories and into the cross-country ski paths of the forest. Needless to say, Stockholm, Oslo, and Copenhagen are perfect walking cities. If you are staying at a centrally located hotel, you may be able to get around on foot and not worry about catching a train or bus unless you want to get to an area outside of town.

Weather and Clothing

The most important thing to remember about the Scandinavian climate is that it is totally changeable. The summer of 1997 was the warmest in at least 125 years, with almost six weeks of temperatures over 80 degrees. But I have also experienced summers during which the daily temperature dipped down into the 50s and didn't get much above 60 degrees. If you are traveling during the summer season, I would recommend that you take a sweater or two, a lined and waterproof windbreaker, and a travel umbrella. Rain is always a possibility in Scandinavia and some rainwear is good to have in your suitcase. During the late fall and winter months, it is very cold! By November you will need your heavy winter coat or a down jacket. Denmark does not have the snowfall that its northern sisters receive, but the wind off the sea can be very intense and chilly. For Norway and Sweden, the winter months require outerwear suitable for the snow.

I have found that Scandinavians are much less formal than Americans, so you may want to leave your dressier outfits at home. For ladies, a skirt and jacket or sweater is sufficient for any restaurant or evening event. For men, a jacket and tie may be required for some restaurants, although one rarely sees them at private dinner parties or gatherings.

GENERAL INFORMATION ABOUT LODGINGS

Room Rates

The room rates listed in this book may not be the same at the time of your trip. They are listed in order to give an indication of the price range that you can expect. In each hotel listing you will find a range of room rates under the single- and double-room categories. This may represent a range of types of guest rooms, although it usually indicates the difference between weekday and weekend rates. In Scandinavia, prices are much higher during the week because of the business travelers who stay in hotels during that time. On the weekends, the rates drop considerably. Many hotels and inns offer half or full board, allowing the travelers who are staying in one place for several days the opportunity to save some money. At many of the mountain or country hotels in Norway and Sweden, where guests often take hiking or skiing trips during the day, the hotel will pack a lunch that can be taken along in a backpack.

An excellent way to save on the cost of the room is to purchase an inn or hotel check before arriving at the hotel. In Denmark, for example, an organization called *Dansk Kroferie* (Danish Inn Vacations) will sell you an inn coupon, which can be purchased at tourist information offices or travel agencies *before* you arrive at the inn. A catalog can be ordered ahead of time from *Dansk Kroferie* (Dansk Kroferie, Vejlevej 16, DK-8700 Horsens, Denmark; Telephone: 75 64 87 00; FAX: 75 64 87 20) or you may pick one up at the tourist information centers in Denmark. I highly recommend contacting the Scandinavian Tourist Information Board located at 655 Third Avenue, 18th Floor, New York, New York, 10017; Telephone: (212) 885-9700. In addition to all kinds of wonderful brochures and information, they can also tell you where you can buy these coupons in the U.S. before your departure. You can save a substantial amount of money compared to the usual rack rate. The participating inns also offer a special *kro menu* (inn menu) in their restaurants. These are special menu selections offered just for this purpose and you may ask for these whether or not you are spending the night at the inn. There are also special menus and games provided for children.

Meals

Food in Scandinavia is the greatest! There will be very few times, if any, when you will be disappointed with the meals served to you in restaurants or inns. It will become virtually impossible for you to pass by a bakery without going in to buy a little sample of something yummy. Although there is some variation in each country, the dishes served will usually be of a traditional nature but sometimes with some Continental flavor and new ideas. In my conversations with chefs, I have often heard them describe their cuisine as Danish, for example, with a French flair. As you travel into the countryside, you will find that the old inns seem to specialize in what I describe as "old-fashioned inn cooking." By all means try it. You will experience some of the most wonderful food you have ever had. Ask for the specialty of that particular area, as I have, and you will broaden your culinary experiences in a very positive way. A nice alternative to a full meal is a sampling of *smørrebrød* (open-faced sandwiches). Ask for the special list/menu for the sandwiches, which you will usually not find on the main menu, and you will be given a pencil to check off the types of sandwiches that appeal to you. Two or three sandwiches are usually enough for a meal. If you are on the run while sightseeing, a stop at one of the ubiquitous hot-dog wagons is an economical and satisfying alternative. Don't forget to ask for fried onions!

As a general rule, breakfast is included in the price of the room at most inns and hotels in Scandinavia. The few exceptions to this rule have been pointed out in this book, and I have listed the various prices for breakfast when appropriate. If the listing does not mention a separate breakfast charge, it may be assumed that it is included in the room rate. Hotels and inns usually provide a buffet table for breakfast with a number of delicious choices. There is always a selection of various kinds of breads and rolls with jams, cheeses, and some sliced meats, as well as coffee, tea, milk, and juices. There are often cold cereals and yogurt. I have stayed at some of the inns or hotels that also provide warm dishes such as eggs (usually soft boiled) and bacon or sausage. If you are in Denmark, you will probably have the opportunity at breakfast to enjoy some of the wonderful pastries, *wienerbrød*, for which the country is so famous.

Telephoning in Scandinavia

Using the telephone in Scandinavia is a bit different from the U.S. Many of the pay phones only take a calling card, which can be purchased at kiosks and post offices. For those that take coins, the money is placed in a slot on the top of the phone box before dialing. The coins that are needed then drop down into the box as you talk. Most of the phones now have instructions in English to assist the caller.

The telephone and FAX numbers I have listed with each hotel and inn do not include the country codes. They are given this way so as not to confuse the reader when phoning within each country. If you are calling from the United States or from one Scandinavian country to another, you will use the following country codes:

Denmark	45
Sweden	46
Norway	47

Some of the hotels and inns, although not many, now have web sites and E-mail capabilities, making reservations and communication much easier. If they do, I have given those numbers.

DENMARK

Greater Copenhagen

DENMARK

Copenhagen

Greater Copenhagen

Ascot Hotel
Åse and Henrik Hildebrandt
61 Studiestræde
1554 Copenhagen V
Telephone: 33 12 60 00; **FAX:** 33 14 60 40
Rates: Single, 870 to 970 kr.; Double, 1070 to 1330 kr.; Penthouse apartments, 1390 to 1990 kr. **Restaurant:** Only breakfast is served in the hotel's dining room. Free parking is available in one of the hotel's three courtyards.

The current owners of Ascot Hotel, Åse and Henrik Hildebrant, once owned one of the most prosperous car-rental businesses in Denmark. When the opportunity arose to purchase the late nineteenth-century apartment buildings now comprising the hotel, Åse made a deal with her husband. If she could turn the hotel into a bigger success than their other business, then they would both agree to devote all of their time to the hotel. That was in 1972 and now their two children are also a part of the management team.

The hotel stands on 492 wooden pilings recycled from the Aborredam Moat, which was once part of the city's western defense wall protecting Copenhagen for several centuries. Although one of the hotel buildings goes back to 1880, the main part of the hotel was built in 1902 and was designed by the same architect who also designed the town hall. What makes the history of this hotel so unique is that it was once a public bathhouse where the well-to-do of Copenhagen's high society could come for a steam bath or an "icy skeleton" bath. At the same time, they could discuss important business and "network." Counts, barons, bankers, and rich merchants all came to the bathhouse. In fact, even the king's brother was a member. For those in this privileged class, there were private rooms where they were served a meal after their bath. At the turn of the century, few apartments in the city had private bathrooms and even the lower class could come to this building to have a cheap shower in the basement. The word *renlighed,* or "cleanliness," appears on the facade of the building, indicating its original purpose. The bathhouse employed more than 65 people who offered everything from manicures to saunas to the citizens of Copenhagen up until 1972, at which time more people had their own facilities and it was no longer needed.

As you enter the hotel's main reception hall, you can see some of the bathhouse's original artwork and design. There are four black granite columns from the Danish island of Bornholm. On either side of the room are bas-relief sculpture by the artist Hansen-Rejstrup that depict bathing men and women, each with their separate wall. In the classical style, the women are seen as sweet and feminine while the men are tough and muscular. Along the staircase are wall paintings of various sea creatures and delicate seawind flowers. Remnants of the bathhouse can also be found in some of the rooms. For example, Dutch tiles that once adorned the steam room have now become a part of a small kitchen in one of the suites.

The hotel, which has reasonable prices by Copenhagen standards, is conveniently located within walking distance of just about anything. Tivoli Gardens, many museums, and *Strøget* (the walking street) are only five minutes away. When you are ready to leave the city, the SAS terminal is almost directly across the street. If you choose to take the train, the Vesterport station is also right next door.

Bregnerød Kro

Bregnerød Kro
Preben Lund
Bregnerød Byvej 2
3520 Farum
Telephone: 42 95 00 57; **FAX:** 42 95 06 55
Rates: Single, 420 to 660 kr.; Double, 560 to 890 kr.; Guesthouse, 820 to 1,750 kr. **Restaurant:** Lunch and dinner are served in the dining room. Breakfast is served in a cozy loft library.

The official records show that this inn was built in 1683. But the original record books were burned in a church fire started by the Swedes, who also burned down the original inn. The local people have always heard that the inn actually goes back to 1638. That would certainly make it one of the oldest inns in Denmark. What is even more exceptional is that the current building has continuously been an inn since 1702, when it was rebuilt after the fire. The inn is located on the old road between Copenhagen and Hillerød (location of King Christian IV's Frederiksborg Castle). For this reason, the king granted a royal privilege to the inn so that he and his staff could stop there on the way to his castle and receive free accommodations and meals. In return, the innkeeper was allowed to brew beer and make the potent drink called "snaps." The old stall that once accommodated the horses and carriages of travelers has now been incorporated into the inn building. A newer building with bedrooms blends into the style of the architecture perfectly.

Farum, the location of Bregnerød Kro, is actually outside of Copenhagen. It provides a wonderful alternative to the travelers who prefer to be outside of the hustle and bustle of the city but appreciate easy access to the many tourist possibilities there. It takes about 20 minutes by car or about 40 minutes by train to the center of Copenhagen. Its location is perfect if you want to explore Hillerød or the rest of northern Zealand. It is also one of the most beautiful spots you could ever want and has even been called the "garden to Copenhagen." From the back door of the inn you can walk into the Ravnsholt Forest or look out over neighboring farms and fields. There are only 15 old houses in the village, so you will certainly find plenty of peace and quiet. You will also get more guest room for your money than you are likely to get in the city. Our room was large and extremely comfortable, with old style furniture, a separate sitting area with television, and a large, modern bath. It was one of the most tastefully decorated rooms I have encountered in my travels. There is also a lovely, thatched-roofed guesthouse for rent. It can accommodate up to six people and, if you are traveling as a group, can provide a very reasonable alternative to separate rooms.

Bregnerød Kro is one of the original roadside inns in Denmark that will give you personal service and an atmosphere filled with history.

Copenhagen Admiral Hotel

Copenhagen Admiral Hotel
Søren Anker-Ladefoged
Toldbodgade 24-28
1253 Copenhagen
Telephone: 33 11 82 82; **FAX:** 33 32 55 42
Rates: Single, 640 to 950 kr.; Double, 920 to 1,155 kr.; Suites, 1,250 to 1,670 kr. **Restaurants:** Pineafore, located on the ground floor, serves breakfast, lunch, and dinner. The Promenade Cafe is a glassed-in restaurant facing the harbor that serves lunch and dinner, and the Nautilus is a bar and nightclub. Unlike most Danish hotels, breakfast is not included with the price of a room at Copenhagen Admiral Hotel, which allows the guest the option to pay for this meal separately. An additional 90 to 120 kr. is charged for the buffet breakfast. There are 80 private parking spaces available in front of the hotel.

If the traveler is looking for a full-service historic hotel in perhaps one of the most beautiful locations in the city, then the Copenhagen Admiral is an excellent choice. It is unusual to find a hotel with this much preserved architectural history as well as so many modern conveniences. Right on Copenhagen's harbor, where you can look out your window and see tall ships as well as cruise liners, it is just a stone's throw from the royal palace, Amalienborg. Adjoining the hotel is the lovely park, Amaliehaven, which runs along the harbor and is filled with fountains and roses. From here, it is just a few minutes' walk to Nyhavn and its wonderful restaurants and lively nightlife. It is also an enjoyable walk to the beloved *Little Mermaid* sculpture and the wonderful Gefion Fountain.

From the moment you enter the lobby, you are surrounded by nautical history. Display cases with museum-quality models of ships and other objects from Denmark's seafaring past introduce the visitor to the original purpose of the building. Built in 1780 by the Pingel, Meyer, and Prætorius trading company, it was designed to be a granary and warehouse with close proximity to the ships. It has the distinction of having survived the Great Fire of 1795 in which half of the city was destroyed as well as the English bombardment in 1807. The Battle of Copenhagen in 1801 took place right outside the building and many people took shelter within its walls. It is still possible to see these thick brick walls and the large arches. Throughout the 366 rooms of the hotel are the original Pommeranian pine beams, which add warmth and architectural interest. Such attention to the building's eighteenth-century integrity earned the hotel a diploma from the Europa Nostra, an international body for protecting Europe's cultural heritage. Of the 400 projects submitted in the competition, only 20 were awarded this coveted award.

Esplanaden Hotel
Bente Noyons
Bredegade 78
DK-1260 Copenhagen
Telephone: 33 91 32 00; **FAX:** 33 91 32 39;
Web site: http://www.dkhotellist.dk/neptungroup.htm
Rates: Single, 720 to 880 kr.; Double, 955 to 1,040; Executive room, 1,270 to 2,140 kr. **Restaurant:** Gronningen Restaurant serves breakfast only. This hotel is a member of Larsens Hotel and Kroferie.

The main door to the hotel reception area is flanked on both sides by two powerful caryatids, sculptures of muscular men who appear to hold up the columns that stretch to the third floor. Situated on the corner of a street in a very fashionable part of town, the building was originally an elegant apartment house constructed between 1754 and 1755. In the beginning, there were two connecting wings, which were joined in 1820 by a beautifully ornamented staircase that can be seen from the exterior. On the interior, the design is sleek and modern with a predominant use of white. One of the charming aspects of the bedrooms that are part of the original architecture is the large windows that look out over the rooftops and adjacent park.

The original idea for this hotel is that it should be based upon the factors that the guests themselves felt important to their stay. As a result, the hotel prides itself on its goal: guests must sleep and wake up in the best possible way. Bente Noyons, the owner, was ahead of her time when she designed a plan to make Esplanaden a "green" hotel. With a keen interest in environmental and ecological issues, Mrs. Noyons has done everything possible to protect the indoor environmental climate of the hotel and protect the health of each guest and staff member. All allergy-causing substances and materials have carefully been eliminated and there are nonsmoking rooms available upon request. Mrs. Noyons' efforts in this area were so innovative ten years ago that there were a number of newspaper articles written about what she was trying to accomplish.

One of the nicest things about Esplanaden Hotel is its location. Just a short walk from the Queen's residence, Amalienborg Castle, and the Citadel, you can follow the waterfront route along Langelinie and visit *The Little Mermaid*. It is also a few minutes' walk from the Østerport Train Station, as well as bus lines that will take you the short distance to the center of the city.

Gentofte Hotel

Gentofte Hotel
Finn Jensen
Gentoftegade 29
2820 Gentofte
Telephone: 31 68 09 11; **FAX:** 31 68 06 11
Rates: Single, 750 kr.; Double, 850 kr.; there is a special two-for-one daily rate during the off season. **Restaurant:** Le Patron serves breakfast, buffet lunch, and dinner and specializes in Danish/French cuisine. Gentofte Hotel is a member of Dansk Kroferie.

Gentofte is a fashionable suburb of Copenhagen that is located north of the city. In the middle of the eighteenth century, it was still a farming community with 20 farms listed in the census of 1768.

As with so many of the old inns in Denmark, Gentofte Hotel is located next to the church, allowing easy access to the inn for the parties or meals that followed baptisms, weddings, and funerals. Gentofte Church may well have been in its present location as far back as the eleventh century, during the time of Bishop Absalon, because remains of a Romanesque church were discovered several years ago within the present church's walls. King Christian IX and Queen Louise often stopped at the church for Sunday services while staying at their nearby summer residence, Bernstorff Castle. In fact, Queen Louise painted part of the altarpiece, which one can still see today.

Gentofte Hotel probably existed as an inn even before the seventeenth century, but we first read about it when ownership was legally transferred to the widow of the innkeeper in 1667. As was the case with many Danish inns, this one also burned several times. The first fire took place in 1731 and the second in 1844. The building that stands today is from the rebuilding after the last fire. Behind the plain, gold-colored facade is an interior that has been modernized. The light, airy rooms have modern furniture and fabrics. Amenities include private baths, telephone, radio, minibar, and television. Special nonsmoking rooms are available.

One of the advantages of staying in Gentofte Hotel during a visit to Copenhagen is that the prices are lower than in the city and getting to the downtown area is easy and quick. The Gentofte train station is about a five-minute walk away and from there the train ride is less than 15 minutes. The bus stop is almost right outside the door of the hotel. On the other hand, you are in an ideal spot if you wish to take the train or drive to northern Zealand. Hamlet's Kronborg Castle, for example, is only 30 minutes away. The hotel is situated on the main street of shops in Gentofte but is surrounded by lovely, well-kept residential streets, so there are plenty of safe parking spaces for your rental car.

The management of Gentofte Hotel prides itself on personal service to the visitor provided by a staff that has been at the hotel for a number of years. When guests return to the hotel, they are often remembered by name. The restaurant, Le Patron, is located in a cozy, old-fashioned room with an open fireplace and exposed wooden beams and is known locally for its excellent food.

Hotel Kong Arthur

Hotel Kong Arthur
The Brøchner family; Kirsten Brøchner-Mortensen, manager
Nørre Søgade 11
DK-1370 Copenhagen
Telephone: 33 11 12 12; **FAX:** 33 32 61 30
Rates: Single, 980 to 1,100 kr.; Double, 1,180 to 1,300 kr.; Suite, 2,700
kr. **Restaurant:** Breakfast served in the glassed-in courtyard; dinner
served in Brøchner Restaurant, which specializes in Danish/French
cuisine. A Japanese sushi restaurant, Sticks 'n' Sushi, is also on the
hotel property. Sandwiches are available with room service 24 hours
a day. The lobby bar is open 24 hours a day. This hotel is a member
of Larsen Hotel og Kroferie.

   During the last quarter of the nineteenth century, the master car-
penters of Copenhagen decided that they would build a residence
for their many apprentices who came to the capital to learn their craft.

The masters and their respective companies built what is now the main building of the Hotel Kong Arthur. Their precise and accomplished carpentry skills are particularly evident in the double staircase elegantly leading from the lobby to the second floor. It is as though the masters wanted to show their apprentices exactly how it should be done. The king himself opened the building when it was completed in 1882.

In the 1960s, the building was converted into a hotel and was purchased by the Brøchner family in 1982. Appropriately enough, Mr. Brøchner was also a carpenter who spent one year renovating each floor of the hotel, putting his own building skills to work. In 1990 the turn-of-the-century Copenhagen Bicycle Factory next door was bought and is now connected to the hotel by a courtyard. The theme of King Arthur was chosen for the Brøchner's hotel and the lobby; the decor now reflects the feeling and style of the Middle Ages. They even commissioned an artist from the National Theater to create a round table complete with all the names of the knights. The rooms in the center building have medieval-style fabrics on the bedspreads and curtains, and many of the rooms still have the original dark wooden beams. All rooms have modern baths with hair dryers, trouser presses, minibars, televisions with free videos, radios, individual safes, and telephones.

The Hotel Kong Arthur emphasizes personal service to the individual traveler rather than to groups, which is in contrast to many large hotels. Perhaps because of its friendly, relaxed type of service, jazz musicians such as Dizzy Gillespie began coming to the hotel when there was a famous jazz club nearby and they continue to come here to stay each year for the annual jazz festival. The hotel faces the Peblinge Lake, one of a series of lakes in the center of town. Lovely old buildings line the opposite side of the lake and swans can always be seen swimming in the lake. It only takes 15 minutes to walk to the Town Hall Square and Tivoli Gardens. A five-minute walk takes you to Nørreport train station, the city's busiest, and from there you can take a train to the center of town or to destinations in northern Zealand. Within a few years' time, a new station will be completed even closer to the hotel and this will connect with Kongens Nytorv and to Kastrup Airport. Free parking is available.

Hotel d'Angleterre

Hotel d'Angleterre
Else Marie and Henning Remmen; Hanne Klitkou, manager
34, Kgs. Nytorv, Postbox 3044
DK-1021 Copenhagen
Telephone: 33 12 00 95; **FAX:** 33 12 11 18; **Web site:** www.remmen.dk
Rates: Single, 1,845 to 2,700 kr.; Double, 2,050 to 2,900 kr.; Suite, 3,400 to 6,500 kr. **Restaurants:** Restaurant d'Angleterre (an elegant spot for a French-cuisine lunch and dinner), Restaurant Wiinblad (breakfast, lunch, dinner, and high tea; specializes in Danish/French cuisine), D'Angleterre Bar. *Note:* Breakfast is not included in the price of the room.

Three hundred years ago, the Von Gram family built their mansion outside of the city of Copenhagen. They owned the house until 1795 and their coat of arms can still be found in many places in the hotel. It was in that same year that the building began its history as a hotel. There had been an English Club where Copenhagen's famous department store, Magasin du Nord, now stands, a mecca for English-speaking residents and Anglophiles. The English Club was turned into a hotel and relocated to the Von Gram mansion next door. In 1873 the original building was demolished and a new building was constructed. At the time of World War II, during the German occupation of Denmark, the hotel became the headquarters for the German forces. After Denmark's liberation by the Allied forces, the building was once again back in business. Today the Hotel d'Angleterre is the "grande dame" of Denmark's hotel world and is the only member of "The Leading Hotels of the World" in Denmark.

The hotel has hosted famous guests from royalty to rock stars, some of whom have given their names to the elegant suites. There is even written documentation to testify to the fact that Hans Christian

Andersen stayed here at one time. Of course, one of the suites bears his name. The front of the hotel looks out over the trees and old buildings of Kongens Nytorv, a busy shopping and cultural hub in the midst of the city, and across to Nyhavn. It could not be more central to what is happening in Copenhagen. Because the opera house and Royal Theater are just across the park, the hotel offers a special opera weekend package, complete with tickets and a wonderful dinner. The wide corridors of the hotel lead to spacious rooms with tall windows. The paneling and high ceilings attest to the hotel's traditional architecture. Lovely marble baths, with all the amenities one could possibly want, are part of the guest rooms' luxury. The spa and fitness club under the hotel is outstanding. A comfortable lounge, where you can order a sandwich and drink, looks out over a neoclassical-style swimming pool. Sauna, Turkish bath, tanning salon, massage, and beauty salon are also available. For the business traveler, a credit-card operated computer and fax machine are easily accessible.

Hotel Kong Frederik

Hotel Kong Frederik
Else Marie and Henning Remmen; Pia Bjerregaard, manager
25 Vester Volgade
1552 Copenhagen
Telephone: 33 12 59 02; **FAX:** 33 93 59 01
Rates: Single, 1,150 to 1,550 kr.; Double, 1,450 to 1,650 kr.; Suites, 2,100 to 6,000 kr. **Restaurants:** Queens Restaurant serves lunch and dinner with salmon as a specialty; Queens Pub is a British-type pub that offers a lighter lunch and dinner menu; Queens Garden is in the courtyard and is the location of the breakfast buffet, which is served for an additional charge of 100 kr.

Until 100 years ago, Vester Voldagade, the location of Hotel Kong Frederik, was on the outskirts of the city, near the city's western wall. Since the thirteenth century, it has been the location of many of Copenhagen's inns, including the spot on which this hotel now stands. It is commonly thought that the two separate hotels that now form the Hotel Kong Frederik were originally boardinghouses that gradually developed into today's concept of a hotel. Before the West Bank of Copenhagen was demolished in 1880, the two hotels were called Industrihotellet and Hotel de Boulevard. In 1900, after two years of construction, the two hotels were opened as Hotel Hafnia and Hotel Kong Frederik. Denmark has had nine King Frederiks and it is not known after which of them the hotel is named. To compensate for this ignorance, there are portraits of all of them throughout the hotel. For years the two hotels competed with each other; each owner wanted to take over the other hotel. Finally, in 1973, one of the city's worst hotel fires destroyed much of the Hotel Hafnia and it was taken over by the Hotel Kong Frederik. Today the Hotel Hafnia has been totally restored and is joined to Hotel Kong Frederik by a skylighted courtyard.

The guest rooms, decorated with British classical-style furniture, are equipped with all the amenities: room safe, television, hair dryer, trouser press, phone, and minibar. For those wishing to use the Hotel d'Angleterre's spa and fitness center with swimming pool, sauna, Jacuzzi, and tanning salon, it is free to Hotel Kong Frederik's guests.

The hotel is located just off the City Hall Square (Rådhus Pladsen) right in the middle of the city. Just around the corner is the beginning of *Strøget* (the Walking Street) and Tivoli is on the other side of the square. If you wish to take a train, either the Main Train Station or Vesterport is about a five-minute walk away. The bus station is just around the corner.

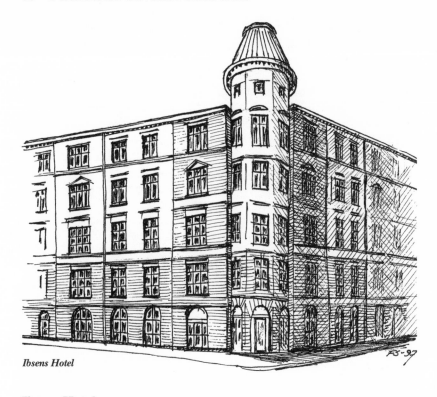

Ibsens Hotel

Ibsens Hotel

Sine Mannicke, Anni Kjær, and Susanne Cordes
Vendersgade 23
1363 Copenhagen
Telephone: 33 13 19 13; **FAX:** 33 13 19 16
Rates: Single, 400 to 450 kr.; Double, 500 to 950 kr. **Restaurant:** None;
only breakfast is served.

History shows that women have always owned this hotel, beginning
with Mrs. Ibsen, after whom the present hotel is named. Now there are
three women who, in 1989, decided that they wanted to manage a hotel
together. They set out to operate a hotel that could offer reasonable
rates in a city known for its high prices. They have accomplished this so
well that they now have a following of guests from all over the world
who often return to Ibsens Hotel. The hotel is now so associated with
the three female managers that callers are disappointed when a man
answers the hotel's phone.

It was built as a luxurious apartment building at the turn of the
century. Mrs. Ibsen converted one floor into a hotel in 1916 and

ran it for the next 33 years. The hotel has now taken over three of the building's floors and will soon include another. In general, the renovation process has been sensitive to the turn-of-the-century style that was the fashion at the time the apartments were built. The owners attended many auctions and purchased furniture, such as four-poster beds, that is appropriate to the time period. Each room, with its warm, Victorian wallpaper, is different and reminded me more of an American Bed and Breakfast establishment than the typical Scandinavian hotel. The traveler should be aware that many of the rooms do not have a toilet or shower, although the hall bathrooms are very roomy and comfortable. Some of the rooms are without carpeting for those who suffer from allergies.

The dining room, which has heavy Victorian draperies and a funky array of objects from paintings and needlework to potted palms, only serves breakfast. There are a number of restaurants of all types within easy walking distance of the hotel. As a matter of fact, if you are willing to take a very short train ride to get to the center of town, it is worth staying here in order to help your travel budget. It is less than a 10-minute walk to Nørreport Station, as well as a number of interesting places, such as Rosenborg Castle, the Botanical Gardens, Davids Collection, and Denmark's National Gallery. The hotel is situated on an out-of-the-way side street that is quiet at night.

Neptun Hotel

Neptun Hotel
Bente Noyons
Sankt Annæ Plads 14-20
DK-1250 Copenhagen
Telephone: 33 13 89 00; **FAX:** 33 14 12 50;
Web site: http://www.dkhotellist.dk/neptungroup.htm
Rates: Single, 1,090 to 1,325 kr.; Double, 1,360 to 1,705 kr.; Executive rooms, 1,985 kr. **Restaurants:** Konkylien is a nonsmoking breakfast courtyard restaurant. The Pearl has a smoking area for breakfast. Gendarmen offers lunch, dinner, and light meals as well as four-course dinners of regional Danish cuisine.

Located on one of the most charming and fashionable streets in Copenhagen, a boulevard of trees and sculpture, the Neptun Hotel has that wonderful combination of international sophistication and cozy warmth. This is due, I am sure, to the excellent skills of the hotel's owner, Bente Noyons. Neptun Hotel is run as a family affair, involving three generations. As Mrs. Noyons was giving me a tour of the hotel, I noted that she was constantly attending to small details, the kind of things that add up to a well-run hotel.

Sankt Annæ Plads, the hotel's address, was first built in the seventeenth century during the reign of King Christian IV. The Naval Hospital was built on the same site. In 1703 the Garnison Church was constructed. It is still in use. On the exact location as the present-day hotel, a malt mill was once situated. There are four buildings that together comprise what is now the hotel. Two of them were built by the same architect, Hans Christian Tybjerg, between 1854 and 1856. He also built the catholic church that is just around the corner on Bredgade. Today the four structures are connected by a skylight that forms a light, airy courtyard without disturbing the architectural integrity.

The lobby, with warm woods and Oriental rugs, is a series of small rooms, including a cozy library. The color schemes of the public rooms change with the seasons. There is also a rooftop garden with lovely teak furniture. The executive rooms are exceptionally lovely. The fabrics used for bedspreads, curtains, and pillows were designed by Bente Noyons and are based on old designs she found in a castle. The same pattern is echoed in the wall stenciling. The special furniture made just for the hotel and the solid ash floor are all without varnish so that those who suffer from allergies can be more comfortable. In fact, the Danish Allergy and Ashma Association was consulted before these special rooms were designed. The standard double rooms are large, simple, and very comfortable, all with two phones, minibar, safe, iron and ironing board, and hair dryer. This is also one of the few hotels in Copenhagen that has air conditioners in each room for those times during the summer when the weather can be rather warm.

When you stay at Neptun Hotel you are almost a neighbor to the Queen. In less than five minutes, you can walk to Kongens Nytorv, where you will find the Royal Theater, Nyhavn, and some of the best shopping and restaurants in the city, as well as the famous walking street, *Strøget*. On the side streets, art and antique galleries are abundant. If you are planning on a trip to Norway or Sweden, the ferryboats leave from the harbor almost next door to the hotel.

Phoenix Copenhagen

Phoenix Copenhagen
ARP-HANSEN Hotel Group; Hlin Jonsson, directing manager
Bredgade 37
DK 1260 Copenhagen K
Telephone: 33 95 95 00; **FAX:** 33 33 98 33
Rates: Single, 1,090 to 1,890 kr.; Double, 1,490 to 2,290 kr.; Suites, 2,800 to 6,000 kr.; Extra bed, 300 kr. Breakfast is 110 kr. extra. There are special weekend rates. Bookings may be made through Supernational Hotels, telephone: 1-800-843-3311 (toll free). **Restaurants:** Restaurant von Plessen serves breakfast and more formal lunches and dinners; Restaurant Gyldensteen serves lunch and dinner; Murdoch's Books and Ale is a Scottish pub named after William Murdoch, an engineer from Scotland who was also an excellent cook and opened an exclusive restaurant in Gyldensteen Palace in 1837; it also serves light meals. During the summer months, meals and drinks are served on the pub's terrace. This hotel is a member of Concord Hotels, Supernational Hotels.

The foundation of what is now the hotel was laid in the 1680s when Col. Samuel Christof von Plessen, commanding officer of the Royal Life Guards, built his new city palace. Den Plessensk Gaard, as it was called, became one of many impressive mansions built around it, and it was joined in 1749 when four noblemen built the four mansions now comprising the queen's royal palace, Amalienborg. A wealthy Frenchman, Jean-Henri Huguetan Gyldenstten, bought Den Plessenske Gaard in 1730 and built a new wing in the rococo style on Dronningens Tværgade. Among the interesting owners in the years following were Brigadier William von Halling, cofounder of the

East-Indian Company, who kept slaves in the mansion's basement, and Urban Jurgensen, the court clockmaker. The 1840s were a time of growth in Copenhagen with the opening of Tivoli Gardens, the founding of the Carlsberg Breweries, and the opening of the first railroad between the city and Roskilde. It was also time for an exclusive hotel in this part of town and a merchant, Joachim Topp, built on to the original mansion and decorated it in the then-popular Victorian style. The landed gentry, as well as the gentlemen of the court, became the frequent guests of this respected hotel. Poet Adam Oehlenschlager became the first permanent resident and King Christian VIII visited the hotel often. King Christian IX often arranged for royal guests to stay here when all the guest rooms at the palace were full. The red sentry boxes for the Royal Life Guards could be seen outside the front entrance. The German Wehrmacht took over the hotel in 1940 for the use of German officers. In 1945 the Allied Forces used it as military headquarters.

The hotel was finally purchased in 1990 by the Arp-Hansen family, owners of a number of other hotels in greater Copenhagen, and it was totally renovated in 1991. Its style is now one of classic elegance. Throughout the entire hotel, soothing colors of peach and pale blue are used in carpeting, walls, and fabrics. Each of the redecorated guest rooms has a desk, minibar, and large private bath with a tub, trouser press, and desk. All of the suites have sitting areas, air conditioners, and fax machines. There is a special business center off of the lobby to assist the traveling businessperson with computers, faxes, a copy machine, and secretarial service. There are nonsmoking rooms for those that request them.

Zealand

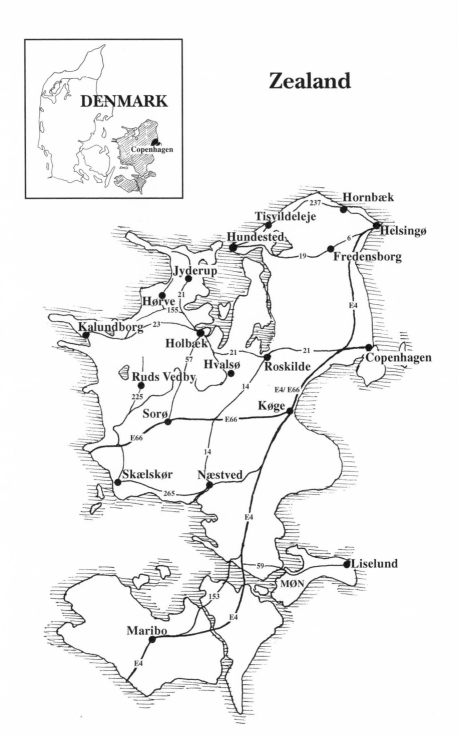

DENMARK

Copenhagen

Hornbæk

237

Tisvildeleje

Hundested

Helsingø

6

19

Fredensborg

Jyderup

E4

21

Hørve

155

Kalundborg 23

Holbæk

21

E4

Hvalsø

21

Copenhagen

57

Roskilde

Ruds Vedby

14

E4/ E66

225

Køge

Sorø

E66

E66

14

Skælskør

Næstved

265

E4

Liselund

59

MØN

153

E4

Maribo

E4

Zealand

FREDENSBORG

Hotel Store Kro

Hotel Store Kro
Hans Christian Basse, manager
Slotsgade 6
DK-3480 Fredensborg
Telephone: 48 48 00 47; **FAX:** 48 48 45 61
Rates: Single, 850 kr., Double, 1150 to 1350 kr.
Restaurant: Breakfast, lunch, and dinner are served in dining room.
There is a bar with billiards.

Hotel Store Kro's history goes back to the beginnings of Fredensborg Castle, the residence used by the royal family seven months out of the year. The King's Inn, as it was originally called, was opened in 1723, only one year after the castle was completed. Built by King Frederik IV, the hotel was to supply overnight accommodations for royal visitors and dignitaries visiting Fredensborg Castle. Apparently the castle was not quite big enough to house everyone who was invited by the king. Today the sights and sounds of the castle are an integral part of life at

Hotel Store Kro. When the queen is in residence, the Royal Guards sound reveille each day at 8:00 A.M. and the changing of the guard takes place at 10:00 A.M. and noon. Impressive works of art and antiques are on view throughout the hotel. Paintings in the reception area, by the Italian theater artist Jacobo Fabis, are similar to those located in the Garden Hall of the castle. A collection of paintings by Oluf Poulsen, depicting scenes from Holberg's comedies, hangs in the hotel's Gallery Hall.

No two rooms in the hotel are alike and are decorated in what the hotel calls "country-house style." All are equipped with bathrooms, telephones, televisions, radios, and minibars. After a day of exploring Fredensborg and the wonderful forest and gardens surrounding the castle, you can treat yourself to high tea served in the Glass Hall or one of the hotel's lovely salons.

Pension Bondehuset

Pension Bondehuset
Karin and Hans Jørgen Larsen
Sørup, Box 6
3480 Fredensborg
Telephone: 48 48 01 12
FAX: 48 48 03 01
Rates: Single, 440 kr.; Double, 715 kr.; Full board available: Single, 690 kr. per day; Double, 1,215 kr. per day. **Restaurant:** Breakfast, lunch (buffet), and dinner (one meal a day if not paying for full board) served in the inn's dining room. **Open:** April 1 to October 15.

Pension Bondehuset is inviting from the moment one turns into the driveway leading up to the inn. We arrived on a day when North

Zealand was in the aftermath of a terrible windstorm. The waves were crashing violently against the seawall in front of the inn, but the two buildings with their thickly thatched roofs seemed to defy the chilling elements of the weather. I could imagine these 200-year-old structures protecting their inhabitants against the two centuries of Danish winters that have passed since they were built. When we entered the front door, my expectations of a friendly and welcoming atmosphere were pleasantly met as I was greeted by the gracious owner of Pension Bondehuset, Karin Larsen. Warm, rich-colored wall coverings, needlework, paintings, antiques, and a book-filled library give one the impression of a well-cared for and cherished home. Our room, number 20, was large and comfortable with a separate sitting area and large, modern bath with the appreciated under-the-floor heating system. The room faces Lake Esrum, Denmark's second largest, and looks out over the lovely lawn and ancient trees toward the water and forests that line the opposite shore. Mrs. Larsen and her husband, Hans Jørgen, have owned the inn for more than 20 years. She told us that it has been functioning as an inn for 75 years. Before that, it was probably a farmhouse.

The town of Fredensborg and Fredensborg Castle is the summer residence of Queen Margrethe II. It is a lovely place that can easily be reached by a 45-minute trip by train or car (38 kilometers) from Copenhagen. If you want to explore the castles of Northern Zealand, Fredensborg is the perfect base as it provides access to Kronborg and Frederiksborg castles as well. From Pension Bondehuset, it is a lovely walk along the shore of the lake to Skipperhuset, an idyllic restaurant in an old building from 1751, and then through the royal forest to the castle. If you like, you may borrow a bicycle or rowboat from the inn and even request a picnic lunch if you will be out exploring the town and surrounding areas during the day.

HELSINGØR

Hotel Hamlet

Hotel Hamlet
Bent Jacobsen, director
Bramstræde 5
3000 Helsingør
Telephone: 49 21 05 91; **FAX:** 49 26 01 30
Rates: Single, 595 to 625 kr.; Double, 795 to 885 kr.
Restaurant: Ophelia (Danish/French cuisine with many fish specialties).

The town of Helsingør (Elsinore in English) has attracted actors and entertainers to its streets and theaters since the sixteenth century. William Shakespeare may have even visited the town before he wrote about the Prince of Denmark and the town's famous castle, Kronborg. In 1586 a woman by the name of Gertrud Clettens Engelskkvinde ("The English Woman") lived in the building now occupied by Hotel Hamlet. Many of these actors frequented her home and two of them fought a duel over her daughter, resulting in the death of both duelers. Her former home now provides comfortable lodgings for tourists wishing to visit this fascinating old town and its castle.

When arriving in Helsingør by either train or by ferryboat from Sweden, the hotel is a convenient two-minute walk away. It is so centrally located that it is part of the core of a walking tour we followed through the oldest part of the town past the cathedral, the Carmelite Monastery of St. Maria, and down the narrow, cobblestoned streets lined with half-timbered buildings beautifully preserved through the centuries. It is also a short walk from the hotel down the footpath leading to Kronborg Castle.

The hotel is now a combination of three buildings, the oldest of which goes back 300 years. When exploring the cellars, now special meeting rooms, one gets a sense of the building's age by looking at the original brick and stone walls. In our room, as in the hallways, the original exposed beams still exist. The smell of old wood helps to create the special ambiance of the hotel. All rooms have modern baths, telephones, and televisions.

HOLBÆK

Langtved Færgekro

Langtved Færgekro
Svend Rinken, manager and chef
Munkhomvej 138
4060 Kirke Såby
Telephone: 46 40 50 53
Rooms: There are no overnight accommodations at this inn. **Restaurant:** Open for lunch and dinner on weekends, other days open at 3:00 P.M. Also outdoor seating next to the fjord.

There are very few inns included in this book that do not offer overnight accommodations, but every once in a while during my travels I came across an inn offering only meals that I just had to include because of its fascinating history and fine food. Langtved Færgekro is such an inn. This is a place as yet undiscovered by many tourists but one that you should know about if you happen to find yourself in the middle of Zealand. Many people from Copenhagen willingly make the 45-minute drive just to eat here. As you leave the town of Holbæk and drive around the southernmost end of Isefjord, you see a thatched-roof inn nestled against the forest next to the fjord. You will immediately get the impression that the building belongs to this place. Actually, it is located there for a practical reason. The bridge that crosses the fjord has only been there since 1952. Prior to that time, the inn's owner was the man who rowed the boat that carried passengers back and forth across the small stretch of water.

The inn is located on the large estate of Count Niels H. R. Schell, whom I had the pleasure of meeting and who was kind enough to relate his family's history in this part of Denmark all the way back to the fourteenth century. "Ryegaard," as the estate is called, means a place in the forest where the trees have been cleared for farmland. On the property, there is evidence of the Vikings as well as kitchen middens and burial places going back much further in time. Count Schell showed me a map from 1757 that shows the inn existed at that time, although it may have already been there even before then. There was originally a tannery, driven by a waterwheel, right next to the inn. It enjoyed brisk business during the Napoleonic Wars when leather was needed for military use. While I was being given a tour by owner Svend Rinken, he pointed out the doors that still remain from 1757 and the drawer in which customers were supposed to deposit the money to pay their bill if the owner was busy ferrying people across the fjord. If the innkeeper was occupied in the kitchen or dining room, all you had to do to summon him was to strike a metal railroad tie with a mallet and use it as one would a gong. Later, the steamship docked right outside the inn.

The inn's atmosphere is typical of the old eighteenth-century Danish inn. Even with my average height, I had to duck a bit to get under the doors between the various small rooms. The ceilings are also low with wood beams and the multipaned windows look out over the lovely scenery of water and lush green forests. Henrik Pontoppidan, one of Denmark's best-known nineteenth-century authors, was so inspired by this location that after an eight-day stay at the inn, he included it in several of his books, including *Vildt* from 1890. You may want to ask to eat in the dining room once used exclusively for members of the city council and other VIPs who were dressed well enough, although you may now relax and come as you are. Svend Rinken is not only a genial host who can tell you wonderful stories about the inn, but he is also an award-winning chef and member of the Cordon Bleu de Saint Esprit, among other distinguished organizations. I had one of my favorite Danish luncheon dishes, a mound of shrimp and fried plaice fish on a bed of puff pastry and fresh vegetables, topped off with a dollop of black Danish caviar. Fresh fish, including eel, is a specialty of the house.

HORNBÆK

Havreholm Slot (Hall)

Havreholm Slot (Hall)
Inge Correll, manager
Klosterrisvej 4, Havreholm
DK-3100 Hornbæk
Telephone: 42 24 86 00; **FAX:** 42 24 80 23
Rates: Single, 950 kr.; Double, 1,350 kr.; Half board, 430 kr. per person;
Lodge for 1 to 4 people, 1,800 kr.; Children under 12 years, half price;
Special weekend package, 960 kr. per person. **Restaurant:** Breakfast,
lunch, and dinner in castle's dining room; French/international cuisine.
There is a wine cellar. The terrace is open for lunch, dinner, and
drinks during the summer. This inn is a member of Danish Castle
and Manor Houses.

Just a 30-minute drive north of Copenhagen, close to Elsinore and
Hamlet's castle, you will find Havreholm Slot, a marvelous combination
of a historic house and a modern resort. In the original, main building
are the reception rooms, a library with games, newspapers, and
magazines, and the dining room with 12 paintings by the well-known
Danish painter Joakim Skovgaard that depict the creation of the
world in a series of works entitled *The Garden of Eden*. The guest
rooms are housed in 16 separate guesthouses located on the sloping
ground of the estate leading down to the River Gurre and a small
waterfall. These modern guesthouses, many of which have their own

kitchenette, house from 1 to 4 persons in each. All are equipped with televisions and videos, minibars, and telephones. Almost any type of sport is available on the grounds, from golf, tennis, horseback riding, billiards, table tennis, and squash to swimming in the indoor and outdoor pools. Bicycles and rowboats are also available. For those who need to relax after an active day, there are saunas, a Jacuzzi, and a solarium.

The house was built in 1872 by Valdemar Culmsee, a paper manufacturer. The Danish poet Holger Drachman was a frequent guest, primarily because of the fact that he fell in love with all seven of the Culmsee daughters, although not at the same time. When Polly Culmsee announced her engagement to one of Drachman's rivals one evening in the castle, Drachman took his hat in hand, said good night to the host and other guests, and jumped out of the second-story window. Not to be deterred by this temporary tragedy, he went on to marry Polly's younger sister, Emmy. Another literary story about the castle connects it with the Danish author Henrik Pontoppidan. He is said to have written his work *Happy Per* in the tower of the castle. He also planted a beech tree next to the entrance to the castle. At the turn of the century, the castle was purchased by Holger Jantzen, the owner of a sugar plantation in Java. His significant contribution to the castle as it stands today was to invite the artist and professor of art Joakim Skovgaard to spend three years here executing his series of paintings about the Creation. These works were exhibited in the Art Academy and later in Stockholm before being permanently installed in the castle's dining room. On the ceiling, Skovgaard chose to paint the motif of the zodiac surrounded by figures depicting the four seasons. The castle stayed in the Jantzen family for more than 70 years until in 1984 it was converted into a hotel.

Hotel Villa Strand

Hotel Villa Strand
Guttermann family
Kystvej 12
3100 Hornbæk
Telephone: 49 70 00 88, in the U.S. call 1-516-239-6792;
FAX: 43 96 97 29, in the U.S. call 1-516-239-7211
Rates: Single, 550 to 785 kr; Double, 385 to 685 kr. per person; Family room, 950 kr.; Full board: Single, 795 to 1,050 kr.; Double, 625 to 950 per person; Family room, 1,685 kr.; Suite, 1,150 kr. **Restaurant:** Kosher meals are served for breakfast, lunch, and dinner in the hotel dining room. **Open:** From April to October.

Hotel Villa Strand has the distinction of being the only hotel in northern Europe with a Kosher kitchen. There are mesuzas on the doors and there is a full-time resident mashgiach. Rabbi M. Jacobs, an American, supervises the hotel, where the standards of Kashrut are observed and all products used are Kosher. Although both Jewish and non-Jewish guests stay at the hotel, smoking is not allowed in the dining room on the Sabbath and hotel bills are not paid from Friday to Saturday evening. With the going down of the sun on Saturday, the hotel is again run as any other hotel in Denmark would be. The Jewish Easter, Pesach, is a busy time for the hotel with more than 80 guests arriving for the main meal. It is because of the keeping of the Jewish holidays and the excellent Kosher kitchen that guests have come from all over the world to stay here.

Hotel Villa Strand was originally built by a wealthy banker at the beginning of the twentieth century, although he later went bankrupt and had to sell his impressive villa behind the sand dunes on the Kattegat. It is located in a charming, small town frequented by summer visitors and owners of summer houses along the northern coast of Zealand. The hotel is located on a quiet residential street with only the dunes to separate it from one of the nicest beaches in this part of Denmark. When we arrived in Hornbæk, the town was celebrating its 500th anniversary and we were lucky enough to participate in its festivities. This location also enjoys a close proximity to the capital, only about 40 minutes away. If you wish to explore Helsingør and its Kronborg Castle, it is only a quick 10-minute drive away. Two new wings have been added to the original whitewashed villa with its red-tiled roof, forming an enclosed courtyard where children can play safely on the hotel's playground equipment. Another separate suite with its own Jacuzzi has been built on the dune side of the hotel. This apartment can be rented by the week or for the whole summer. All of the guest rooms are very basic and simple, although they have private modern baths. Room number 3 has a lovely balcony overlooking the sea side of the hotel.

HUNDESTED

Lynæs Kro

Lynæs Kro
Ole Schjerbeck
Frederiksværksvej 6
3390 Hundested
Telephone: 42 33 86 66
Rates: Single, 650 kr.; Double, 800 kr.; Suites, 950 kr. **Restaurant:**
Breakfast is served in special breakfast room or on the terrace; dinner
is served in one of several dining rooms. Outdoor dining is offered
during the summer months. **Open:** April through December. The
inn is a member of Romantik Hotels and Restaurants.

Located in a very tiny village where Roskilde Fjord and Ise Fjord meet,
Lynæs Kro has a popular restaurant known among Scandinavians
traveling along the northern coast of Zealand. There are also five cozy
guest rooms for the traveler. Rooms 1, 2, and 3 have wonderful views
out over the fjord and the harbor. The hotel is a marvelous starting point
for walking tours along its small lanes and down to the harbor, and
then on to Hundested, a place in the nineteenth century where seals
were hunted and where fishing has been the major occupation for
several centuries. A little farther is the oldest fishing village, Kikhavn,
which dates back to the thirteenth century.
     Ole and Kirsten Schjerbeck have owned the inn for 25 years, but
its history originated in 1782 when the navigator of the ferryboat,
Jens Erichsen, applied for permission to start an inn with stables for
the horses. It was denied because another inn already existed at the
time. In 1810 the town of Frederiksværk granted another ferry operator
permission to serve snaps or aquavit to travelers. In 1822 Jens Erichsen's
son finally received permission from King Frederik VI to have an inn,
especially because of the storms and winds that plagued the area, which
often made it difficult for travelers to reach home without stopping

along the way. The only stipulation was that the inn should be open to those traveling from other places, not to the local farmers and fishermen. The current inn has an interesting mixture of various antique pieces, including a table that was originally the door from a women's prison in Copenhagen. The first dining room has a medieval theme with a stained-glass window, dark wood paneling, and a large, carved wooden table. Another dining room, known as the Gobelin Room, has a series of gigantic paintings that once hung in Mr. Schjerbeck's grandfather's *herregaard* (manor house), each illustrating a different scene from Shakespeare's *The Tempest*. The menu is typically Danish with a Continental flair. There is always fresh fish, and salmon on an oak plank is a specialty of the house.

HVALSØ

Sonnerup Gods

Sonnerup Gods
Birgitte Israelsen
Tølløsevej 55
DK-4330 Hvalsø
Telephone: 42 40 82 55; **FAX:** 42 40 70 46
Rates: Single, 300 kr.; Double, 500 kr. **Restaurant:** The only meal is breakfast, served in the dining room; but large parties can be arranged.

Sonnerup Gods (Manor) was first mentioned in 1341, although it is possible to trace the names of its owners beginning in the sixteenth century. Perhaps one of its more illustrious residents was Manderup Parsberg and his second wife, Anne Brahe, who lived there beginning in 1621. He was a royal counselor who, from 1588 to 1596, was one of the four regents during the years before King Christian IV came of age and ascended the throne. Often engaged in duels with his various opponents, his most famous fight was with the famous Danish astronomer Thyge Brahe, who lost his nose as an unpleasant result of the confrontation. After Parsberg died, his widow owned the estate until 1633.

From the middle of the seventeenth century, the ownership of the estate went from the hands of the nobility to that of the commoner. One of its owners was Rasmus Vinding, the main author of King Christian V's *Danske Lov (Danish Law)*. Severin de Junge, a director of the West Indian-New Guinea Company, was responsible during his ownership for reconstructing the main building after a terrible fire in 1731. The original building is now in ruins behind the present main house in an area commonly known as the "Burnt Grave." On a hilly mound surrounded by a moat, the ruins are said to be haunted by a maid who drowned in the moat's water after the fire. Also near the manor house is Tadre Mill, the only overshot water mill in this part of Denmark that still works. The mill goes back to 1405 and the present mill was built in 1840. Corn is still milled and wood sawed here from time to time.

Sonnerup Gods is located near the larger town of Roskilde, only a 45-minute drive from Copenhagen, Today the manor house is used primarily as a course and conference center, although it is possible for the individual traveler to spent one or more nights here. If you are traveling with a group, it is also possible to rent the whole manor house just for the group. An American and a Dane recently had their wedding here and guests came from both countries for the celebration. The woods on the estate, filled with beech, maple, and 300-year-old oak trees, are well worth exploring. Wild game, such as pheasant and gray ducks, roam the grounds and there is a wonderful hunting lodge dating from 1600, which, according to the National Museum, makes it the oldest country building in Zealand.

HØRVE

Dragsholm Castle

Dragsholm Castle
Merete Bøttger and Flemming Bøttger, owners;
Annette V. Petersen, director
DK-4534 Hørve
Telephone: 59 65 33 00; **FAX:** 59 65 30 33
Rates: Prices are per person for a weekend. Single without bath, 650 kr.; Single with bath, 775 kr.; Double without bath, 750 kr.; Double with bath, 875 kr.; weekly rates and half and whole board are available.
Restaurant: There are several rooms where all meals are served.

The history of Dragsholm Castle goes back to the twelfth century when it was built by the bishop of Roskilde. Because it was situated on the Bay of Nekselø and Lamme Fjord, it was a perfect place to provide defense for that area. All four sides were protected by a moat and it could only be entered on the northern side. After the Reformation in 1536, the castle passed into the hands of the king. During the Swedish War of 1658 to 1660, it was bombarded and suffered a great deal of damage. After being owned by several wealthy men, it finally underwent extensive renovation under the ownership of Frederik Christian Adeler (Counselor, Judge of the High Court, and Groom of the Chamber). He later married a noblewoman and their heirs owned the castle until 1932. In 1843 the estate was raised to a barony. The first baron, George Frederik Otto Zytphen Adeler, was known as a humane aristocrat who started a cooperative for the local farmers. The last baroness died in 1932 and her heirs were unable to pay the death taxes. In 1937 Johan

Bøttger bought the castle and its 475 acres of farmland and forests. It is his children who today own and run the castle as a hotel.

The 800-year-old castle has more than 100 salons and guest rooms filled with antiques and art, including Denmark's oldest wine cellar. It is also known for its ghosts. The "White Lady" is supposed to be the most frightening of the group. As the story goes, she was the daughter of the king's county director. She fell in love with a lower-class young man. As a punishment, she was buried alive within a brick wall and left to die. It is said that she now appears to seek revenge for what happened to her. For the brave, it is possible to stay in Room 20, across from where this tragic event was supposed to have taken place.

JYDERUP

Bromølle Kro

Bromølle Kro
Bettina Bresnov
Slagelsevej 78
4450 Jyderup
Telephone: 53 55 00 90; **FAX:** 58 25 02 38
Rates: Single, 300 to 425 kr.; Double, 400 to 650 kr.
Restaurant: Breakfast, lunch, and dinner are served in the dining room.

In 1998 Bromølle Kro celebrated its 800th anniversary as an inn. Bettina Bresnov and her husband, Jan (Bettina's parents Anne and Hugo Bresnov ran the inn for 21 years before Bettina and Jan took over), chose to commemorate the occasion with the publication of a book about the inn's history and the production of a play performed in August 1998.

Evidence of people inhabiting this particular place goes back 7,000 years. We know this because an amulet was discovered here, dropped by a hunter who probably used it to protect himself from evil spirits. During Denmark's medieval history, Bishop Absalon, who founded Copenhagen, inherited Bromølle from his parents. In 1198 he then gave it to Sorø Monastery. By 1400 the monastery was no longer interested in owning this property and it was given back to the bishop of Roskilde. The *Chronicles of Zealand*, from the middle of the fourteenth century, tell us that there was a mill here, one of the five King's Mills. The spot was an important place for the farmers' traffic that traveled back and forth with wheat and animals on the way to market.

During these years, it was sometimes dangerous to stay at the inn. One of the innkeepers used rather violent methods to steal money from his guests. A number of skeletons belonging to these unfortunate lodgers turned up in the graveyard of the nearby church. When discovered, the innkeeper and his wife were arrested and later hanged just 500 meters north of the inn. Happily, the modern guest doesn't have to worry about being submitted to the same treatment.

In the eighteenth century, a general store was incorporated with the inn, the walls of which are now part of the public rooms on the first floor. Today the inn is next to a nature park with animals and a playground for children. In the garden of the inn stands what is known as the "oldest tree in Denmark," mentioned in several books by the famous Danish author Martin A. Hansen. The inn's kitchen prepares traditional Danish inn fare as well as nouvelle Danish cuisine.

KALUNDBORG

Ole Lunds Gaard

Ole Lunds Gaard
Kordilgade 1-3
4400 Kalundborg
Telephone: 53 51 01 65
Rates: Single, 240 to 460 kr.; Double, 575 to 660 kr. **Restaurant:** Breakfast, lunch, and dinner are served in the inn's dining room.

If the traveler is interested in seeing the many interesting sights of Kalundborg, including its famous five-towered church, Kaalund Cloister, the ruins of Kalundborg Castle, the Old Stone Park, and Kalundborg Museum, then Ole Lunds Gaard is within walking distance (5 minutes). It is also near the part of town called Røsnæs, near the water. Amidst the picturesque houses of this harbor town with its fishing boats, this inn is a traveler's bargain, to be sure. The word *gaard* in Danish may mean "farm" but in this case it refers to a large house in town that has a courtyard in back. There was often a small barn on the other side of the courtyard where the family's horses and perhaps a few animals such as a cow and pig were kept just for the use of that household. Today Ole Lunds Gaard (Ole Lund's Residence) is located off the town's walking street but the courtyard is now a garden where visitors can enjoy a quiet moment. There was probably an Ole Lund who existed at one time, although we don't know anything about him. But it is certain that a merchant constructed the building around 1777.

All the rooms in this half-timbered old house have televisions, minibars, and telephones, although some do not have a private bath. On the walking-street side of the building is a sidewalk cafe and the inn's restaurant inside offers a typical inn menu at extremely reasonable prices.

KØGE

Vallø Slotskro

Vallø Slotskro
Benny Jeppesen
Slotsgade 1
4600 Køge
Telephone: 56 26 70 20
Rates: Single, 495 to 585 kr.; Double, 575 to 740 kr. **Restaurant:** Breakfast, lunch, and dinner are served in the inn's dining room.

After a 35-minute train trip from Copenhagen to the historic trading town of Køge, we took a small, regional train, called "The Pig," to the fairy-tale setting of the tiny hamlet of Vallø. From the train stop, which one could hardly call a station, we walked down one of the loveliest country roads one could imagine to the sixteenth-century Vallø Castle. Surrounded by forests and farmland, the castle's towers can be seen from a long distance. It shares the town's cobblestoned streets with just a handful of charming, half-timbered buildings and the Slotskro (Castle Inn), which is located directly opposite the Renaissance castle. My daughter and I spent a glorious spring afternoon walking through the castle's gardens and around the many small ponds filled with ducks and swans—always with the incredible castle enhancing the scene from every angle.

The first castle was built in 1581, although mention of the property goes back to 1319. Several of the Danish queens, together with a famous royal mistress, occupied the castle for a number of years. Since the eighteenth century, it has existed as a residence for older unmarried or widowed ladies of noble birth. It was the abbess of this group of women that originally requested of King Christian VII, in 1781, that an inn be built across the street. When the permission was finally given, it was with the restriction that the inn only be allowed to brew beer, not anything stronger, and that local farmers not be served alcoholic drinks. Most of the guests who stayed there in times past had some association with the castle. It has been a common occurrence throughout Danish history that an inn be located near a castle.

Room number 5 of Slotskro has the most enchanting view of any hotel or inn room in which I have stayed in Denmark. From the window, you look down on the moat and across the bridge to the two front towers of the castle. As the street lights and a few of the castle's lights begin to come on in the evening and the swans fly across the sky, it is a scene straight from a Hans Christian Andersen story. In the inn's restaurant, which has a very economical menu, I recommend the local regional specialty of smoked eel cooked in beer.

MARIBO (ISLAND OF LOLLAND)

Hotel Strandbechgaard
Kurt Strandbech
Maribovej 54
4930 Maribo
Telephone: 54 75 54 19; **FAX:** 54 75 54 19
Rates: Double without bath, 350 kr.; Double with bath, 475 kr.
Restaurant: Breakfast and dinner (the day's meal) are served in the dining room.

Although Lolland and Falster are islands separated from the larger island of Zealand, I have included them in this chapter. Both islands are south of Zealand and are just a bridge away, making access to them very easy. Maribo, in the center of Lolland, is a wonderful place to visit and a delightful place for those who like to explore on foot. The lake Sønder Sø provides a lovely setting for the town, with paths that allow the visitor to walk all the way around the lake. On one side is the cathedral of Lolland and, next to it, the ruins of the convent of the Order of St. Birgitte.

Hotel Strandbechgaard is just 4 kilometers outside of town, making it an ideal and less expensive place to stay in order to enjoy Maribo and the rest of the island. It is difficult to understand how this large, dignified yellow building began its history 150 years ago as a workhouse for the poor. At that time, 37 poor men worked the land belonging to the house. Later, it was a home for older people for 45 years. After that, the building became part of the famous Danish Folk High School movement and was devoted to the teaching of art.

Kurt Strandbech, the present owner, bought it in 1990 with the intention of making it his private home. It was that until he decided that it should be opened as a hotel. The 15 guest rooms are cozy and warm. The common rooms are more like those found in a very nicely decorated and cared for private home. The dining room, with its chandeliers and fireplace, provides a pleasant setting for the hotel's meals.

MØN

Liselund Ny Slot

Liselund Ny Slot
Anne and Bent Mathiesen
Langebjergvej 6
4791 Borre
Telephone: 55 81 20 81; **FAX:** 55 81 21 91
Rates: Single, 650 kr.; Double, 890 kr.; Extra bed, 300 kr.; Tower room,
1,450 kr.; Children to age four are free and children from age four to
twelve are half price; special weekend, holiday, and extended-stay rates;
if you want to rent the whole castle, 9,900 kr. per day. **Restaurant:**
Breakfast is 70 kr. extra; lunch and dinner are in the dining room. A
cafe serves light meals, coffee, pastries, and drinks during the summer
months. The inn is a member of Danish Heritage Castles and
Manor Houses.

   The cliffs on the island of Møn are perhaps the most dramatic
scenery in Denmark. Dropping straight from the green forests
down to the sea, the white chalk cliffs provide one of the country's
landmarks that should be seen at least once. The island itself is just

off the southeastern coast of the larger island of Zealand and is 120 kilometers from Copenhagen. On the western end of the island is the largest town of Stege and the castle is situated on the eastern tip. Liselund was created by De Bosch De La Calmette in 1790 during the time of the French Revolution. A fairy-tale park was built with the idea that something exciting and different could be seen at every turning point in this natural setting. Trees, bushes, and flowers were carefully laid out and small buildings such as a Swiss House, Norwegian Mountain Cabin, chapel, several farmhouses, and a Chinese Tea Pavillion helped to provide a feeling of fantasy. The small thatched-roof of Liselund Gamel (old) Castle is also one of the architectural gems. For the modern guest at the castle, the unbelievable park and the natural beauty of this area provide endless opportunities for exploring on foot and just sitting and relaxing amid enchanting beauty.

The castle as it exists today was built in 1887 by Baroness Oluffa Krabbe and Baron Fritz Rosenkranz. On one side, the yellow and white exterior's two anchoring sections are broken by two levels of arched, columned porches. From the other side, a tall tower begins with the columned entrance on the ground level and continues through three more floors to its pointed top. The result is a balanced and yet fanciful building with much charm. Inside, light pastel-colored walls contrast delicately with the white wood molding and the ceiling-high, white porcelain stove. The guest rooms are each named after one of the stories by Hans Christian Andersen. The dining room serves traditional Danish dishes inspired by French cuisine, always with fresh, quality ingredients.

NÆSTVED

Hotel Kirstine

Hotel Kirstine
Bo Nielsen
Købmagergade 20
4700 Næstved
Telephone: 55 77 47 00; **FAX:** 53 72 11 53
Rates: Single, 545 kr.; Double, 745 kr. **Restaurant:** The hotel's dining room serves lunch and dinner. The special Arcade restaurant is used for breakfast. The hotel is a member of Larsens Hotel and Kroferie.

When I arrived at Hotel Kirstine, it was one of those gray, drizzly, cold days typical for Denmark in the month of November. The cheery red-and-white, half-timbered building was like a welcoming beacon in this dreariness, although what awaited me within the cozy lobby was totally unexpected. Every available tabletop in the reception room was covered with the warming light of candles to compensate for the autumn darkness. It was a perfect example of what the Danes call *hyggelig*. The word symbolizes the almost national pursuit of coziness and an atmosphere that makes you feel relaxed and happy. Hotel Kirstine certainly accomplishes that.

The building's history can be traced to Mathias Hansteen, an alderman who built it as his home in 1745. From 1809 until 1876, it was lived in by a series of mayors, who utilized the ideal location on the top of a small rise to look down on the ships carrying important trade to and from this very old market town. The present owner, Bo Nielsen, entered into the hotel business with plenty of experience, including the ownership of three restaurants in Copenhagen's world-famous Tivoli Gardens. He named the hotel after a small river running near the hotel that originates from a spring said to have been holy in ancient times.

Our room, although with modern furniture, had retained its feeling of a past era. It looked out onto a lovely garden and onto a park across the street. Of special note is the remarkable House of the Apostles on the other side of the hotel, a medieval building with carved heads of the Twelve Apostles on the exterior. The breakfast we had at this hotel was among the best we have encountered. The selection was particularly appealing to the American palate and included, among other items, scrambled eggs, sausages, cereals, rolls, and pastries.

Even if you are spending most of your visit in Copenhagen, Næstved, with Hotel Kirstine as your base, provides an excellent side trip into the Danish countryside. It is an historic town with much to offer for a visit of one or two days. Close by are the Holmegaard Glass Factory, Herlufsholm Castle, Gisselfeld Manor House, and Gavnø Castle.

Hotel Vinhuset

Hotel Vinhuset
Per Couriol Hansen
Sct. Peders Kirkeplads 4
4700 Næstved
Telephone: 53 72 08 07; **FAX:** 53 72 03 35
Rates: Single, 590 kr.; Double, 740 to 1,200 kr.; Extra bed, 200 kr.; a complete pension with three meals is also available for an extra charge of 275 kr. per person. **Restaurants:** Bytinget (Danish and international cuisine); Les Baraques (specialties from the New French Cuisine); outdoor cafe is available during the summer months. The inn is a member of Larsens Hotel og Kroferie.

If you want to trace the roots of this building to its beginnings, you must travel down to the cellar, which dates back to the 1400s. Although it isn't completely certain, this part of the structure is believed to have been the wine cellar for the Order of the Black Friars. Legend has it that a secret passage lead from this cellar to the castle of Herlufsholm, several kilometers away. Today it is still possible to enjoy an aperitif before dinner in this medieval portion of the building. The hotel itself goes back to 1766 when owner Niels Lynge was given permission from the king to serve alcoholic drinks and accept overnight guests. It has existed as a royal privileged inn ever since and has continuously served as a hotel for more than 200 years. In more modern times, it was considered one of the "great" hotels in Denmark, an established hotel where people came to eat and dance as well as hold wedding and christening parties. The Gothic St. Peter's Church is situated in the middle of the square that Vinhuset frames on one side. As with so many towns in Denmark, the inn or hotel is built next to the church so that the parties associated with these important religious occasions can easily be held nearby. Another medieval church, St. Mortens, is just a five-minute walk away.

The hotel had fallen on a few years of hard times when the current owner, Per Couriol Hansen, literally saved it from the wrecking ball in the 1980s. After two years of extensive renovation, the local citizens of Næstved are happy that the building was saved. If you happen to be awakened by the bells of St. Peter's Church, consider the experience as part of the charm of staying in this old hotel.

Menstrup Kro

Menstrup Kro
Johannes Christoffersen
Menstrup, 4700 Næstved
Telephone: 53 74 30 03; **FAX:** 53 74 33 63
Rates: Single, 498 to 598 kr.; Double, 688 to 788 kr.; Extra bed for a child, 60 kr.; Suite, 1,200 kr.; half and whole board available; discounts for longer stays; special weekend prices. **Restaurant:** Breakfast, lunch, and dinner are served in the dining room. This inn is a member of Dansk Kroferie.

I have chosen to list the four inns and hotels in the area of Næstved in this book for two reasons. First, all four are excellent lodgings where the traveler just cannot go wrong by staying in one of them. Secondly, Næstved is an excellent choice as a location for exploring the southern part of Zealand. It is a mere one hour's drive by car to Copenhagen and yet the visitor gets a wonderful sense of the beauty of rural Zealand. Some of Denmark's most beautiful castles and manor houses are within a few kilometers (Borreby and Gavnø castles and Holsteinsborg, for example).

Menstrup is actually a country village between the two medieval towns of Næstved and Skælskør, which is why it was chosen as the location for a royal privileged inn. This location provided the needed place to rest for merchants and other travelers going between these two important trading points. The Royal Guards Hussars, who accompany Queen Margrethe on state occasions, also play an important role in the history of this area. In fact, one room at Menstrup Kro is devoted to the regiment's history and displays a collection of uniforms, photographs, and other memorabilia.

The exterior of the inn is rather distinctive. The half-timbered, black-and-white facade is broken by the A-shaped roof over the front door with its yellow woodwork. The inn has been owned since 1962 by the Christoffersen family and has been added to extensively. The guest rooms are basically modern in style, and an indoor swimming pool, sauna, tennis court, and billiards and Ping-Pong room have been added. The owner, however, has tried to maintain the atmosphere and feel of the old inn tradition. All guest rooms have private baths, hair dryers, minibars, televisions, and videocassette players. The inn is known for its excellent food and an extensive wine cellar is available. Nearby are opportunities for golf, sailing, riding, and fishing, all of which can be arranged by the inn.

Mogenstrup Kro

Mogenstrup Kro

Lars Nelsson, owner; Lars Pallesgaard, manager
Mogenstrup, DK-4700 Næstved
Telephone: 53 76 11 30; **FAX:** 53 76 11 29
Rates: Single, 795 kr.; Double, 895 kr.; "Manor house" rooms, 995 kr.
Restaurant: Breakfast, lunch, and dinner are served in the inn's dining room. There is a discotheque.

The history of this particular place in southern Zealand goes back to the Middle Ages when pilgrims sought the healing powers of the waters of Saint Mogens Spring. Next to this spring a church was built during the time when so many were traveling from all over Zealand to this special place. It was in 1829 that Birgitte Sophie Christiane Kaas received the royal permission from King Frederik VI to build an inn in Mogenstrup. The reason for this inn was that a new road had been built between Næstved and Præstø and there was a need for a place where travelers could stop for the night. The inn still has Denmark's only existing "basement baths," a vaulted space where large tubs were placed and hot water was brought to the guests who wished to take a bath. Of course there is no longer a need to use them, since all the guest rooms now have private bathrooms, but it was a luxury at the time. Other modern amenities today include a sauna, solarium, and an 18-hole golf course. The white two-story inn with the red-tiled roof now has 107 rooms. The guest rooms are decorated simply with dark wood furniture, some with canopied beds. All have French doors looking out over the parklike setting surrounding the hotel. The oldest part of the inn is the dining room, where one finds dark wood paneling and wooden beams. The inn serves a large breakfast and lunch buffet and the menu always includes fresh fish dishes.

ROSKILDE

Hotel Prindsen

Hotel Prindsen
Martin Bank and Ole Andersen, directors
Algade 13
4000 Roskilde
Telephone: 46 35 80 10; **FAX:** 46 35 81 10
Rates: Single, 725 kr.; Double, 825 to 875 kr. **Restaurant:** La Bof
(specializing in steaks). This hotel is a member of Best Western.

Roskilde is Denmark's oldest royal city, and an absolute must if you are staying in the capital and want to venture out to see something else of the island of Zealand. It is a mere half an hour by train from Copenhagen's main train station, and Hotel Prindsen is the historic place to stay in this historic town. It is so well located that many travelers can walk from the train station to virtually all the attractions. The famous cathedral (where most of the royalty of Denmark has been buried through the centuries) is close by, and a pleasant 15-minute walk will take you to the Viking Ship Museum and the beauty of the Roskilde Fjord.

We stayed in one of the attic rooms on the top floor and it was warm, cozy, and nicely decorated with a lovely modern bath and all the amenities. One of the most impressive aspects of this hotel is the careful attention given to environmental efforts. No chemicals or toxic sprays are used in or around the building, there are smokefree zones in the restaurant and hotel, and an organic breakfast is served. Of course, when you stay in the Hotel Prindsen, you are in good company. Other famous guests have included Hans Christian Andersen and King Frederik VII.

In 1995 the hotel celebrated its 300th anniversary, an appropriate time for the printing of a book about its history. From this publication

I learned that, by royal decree, the hotel opened in 1695. The history of the hotel is a little foggy until 1721, when we read that several important guests attending the funeral of Queen Louise at the cathedral were housed at the hotel. The Great Fire of 1731 destroyed almost all the buildings on either side of the main street, including the hotel. The widow of the original owner set about the task of rebuilding, downsizing a bit due to the higher costs of construction at the time. In the 1780s another widow, Mrs. Rosted, took over the running of the hotel and provided such good food that the people of Copenhagen were said to have traveled to Roskilde just to eat in the restaurant. In 1874 a group of citizens formed a company, tore down the original hotel, and commissioned a well-known architect to design a new building in the style of sixteenth-century France. It is this building that serves as the hotel today. It is the most distinctive and beautiful building facade on the main street that runs through Roskilde.

Skjoldenæsholm

Skjoldenæsholm
Mr. and Mrs. Bruun de Neergaard
Skjoldenæsvej 106
4174 Jystrup
Telephone: 53 62 81 04; **FAX:** 53 62 88 55
Rates: Single, 780 to 1,010 kr.; Double, 975 to 1,195 kr.; Extra bed, 210 kr. **Restaurant:** All meals are served in the dining rooms of the manor house. Skjoldenæsholm is a member of Danish Heritage Castles and Manor Houses.

If there is such a thing as a utopia in Denmark, a candidate would surely be this unbelievably beautiful manor house. In fact, the great Danish author Johan Herman Wessel once wrote, "Should the Gods wish a pleasant sojourn on earth, they would choose Skjoldenæsholm." Our own visit was nothing short of perfection. We arrived on a very cold February day when the gorgeous grounds and forests surrounding the manor house were covered with a light dusting of snow. The lake next to the buildings was covered with ice and there was a lovely quietness to everything. This experience proved that Skjoldenæsholm can be enjoyed during all the seasons of the year.

With a history dating back to the Middle Ages, the present neo-classical building was built in 1766 by Anna Joachimine Ahlefelt, a brave and self-sufficient woman whose husband had been a wealthy shipbuilder. Her tapestries depicting the shipbuilding yards in Copenhagen that her husband owned still hang in one of the house's large drawing rooms. Her husband died just as the house was being completed and she lived out the rest of her life here, devoting much of her energy to the liberation of the peasant class. Rumors abound that Anna still haunts the grounds, but we did not see her.

The estate was sold to the Bruun de Neergaard family in 1794 and it is now in the possession of the seventh and eighth generations of that family. The running of the hotel is now in the capable hands of Susanne Bruun de Neergaard, a young woman whose love for her ancestral home and its history was evident as she took us on a tour of the manor house. The family has taken great pains to preserve the original architectural character of the building. Much of the artwork and furniture is original to the estate. I was particularly impressed by the Peacock Room and its original wall paintings and another set of twin rooms containing sets of baroque prints, some of which are by Peter Paul Rubens. The room in which we stayed, for example, was decorated with an impressive set of eighteenth-century furniture that had been in the house for generations. As I sat at a writing desk in our room and looked out through the old glass panes of the window at the garden and woods beyond, I fantasized about what it might have been like to have lived in this wonderful house several centuries ago. I decided that the luxurious bath with its Jacuzzi tub and the lovely central heating that kept the room toasty warm probably made the experience even better today. Skjoldnæsholm is also a working estate, involved in the forest industry and farming, with all the farm buildings needed for this operation.

Dining at Skjoldnæsholm is an experience in itself. We were served a three-course meal beginning with native Danish fish and seafood, followed by an entree of venison prepared to perfection, and ending with a chocolate mousse cake to die for. The breakfast was equally well prepared and presented. For the golfer, there is an 18-hole course meandering along the peaceful forests. The trails through the forests and along the lake provide the walker with hours of pleasure. You can even hike all the way up Gyldenløves Høj, the highest point on the island of Zealand, named after the half-brother of King Frederik IV who once owned Skjoldnæsholm around 1700.

Svogerslev Kro

Svogerslev Kro
Hanne and Flemming Petersen
Svogerslev, DK-4000 Roskilde
Telephone: 46 38 30 05; **FAX:** 46 38 30 14
Rates: Not available. **Restaurant:** Breakfast, lunch, and dinner are
served in the dining room. Outdoor dining is offered during the
summer months.

On the country road between Roskilde and Holbæk you will find
this old post (mail) inn. The cheerful pink walls and thatched roof of
the original building dating back to the end of the seventeenth century
greet the visitor with charm and make him feel welcome. Flemming
Petersen, the present owner who began his career at the inn as a waiter,
has built on to the inn to accommodate the need for more rooms over
the years. On the occasion of the inn's 250th anniversary in 1977, a
new guest wing was completed. Another small building with 5 modern
rooms and private baths was added, creating a cozy grouping around
a parklike courtyard. The old dining room still retains the charm of
yesteryear with warm green walls, beams with seasoned sayings written
on them in old script, a fireplace, and a grandfather clock.

This location between Horns and Roskilde was where the carriage
carrying the mail stopped to rest and change horses. According to
the law, there should be two rooms where the traveler could rest for
the night, as well as a stable for the horses. For this reason, the inn was
given its royal privilege in 1727, although the inn already existed then

and there was probably another inn before this one. As was the custom, the owner was given permission by the king to brew beer but not to make anything stronger. The stable was torn down in the 1920s, but the inn's original structure still stands. It is only three kilometers to Roskilde, making this a wonderful choice for excursions around southern Zealand.

RUDS VEDBY

Nørager Herregårdspension

NØRAGER HERREGÅRD

Nørager Herregårdspension
Kim and Rikke Gorm Hansen
Nøragervej 23
4291 Ruds Vedby
Telephone: 58 25 01 51; **FAX:** 58 25 03 51
Rates: It is possible to visit the manor house just for the day or stay overnight. The overnight accommodations are for groups only. Special half or full board available. Please contact Nørager Herregårdspension for the exact room rates. **Restaurant:** Meals by prior arrangement. This manor house is a member of Danish Heritage Castles and Manor Houses.

Although only groups may stay in this nineteenth-century manor house, it is also possible to come just for the day. To see the house and explore the grounds is quite an experience. The history of Nørager goes back to 1429 and the inn has been in the hands of 13 different owners, including the Moltke family, who owned the estate for more than 100 years. The present owners, Rikke and Kim Gorm Hansen, a brother and sister, are the third generation of their family to be at the manor house. The main structure of today was built between 1868 and 1873. Some of the house's famous visitors were Hans Christian Andersen and the polar explorer Knud Rasmussen. Nørager Manor House is just an hour's drive from Copenhagen, but you can also get there by train to Jyderup and then by bus to the house. A trip here could be included with a visit to Trelleborg, the Viking castle that has been excavated.

The manor house grounds are unique, especially the older part with weeping beech, chestnut, and plate trees from 1800. The "Soup

Tree" is said to be the spot where superstitious souls "stir the pot." As with other places in Denmark, there is a special tree with a large hole in its trunk. An old legend claims that if one climbs through the hole, he or she will be spared certain illnesses. "The Temple" is formed in another spot by nine linden trees that seem to form a room or temple. The wildlife on the estate is abundant and includes wild deer, hawks, pheasants, and bats, which come out during the twilight hours. For those groups who spend the night here, there is the possibility of staying in Earl Moltke's bedroom, essentially unchanged since his time. The enormous wooden bed with the headboard that stretches almost to the ceiling is a bit shorter than today's beds, but it provides an impressive setting for a night's sleep.

SKÆLSKØR

Villa Fjordhøj
Ena Wendt
Rådmandsvej 23 b
4230 Skælskør
Telephone and **FAX:** 58 19 14 51
Rates: Single, 300 kr.; Double, 450 kr.; Small apartment can be rented
for the week; Full board is available. **Restaurant:** Hotel has a small
dining room where breakfast is served but lunch and dinner can be
ordered a la carte with prior arrangement.

On the brass plate outside the hotel one finds the word *refugium*
next to the name of the hotel. This could not be more apropos, since
I cannot imagine a better refuge or a place more conducive to peace
and relaxation then Villa Fjordhøj. This turn-of-the-century mansion
is on the outskirts of the small fishing and harbor town of Skælskør, a
charming place of old buildings and fishermen's houses on the waters
of Skælskør Fjord. A 10-minute walk from the center of town past the
old church and the medieval-looking town hall brings the visitor to
the massive wall surrounding the hotel. Built by the town's richest
businessman who owned most of Skælskør, J. J. Lotz, it was his private
residence until his death in the late 1950s. His grandchildren still
come to the hotel to stay from time to time and to recall their childhood
visits. For the next 30 years it served as a convalescent home for the
county of Sorø. Three years ago, Ena Wendt fulfilled a 20-year dream

of owning a hotel and bought the house. During the renovation process, she invited each of her friends to "adopt" one of the guest rooms and decorate it in any style he or she chose. They were responsible for the design as well as the work, and the result is a wonderful collection of cozy rooms, each in an entirely different style. They range from a Danish-modern room from the 1950s to a country-style room with a photograph of the designer's great-grandmother on the wall. All of the rooms are basic but comfortable. Some have sinks but the toilets and baths are off of the hall. Room number 6 has a private balcony and a gorgeous view of the fjord and the lovely flower-filled garden that stretches down to the water. Room number 4 also has a wonderful view over the fjord and is the only room with a private shower.

Villa Fjordhøj is a friendly, laid-back kind of place to stay, thanks to the warm hospitality of Mrs. Wendt. It is often possible to find a group of people singing around the piano, with Mrs. Wendt playing the accordion. Breakfast is a special treat, with different types of cheeses and meats, as well as the fruit, bread, and eggs that Americans prefer. In the evening, one can take a walk down the path that extends from in front of the hotel and along the fjord, past fields of red currant bushes and through the trees that line the water. If you care to go out on the fjord, the hotel owns two small boats you may borrow. For those who wish to explore by bicycle, those are available as well.

SORØ

Hotel Postgaarden

Hotel Postgaarden
Gorm Oldorf
Storegade 25
DK-4180 Sorø
Telephone: 53 63 22 22; **FAX:** 53 63 22 91
Rates: Single, 395 to 595 kr.; Double, 595 to 850 kr. **Restaurants:**
Mimrelund (a Chinese restaurant serving lunch and dinner); De Små
Stue (a lighter lunch menu, steak and fish specialties for dinner).

The oldest part of the hotel, dating from 1664, was originally built
as a farm house. The farmer soon received a license to serve beer. By
1682 the first guest rooms were added and it officially became a royal
privilege inn during the reign of King Christian V. The stall, used to
house the horses and carriages and provide lodging for the drivers, is
now the location of the Mimrelund Restaurant. By 1800 more guest
rooms and a reception area were built, creating the hotel building you
see today.

Two of Denmark's most famous authors stayed for extended periods
in the hotel. B. S. Ingemann (1789-1862), a poet and writer of many
of the hymns sung in the Danish Lutheran Church, lived here on a
full-time basis before moving into Sorø Academy, a school founded by
King Frederik II in 1586. If you visit Sorø Academy, one of the town's
most beautiful buildings, you will see Ingemann's house on the
grounds. A stop at the County Museum, housed in a wonderful red,

half-timbered house from the early seventeenth century, gives the visitor the opportunity to see a room arranged with furniture and belongings from Ingemann's house. Hans Christian Andersen was a friend of the poet's and a frequent houseguest. The other author who lived in Hotel Postgaarden was Ludvig Holberg (1684-1754). His strong interest in education led him to become a supporter of the academy. He spent the last nine summers of his life at Tersløsegård, now a museum in Sorø and open to the public.

While the exterior of the hotel reflects its 300-year history, the traveler should be aware that the interior has been modernized through the years. The rooms are very basic with modern furniture. Our room, which was classified as a "normal" room (the least expensive category), was rather small, so you may want to splurge a bit and take one of the larger rooms. The cobblestoned courtyard in back of the hotel provides a lovely setting in the summertime for refreshments.

Hotel Postgaarden is centrally located on the main street of Sorø, only a five-minute walk to the medieval monastery gate, Sorø Church, the academy, and its breathtaking gardens alongside of one of the three Sorø lakes. If you are a nature lover, there are miles of paths around the lakes that take you through forests and allow you to see some of the loveliest scenery in Denmark. If you are interested in early Danish architecture, a walk through Sorø's streets will reward you with numerous examples of some of the best-preserved houses in the country. If you are traveling west through Zealand and want the experience of a quiet, fairy-tale town, Sorø will not disappoint you.

TISVILDELEJE

Havgården

Havgården
Lilly and Claus Wiegand Larsen
Strandlyvej 1
3210 Vejby Strand
Telephone: 48 70 57 30; **FAX:** 48 70 57 72
Rates: Single, 650 kr.; Double, 750 kr.; Half board, 200 kr. extra.
Restaurant: Breakfast and dinner are served in the inn's dining room.
The restaurant is open from June 1 to the third week in August, although
guests during the other months can always eat in the restaurant.

Every once in a while during my travels around Scandinavia, I have
been lucky enough to just serendipitously come across an inn I had not
known about before. Havgården was just such a find that we discovered
while driving along the northern coast of Zealand. It is an absolutely
wonderful inn in a location I would choose if I wanted to be in a quiet
location and experience some of Denmark's loveliest natural scenes.
On a peaceful lane of summer houses, Havgården is a thatched-roofed
farm building originally built in 1825. After going through a thorough
renovation process, the inn was given an award from the county for
its beautiful restoration.

Claus Larsen is a third-generation innkeeper and restaurateur
whose training took him to Switzerland and Germany. Lily Larsen is
the inn's competent chef who took her culinary training under Claus's
uncle at Hotel Store Kro in Fredensborg. Together, they bought the
old farmhouse, whose land had been gradually sold off after 1920, and
turned it into an inn in 1986. In 1990 a new building was constructed
in keeping with the original style. The two buildings together enclose
one of the loveliest gardens I have seen. The low-ceilinged rooms with

modern baths are all in the country style with blonde-wood furniture and floral fabrics. There are purposely no televisions or radios because the guest is supposed to enjoy the quiet of the countryside rather than the noisy reminders of a faster-paced world. The reception rooms and dining room are cozy, as one would expect in an old farmhouse, although the paintings and furniture are sophisticated and in perfect taste.

If you follow the narrow road in front of the inn down toward the Kattegat, you come to a small path that leads between two summer houses. When you come to the end you are in for an enormous surprise. Stretching before you is a spectacular vista of sea. Leading down to the beach are three almost endless staircases descending what must be one of the steepest cliffs in Denmark. In a country as flat as this, it is certainly unexpected to find such a dramatic descent. If you are not afraid of heights, it is well worth the climb down to the beach for a walk along the shore.

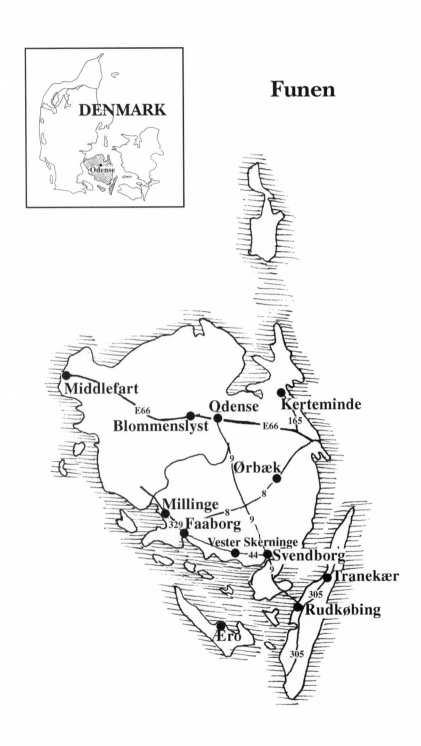

Funen

DENMARK

Odense

Middlefart

E66

Odense

Blommenslyst

Kerteminde

E66   165

9

Ørbæk

8

Millinge

8

329 Faaborg

9

Vester Skerninge

44

Svendborg

9

Tranekær

305

Rudkøbing

Ærø

305

Funen

BLOMMENSLYST

Blommenslyst Kro

Blommenslyst Kro
F. C. Hertz, manager
Middelfartvej 420
DK-5491 Blommenslyst
Telephone: 65 96 70 12; **FAX:** 65 96 79 37
Rates: Single, 435 to 560 kr.; Double, 640 to 700 kr.; Extra bed, 140 kr.
Restaurant: Breakfast, lunch, and dinner are served in the inn's dining room. This inn is a member of Dansk Kroferie.

This inn, built in 1800, received its royal privilege from King Frederik III in 1853. It was named after Anders Bluhme, a butcher and trader in cattle. He originally named the inn Bluhmeslyst, which was then translated into Blommenslyst, the closest Danish word. Throughout its history, the inn has served as a stagecoach stop and lodging for everyone from peasants to businessmen. In its almost 200-year existence, it has burned down twice and been rebuilt. Modern guest rooms, all with private baths, televisions, radios, and minibars, have been added in a new wing. Most of the rooms look out over the garden. Middelfart is located on the western end of Funen at the point where the bridge crossing the Lille Bælt begins. It is a good location that allows the traveler access to both Funen and western Jutland.

FAABORG

Hvedholm Slot

Hvedholm Slot
Ann Vibeke and Gorm Lokdam
Hvedholm Alle 11, Horn
DK-5600 Faaborg
Telephone: 62 60 22 57
Rates: Single, 650 kr.; Double, 775 kr.; Suites available. **Restaurant:** Breakfast and dinner (served from 5:00 to 10:00 P.M.) are provided in the castle's dining room. The castle is a member of Danish Heritage Castle and Manor Houses.

Hvedholm Slot (castle) opened its doors as a hotel in 1997. Located on the outskirts of Faaborg, it overlooks the town's harbor and the South Funen islands from the large park surrounding the castle. The property is mentioned as early as 1231 when it is listed as belonging to the king. By 1475 it was taken over by the Hardenberg family, in whose hands it remained for the next 500 years. One of Denmark's few female vassels, Sophie Lykke, was one of the owners during these centuries. Jørgen Brahe, who owned nine large estates in all, inherited Hvedholm Castle in 1611 and became known as "the little king of Funen" because of his large property holdings. When you visit the castle today, you can see the portal over the entrance to the castle built by Brahe. The castle was tragically burned at the end of the seventeenth century but was rebuilt during the middle of the eighteenth century. A young teenager named Preben Bille Brahe inherited the castle in 1788 and began a large collection of art and rare books there. You can see a bust of Brahe by the famous Danish sculptor Bissen as you enter the castle grounds. Count Bille Brahe Selby rebuilt much of the castle in 1880.

Today the red-and-beige, 5,000-square-meter castle is impressive to say the least. A high tower at the end of one wing rises high above the rest of the Dutch Renaissance-style building. All of the guest rooms in the castle have four-poster beds and lovely decor. Many of the high-ceilinged reception and dining rooms have gilt decorations and carvings, as well as oil paintings. The parklike grounds have a number of rare trees, including the Hans Christian Andersen plane trees.

Steensgaard Herregårdspension

Steensgaard Herregårdspension
Anne Brahe
Millinge DK, 5600 Faaborg
Telephone: 62 61 94 90; **FAX:** 62 61 78 61
Rates: Single, 815 kr.; Double, 990 to 1,190 kr.; Special "manor house" stay including three-course dinner, welcoming drink, evening coffee with pastry, and breakfast, 930 kr.; Half and full board available.
Restaurant: Breakfast, lunch, and dinner are served in the manor house's dining room. The Yellow Room has dining and dancing. The manor house is a member of Danish Heritage Castle and Manor Houses.

Steensgaard Herregårdpension is exactly as one would imagine a manor house to be whose history dates back to the fourteenth century. The main building, with its red-brick, half-timbered exterior, embraces visitors as they arrive in its cobblestoned courtyard. Gracing the front entrance is an elaborately decorated door with stone carvings and caryatids guarded on each side by small cannons. Situated on the southwestern corner of Funen, close to the town of Faaborg, it lies at the foot of the so-called "Funen Alps." The 24 acres of parkland and game reserve surrounding the manor house, as well as the lake and manicured grounds directly next to the house, are a walker's paradise. There are only 12 bedrooms in the manor house, and each visitor feels as though he or she is actually experiencing this historic building as it was long ago.

From the two-story main hall, the staircase leads up to the second-floor balcony past large paintings and a suit of armor. The library is a warm, book-lined room of dark wood, overstuffed velvet furniture, and a brass chandelier. Everywhere, there are antiques, original works of art, and lovely Oriental carpets. In the wood-paneled dining room with stucco-decorated ceilings, everything is as it should be. The front of the fireplace is decorated with coat-of-arms designs and the chairs are wood carved and upholstered in leather. The beautifully decorated guest rooms reflect a manor house atmosphere. The dining room serves traditional food appropriate for an old manor house.

According to documents found in the Royal National Archives, Steensgaard estate was first mentioned in 1310. Through marriage with the Dutch family von Reventlow, the Emmiksen family came to live there in the fifteenth century. One of the members of this family, Otte Emmiksen, became known as "the Evil One" and was said to have terrorized the local peasants. He was just as hard on his third wife, Dorte, who, in order to get out of the nightmare she was living, arranged to pay 44 *daler* to a man to kill her husband. This he did late one night in 1594, hitting him in the head with the large kitchen axe. It took more than 24 hours for Otte to die. The killer fled and was later captured and executed. Dorte was able to return to her hometown but was never able to live in the peace she had hoped for. She is still said to return each night at two minutes past midnight to try to clean the blood stains off the floor, although the original wooden floor was replaced many years ago.

KERTEMINDE

Tornøes Hotel

Tornøes Hotel
Morten Birkerød
Strandgade 2
DK-5300 Kerteminde
Telephone: 65 32 16 05; **FAX:** 65 32 48 40
Rates: Single, 395 to 495 kr.; Double, 495 to 895 kr.; Suites, 895 to
995 kr.; Weekend and senior citizen rates available.

Kerteminde lies on the Kerteminde Fjord on the northeastern
tip of the island of Funen. There are many old houses to see along
its narrow cobblestoned streets, and the beaches are within easy
walking distance of the town's center. Just north of Kerteminde is
the peninsula of Hindsholm, where the traveler can explore some
lovely countryside and small villages. In Kerteminde itself is the
Fjord and Bælt Center (connected with the University of Odense),
a place for children and adults alike where a 160-foot tunnel takes
the visitor under the water to study marine fauna and flora. The
three-story red brick building of the Tornøes Hotel faces the harbor
and looks out over Kerteminde.

The hotel's history began in 1643 when the deputy mayor from
Odense, Erik Jørgensen, lived in this merchant's house where food
and other necessities were sold. There was actually a combination of
several types of buildings that make up the present hotel. In 1870
Wentzel Heinrich Tornøes, a brewer, also opened his place to guests, and
it is from him that the hotel received its name. The building has been
totally restored inside but still maintains its traditional atmosphere. The
guest rooms all have private baths and televisions. The restaurant, which
specializes in fresh fish, overlooks the fjord.

MIDDELFART

Hindsgavl Slot
Annette Brødsgaard, manager
Hindsgavl Alle 7
5500 Middelfart
Telephone: 64 41 88 00; **FAX:** 64 41 88 11;
E-mail: SLOTSBOOK@INET.UNI-C.DK
Rates: Single, 595 kr.; Double, 895 kr.; Extra bed, 175 kr.; Children under the age of 12 are given a 50 percent discount. **Restaurant:** Breakfast, lunch, and dinner are served in the castle's dining room. This castle is a member of Nordisk Hotel Pas.

Surrounded by more than 125 acres of forest and parklike grounds, Hindsgavl Castle's red-brick exterior is stately and yet welcoming. Located just where Funen ends near the Lillebælt (body of water between Funen and Jutland) and Jutland begins on the other side of the sound, the castle is just a bit outside of Middelfart on a little peninsula. The estate was first mentioned in the twelfth century on a list of properties owned by King Valdemar II. The first castle built on the property is now in ruins but can still be found on the top of a steep hill nearby.

This castle was the location of a cease-fire agreement between Danish king Erik Menved and Norwegian king Erik Magnusson in 1295. In 1658 Swedish king Karl Gustav X made his famous trip over the frozen Lillebælt here, and a cannon from that period still sits in the castle's park. As it stands today, Hindsgavl Castle was built in 1784 by Captain, Lord of Chamber, Christian Holger Adeler. After he died at the age of 58, his widow lived on in the castle. She also had to live through the occupation of 40,000 French and Spanish troops who kept their quarters nearby.

In 1808 when the famous Danish castle Koldinghus burned down, Marchal Bernadotte, his wife, and son—the future King Oscar I of Sweden and Norway—went to live for a time at Hindsgavl. In 1814 King Frederik VI of Denmark and Norway was at Hindsgavl when he signed the peace treaty that divided Norway from Denmark. During World War II, the castle was used by the German troops as their quarters and suffered considerable damage during that time. After the war, one of Denmark's best-known architects, Steen Eiler Rasmussen, was in charge of the restoration of the buildings.

All of the 73 rooms of the castle were renovated in 1995. With respect to both colors and materials, the old manor house tradition was taken into consideration. Perhaps some mention should be made, however, of the "White Lady." Although she confines her appearances to the parks around the castle, she has only shown herself to the male guests. She is said to approach them with open arms but, as she gets close, she disappears. Some have speculated that she may be the young bride who came to Hindsgavl to be married. As she approached the castle in her carriage drawn by four horses, the carriage overturned and she was thrown into the water, where she drowned. This is but one of the many tales that surround this old castle.

MILLINGE

Falsled Kro

Falsled Kro
Sven Grønlykke, owner; Jean-Louis Lieffroy, chef and joint owner
5642 Millinge
Telephone: 62 68 11 11; **FAX:** 62 68 11 62
Rates: From 730 to 2,570 kr.; Extra bed, 175 kr. **Restaurant:** Breakfast
is served in the Breakfast Room. Lunch and dinner are served in the
inn's dining room. Breakfast is an additional 130 kr.

Located on the southern side of the island of Funen facing the
beautiful collection of islands that form the Funen Archipelago,
Falsled Kro is a luxurious inn where everything from decor to cuisine
is top of the line. Its history began in the sixteenth century when it was
a smugglers' inn. It gained its royal privilege or charter in the middle
of the eighteenth century when Morten Jensen was given permission
to run an inn and distill spirits. In 1970 Lene and Sven Grønlykke
bought the inn and put together a beautiful and creative assemblage
of three buildings with thatched roofs and various courtyards. The
fame of the inn has spread because of the superb kitchen, directed
by the French chef Jean-Louis Lieffroy, a member of the French chain
Traditions et Qualite. One of the trademarks of his various dishes is the
use of the freshest available ingredients from the island of Funen.
Fresh plums, asparagus, strawberries, apples, pears, nuts, and even wild
mushrooms are added to wild game supplied by the castle huntsmen
and fresh fish from the harbor. An extensive herb garden at the inn
also is used by the chefs.

The rooms, many with fireplaces, balconies, and canopied beds, are all different. Beautiful fabrics, tiles, and old-style furniture create an elegant ambiance. Room number 1, for example, has two floors, while room number 15 is half timbered with quilted beds and a separate sitting area with a fireplace. Breakfast can either be taken in the sunny, cheerful Breakfast Room or on the luxurious terrace. From the inn it is a short trip to the islands of Ærø, Tåsinge, and Landland, as well as north to Odense, the birthplace of Hans Christian Andersen.

ODENSE

Kongelig Privilegeret Sortebro Kro

Kongelig Privilegeret Sortebro Kro
Den Fynske Landsby (Funen Country Village)
5260 Odense 5
Telephone: 13 28 26
Restaurant: This inn is only a restaurant and is open during the season from June 15 to September 1. It is open from 9:00 A.M. to 9:00 P.M. Monday through Friday and from 10:00 A.M. to noon and 5:30 to 9:00 P.M. on Sundays.

Sortebro Kro is the only museum building in Denmark that serves as a restaurant. Den Fynske Landsby is an open-air museum operated as one of the city of Odense's museums and consists of more than 20 different historic buildings brought from other locations and put together into a simulation of a small village in Funen. The inn had originally been built near the village of Lakkendrup on the Nyborg-to-Svendborg road, an old link between Zealand, Funen, and South Jutland. It was built in 1807, the same year it was given its royal privilege or license to operate by the king. Its first innkeeper was Christoffer Rasmussen. It was a perfect spot for an inn since the mail coach stopped there and the passengers needed a place to sleep and eat. The less prestigious travelers, such as the journeymen, stayed in the stalls with the animals while the gentry stayed in the inn. The inn finally closed in 1926, a victim of new railroad routes and new highways that took travelers elsewhere.

The city of Odense bought the inn in 1943 and it became part of the open-air museum collection of buildings. In the restaurant today, one can either order a la carte or enjoy the three-course meal of the day. The food includes both traditional Danish inn fare as well as more sophisticated Continental dishes. The traditional *natmad*, or "night food," is yummy and reasonably priced.

RUDKØBING

Lindelse Kro

Lindelse Kro
Jørgen Hedegaard
Langegade 21, Lindelse
5900 Rudkøbing
Telephone: 62 57 24 03
Rates: Single, 400 kr.; Double, 535 kr.; Extra bed, 150 kr.; Special weekend, weekly, and half-board rates are available. **Restaurant:** Breakfast, lunch (also a luncheon buffet), and dinner are served in the inn's dining room. During the summer months, meals are also served outdoors in the inn's courtyard.

Once called *Landevejskroen* (the Country Road Inn), Lindelse Kro is located on one of Denmark's best beaches on the eastern side of the lovely island of Langeland. With 140 kilometers of coastline, it is called the Long Island. Its scenery ranges from farms with meadows and forests to cliffs and sandy beaches. Rudkøbing is the charming main town and has wonderful old houses, idyllic small squares, and the local history museum. You can get to the island by bridge from the town of Svendborg on Funen. If you want to get to Germany from Rudkøbing, it is only a 2 ½-hour boat trip to the city of Kiel.

In 1997 the hotel celebrated its 107th year, although there have been times in its more recent history when it was auctioned several times. Thanks to the present owners who bought the inn in 1989, it has been thoroughly renovated. The menu in the inn's dining room is typically Danish with a big emphasis on the fresh fish so readily available on the island. In fact, during the summer months, a special fish and seafood buffet is offered every Thursday with 30 different dishes from which to choose. If you really want to experience some excellent old-fashioned Danish inn food, then try the Egg Cake, which, although it sounds like a dessert, is actually a main dish prepared with bacon and chives.

SVENDBORG

Det Lille Hotel

Det Lille Hotel
Badstuen 15, Troense
5700 Svendborg
Telephone: 62 22 53 41
Rates: Single, 300 kr.; Double, 450 kr.; Two-room suite for four, 760 kr.;
Extra bed, 120 kr.; special prices for longer stays. **Restaurant:** Breakfast
is served in the dining room. Dinner can be arranged. A coffee room
serves cake and coffee.

Troense is the charming little town on the island of Tåsinge, just 4
kilometers from the larger city of Svendborg. The street where Det
Lille Hotel (the Little Hotel) is located, Badstuen, and the street next
to it, Grønnegade, are said to be among the loveliest in Denmark. The
hotel borders on the fields surrounding Valdemars Castle and there
is a beautiful old garden. From the late 1600s, Troense has been a
seafaring town as well as a center for shipbuilding. Even today, there is
much going on in the way of boating and a museum is devoted to the
subject of merchant shipping. At the end of Badstuen is the area used
for winter anchorage and old skipper houses still line the street. The
name Badstuen, which means "sauna," is thought to have come from
a group of Finnish shipbuilders who lived here at one time. The house
that is now Det Lille Hotel is a perfectly charming red half-timbered
building with a thatched roof that was probably built in 1823,
although there was a house on the same spot as far back as 1757. It
was originally part of the estate of Valdemars Castle and lived in by a
tenant. It was also known to have been the home of sailors and there
was a cowshed. One of the later owners of the house was the founder
of the Troense Museum of Merchant Shipping.

Valdemars Slot

Valdemars Slot
Per Hansen
Slottsalleen 100, Troense
DK-5700 Svendborg
Telephone: 62 22 59 00; **FAX:** 62 22 69 10
Rates: Single, 450 kr.; Double, 790 to 1490 kr. **Restaurant:** Restaurant
Valdemars Slot has French cuisine; Restaurant The Gray Dame offers
traditional Danish cuisine; Bistro Æblehaven serves light meals and
snacks; there is also a tea pavilion.

Valdemars Slot (castle) is one of the largest privately owned palaces
in Denmark. The castle is located on the beautiful island of Tåsinge,
connected by bridge to the south side of the major island of Funen.
The castle, which has been owned and lived in by 10 generations of
the same family, was originally built by King Christian IV between 1639
and 1644. The king had a mistress, Kristine Munk, with whom he
fathered 10 children. Valdemars Slot was built for the only son that
came out of this relationship.

It was Niels Juel, a navy admiral who defeated the Swedes in the
battle fought at Køge Bay, who bought the estate in 1677 and made it
into the castle that exists today. In the middle of the eighteenth century,
one of Niels Juel's descendents built the two gatehouses, stables,
carriage houses, and tea pavilion that looks out over the sea and serves

today as a place for pastries and tea. The vaults built during King Christian IV's time were constructed with bricks and stones from a nearby medieval castle after it was torn down. Today these vaults are the location of the Restaurant Valdemars Slot, the only restaurant in the world located under a church. The church has been the choice of many brides for their wedding ceremonies. In the castle are a number of rooms filled with artworks and impressive interiors. Among them are the King's Hall with the equestrian portraits of Danish kings and princes; the library with a collection of several thousand books; the Knight's Hall with the full-length portraits of King Frederik V and his two queens; the Baroness's Bedroom; and several rooms filled with beautiful tapestries.

The castle itself is open to the public as a museum, but it is possible to stay on the grounds of the castle in one of the seven rooms in the northern gatehouse that was built in 1753. From the gatehouse it is only 50 meters to the beach and the outstanding estate is yours for the exploring. You may choose to have your breakfast in your room, in the restaurant, on the terrace, or in the tea pavillion. An antique ferryboat travels between the island and the larger city of Svendborg several times during the day; it makes for a nice day trip.

TRANEKÆR

Nedergaard

Nedergaard
Bodil and Jørgen Sander
Nedergaardsvej 10
DK-5953 Tranekær
Telephone: 62 59 13 16; **FAX:** 62 59 15 15;
E-mail: sander-u@post4.tele.dk
Rates: Single, 400 to 500 kr.; Double, 550 to 700 kr.; children under
age 3 are free. **Restaurant:** Breakfast is included in the room rates.
Dinner is served on Friday, Saturday, Sunday, or holidays. Meals are
served on the other days by prior arrangement.

Nedergaard is located toward the northern end of the island of
Langeland among fields and forests close to the sea. It is about an
hour's drive from Nyborg or one can take the ferryboat from Tårs on
the island of Lolland. It is only a fifteen-minute drive from where the
boat docks at Spodsbjerg. The manor house's origins go back to the
fifteenth century and it is the oldest estate on Langeland. The main
building, from 1867, is a red-brick, three-level structure with a
three-arched porch on the front side. The other side of the building
overlooks sloping lawns down to the edge of the water. From the
terrace of the manor house is a wonderful view of the natural park
and the large ships that sail by. To get to the beach and the little
hunting lodge, it is just a ten-minute walk. The interior of the house is
as one would imagine it to be—not as a hotel, but as the private
residence of someone who has collected beautiful furniture and
paintings. One impressive room follows another, each with a high
ceiling, tall windows, chandelier, and warm wood floors. There are
only four guest rooms, allowing the visitor to feel as though he or
she has almost the whole house to experience alone.

VESTER SKERNINGE

Rødkilde Herregaard

Rødkilde Herregaard
Inge Marie Rasmussen
Rødkilde, Rødkildevej 15, Ulbølle
5762 Vester Skerninge
Telephone: 62 24 10 45 or 40 14 99 45; **FAX:** 62 24 10 77 (advance booking requested)
Rates: Single, 440 kr.; Double, 580 to 780 kr. **Restaurant:** Breakfast only is served in the old cellar kitchen.

Rødkilde (which means "Red Spring") was mentioned as early as the fourteenth century and was then owned by a series of Danish nobility until it was acquired in the eighteenth century by Bailiff Jens Lange, who is said to still haunt the manor house at the time around the equinox. Today's lovely white manor house seems too bright and cheerful to provide a residence for an unhappy ghost roaming the house's old cellar. Its owner, Inge Marie Rasmussen, had always dreamed of owning a little hotel and it has now become a reality for her. She and her husband have run this large estate for many years as a working farm. Many agricultural students have lived and worked here in order to learn the skills of farming, including Prince Ingolf, who now has one of the guest rooms named after him. After their two children were grown, they decided to turn the main building into a Bed and Breakfast hotel. Many years of traveling the world in the retail business have also given Mrs. Rasmussen a wonderful sense of taste, which she has used in the decoration of the many rooms. In one guest room, she has placed a quilt she bought in China, while in one of the bathrooms, Laura Ashley fabrics and wallpaper have turned it into an inviting space. On the grounds are other buildings, several of half-timbered construction, including the Rødkilde Water Mill. The mill with its large waterwheel was built originally in 1754 by His Royal Highness' Minister of Justice Jens Lange. The mill was used to grind flour up until 1960 when new technology made it obsolete. A terrible storm in 1989 downed a tree, which fell on top of the mill. This event put into motion a restoration project that was a collaboration between the Rasmussens and the Forestry Service. The preservation was so well accomplished that it received the acclaimed Europa Nostra Prize, awarded to only 30 buildings in Europe each year.

The manor is located only 1 kilometer off Highway 44 between Svendborg and Fåborg. It is not far to the castle Egeskov or the island of Langeland. It is also easy to explore many of the small islands of Funen and the beautiful countryside. A golf course is nearby and Rødkilde Herregård has a special green-fee arrangement with it.

ÆRØ

Hotel Ærøhus

Hotel Ærøhus
Birthe and Svend Christensen
5970 Aejrøskøbing
Telephone: 62 52 10 03; **FAX:** 62 52 21 23
Rates: Single, 225 to 440 kr.; Double, 380 to 650 kr.; Half board and special weekend packages are available. **Restaurant:** Breakfast, lunch, and dinner are served in the hotel's dining rooms: Marinestuen (a room with a collection of maritime objects and paintings by Schossler-Pedersen); Sigvard's Stue (the hotel's oldest room, which earlier served as a tavern—now it is a cozy room with antiques); Bormesterstuen (a more modern room with a lovely view over the harbor). They serve in the courtyard during the summer. **Closed:** From the end of December and through the month of January.

An advertisement from the June 18, 1954, edition of the local newspaper announced the re-opening of a hotel previously known as Hotel Skandinavien. At that time newly renovated, it claimed to have delicious food and reasonable prices. This definitely still holds true today. The room rates in this charming half-timbered inn are bargains. With its dark rose-colored exterior and welcoming courtyard and garden, it echoes the charm of the island of Ærø, a favorite summer spot for Danes.

Going back in time, the building was originally bought in 1773 from the town of Ærøskøbing by a man named Bonsack from Slesvig. The deed for the purchase still hangs on the wall of the inn. Mr. Bonsack's main profession was that of a barber, although in those days barbers also performed surgery and he was known as a surgeon. The inn then went through some difficult years until it was purchased in the 1930s by Sigvard Bang Hansen and his wife, Mie. It is their daughter, Birthe Bang Christensen, and her husband, Svend Mumm Christensen, who now own and run the inn.

With a reputation as a family inn, it is only a few minutes' walk from a beautiful beach. In the main building, the older guest rooms are located on the third floor, while the second floor is the location of more newly renovated rooms with private baths, televisions, and telephones. For those who prefer a small apartment more suitable for families, those are also available in a modern wing, each with kitchen and a small terrace. Guests have access to two tennis courts and a swimming pool.

ØRBÆK

Lykkesholm Slot

Lykkesholm Slot
Amalie Sehestedt Juul, manager
Lykkesholmvej 20
5853 Ørbæk
Telephone: 62 29 29 62; **FAX:** 62 29 29 61; **Mobile phone:** 20 87 20 30
Rates: 16,000 kr. to rent the entire castle with 13 double rooms for 24
hours. If you wish to rent only half of the castle, the price is 8,000 kr.
for one night. **Restaurant:** Breakfast is included in the cost, although
other meals must be arranged in advance. This castle is a member of
Danish Castle and Manor Houses.

If you have ever wanted to have an entire castle all to yourself, this
might be the place where your dream could come true! Lykkesholm
Slot can be rented for one day or for longer periods, if you wish. If you
are coming to Scandinavia in a group, whether it be with friends, family,
or a prearranged group trip, it would be unforgettable to experience
this castle as did those who have called it home since the seventeenth
century. Because the castle has its own chapel, it is a place where a
marriage and the family celebrations that follow can be arranged in a
very special style.

Hans Christian Andersen, who stayed at Lykkesholm Slot for a long
period in 1830, called it "the most beautiful place I know in Funen."

The history of the castle goes back to the year 1329 when it was recorded as being owned by Mrs. Christine. In its early history, the property was named Magelund and was known as a very strong fortification during the Middle Ages. At another point during its ownership, it was believed to have been owned by Queen Margrethe I, the famous monarch who united all three of the Scandinavian countries. The original castle walls remained until the beginning of the eighteenth century, when the ruins were finally destroyed. The present castle, built in 1668, was named after an earlier owner, Kaj Lykke.

The main building is comprised of three wings built together that are open to the water and the surrounding park. The middle one, the oldest part built in the seventeenth century, is higher than the other two, built in the eighteenth century. The renovation has provided eleven double rooms with private baths and two double rooms that share a bath. All of the guest rooms have beautiful views of the lake and forest. For those who want to enjoy the outdoors, there are walks through the parks and grounds, as well as fishing in the lake. At nearby Nyborg (16 kilometers), it is possible to putt at the Skt. Knuds Golf Course.

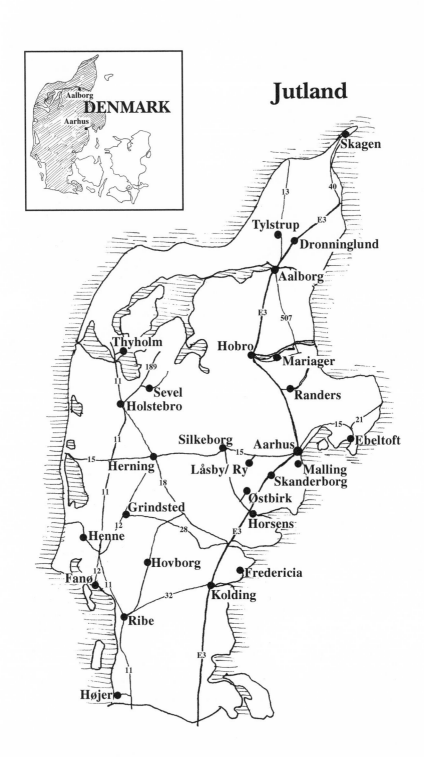

Jutland

DENMARK

Aalborg

Aarhus

Skagen

13   40

Tylstrup   E3

Dronninglund

Aalborg

E3   507

Thyholm   Hobro

Mariager

189

11   Sevel   Randers

Holstebro

15   21

11   Silkeborg   Aarhus   Ebeltoft

15   Herning   Låsby/ Ry   Malling

18   Skanderborg

11   Østbirk

Grindsted

12   28   E3   Horsens

Henne

Hovborg   Fredericia

Fanø   12

11   32   Kolding

Ribe

E3

11

Højer

Jutland

AALBORG

Helnan Phønix Hotel

Helnan Phønix Hotel
Enan Galaly
Vesterbro 77
DK-9000 Aalborg
Telephone: 98 12 00 11; **FAX:** 98 16 31 66
Rates: Single, 900 Kr.; Double, 1,100 kr. **Restaurant:** Halling Restaurant is the main dining room and member of the Cordon Bleu. Brigaderen is a less expensive English-style restaurant. Breakfast, lunch, and dinner are served. There is a bar. They offer outdoor terrace dining during the summer months.

The Helnan Phønix is right downtown in the city of Aalborg and centrally located for walking to everything there is in the way of shopping (the walking street with shops), Jomfru Ane Gade (the street with many restaurants), and sightseeing. The red-brick, gabled facade has been an institution since it became a hotel in 1853. Before that, it was the home built by Brigadier William von Halling when he returned to Denmark from India in 1770. He brought slaves, who were housed in the cellar of the house. He was not known as a very nice person: he openly mistreated his servants and slaves as well as his own wife. He arranged the marriages for the peasants under his control and even demanded that he spend the wedding night with the bride before she could be with her new husband. Many unsuccessful attempts were made on his life and, when he finally died, the church bells were rung in celebration instead of mourning. A large number of people came to his funeral in Aalborg just to make sure that he was really dead and buried.

He paid enormous sums of money to the king for the title of "white knight," given to those with the Grand Cross of the Order of Dannebrog. He also bought the military rank of brigadier and a noble rank. All these payments provided enough cash for the paving of Kongens Nytorv (the King's New Square) in Copenhagen.

Halling's legacy was apparently not all bad, although his only contribution was a monetary one. His mansion in Aalborg still remains the largest part of the hotel and there are art objects, of which he had collected many, which are still part of the hotel's collection. Enan Galaly, from Heliopolis, bought the mansion and converted it into the hotel. It is named the Phønix, or Phoenix, after the mythical bird that rose again in the Sun Temple of Heliopis. It is interesting that the present owner comes from the place where this story was supposed to have taken place, although the hotel already had the name at the time Mr. Galaly bought it. The hotel was renovated in 1995 and a section was added with 30 new guest rooms, each with its own kitchen and entrance.

Kokkedal Slot

Kokkedal Slot
Ann Vibeke and Gorm Lokdam
Kokkedalvej 17
9460 Brovst
Telephone: 98 23 36 22
Rates: Single, 650 kr.; Double, 775 to 975 kr.; special castle visit with afternoon coffee and pastry, three-course dinner with hors d'oeuvres, and morning buffet, 735 kr. per person, per night. **Restaurant:** Breakfast

and dinner are served in the castle's dining room. This castle is a member of Danish Heritage Castles and Manor Houses.

The imposing white fortresslike exterior of this castle, sometimes called the white "Sleeping Beauty," overlooks the lovely waters of the Limfjord. The nearest town is Brovst, although it is located only 30 kilometers from the large city of Aalborg in northern Jutland. Going back in history to the Middle Ages, this fjord, which at that time reached all the way to the castle, was where the Viking ships often formed a flotilla before setting out on their various expeditions. In 1016 a group was lead to victory under Kokkedal's banner or standard and the family was called Banner after that time.

The castle that exists today was built in the middle of the sixteenth century by Lord High Constable (vassal) Erik Banner as a fortification with the moat, three-feet-thick walls, and a drawbridge for the purpose of securing it from its potential enemies. If all of this didn't work, one could still resort to the underground tunnel.

Erik Banner played an important part in history when he became responsible for a prisoner, Gustav Vasa, whom King Christian II had entrusted to his care at the castle. What the king did not plan on was that the two men would become such good friends. Banner eventually freed Vasa and he escaped to Sweden where he started the new Swedish monarchy. During the Reformation, the church's land was confiscated and much of it at that time became a part of Kokkedal Castle. In the 1920s, Prince Erik, King Christian X's cousin, owned the castle. The king often came by ship to visit Prince Erik and today one can still see a doorknocker in the shape of the royal Order of the Elephant showing this royal familial connection. Prince Joachim, the son of the present monarch, Queen Margrethe, was the protector for the castle during the recent restoration process.

There are now 16 guest rooms for visitors, all with private bath and telephone, as well as 10 apartments on the castle grounds. A sauna, swimming pool, and tennis and badminton courts are available, as well as a nearby golf course and bird sanctuary. Of special note is the Rumanian wine, Royal Classic, made especially for the castle. Each Saturday, from 1:00 to 4:00 P.M., there is wine tasting in the castle's wine cellar. In addition to the charming rooms with their canopied beds, there are also hidden rooms and alcoves. In one of these rooms, a knight's daughter had an illicit affair and became pregnant 400 years ago. As the story goes, she was buried alive in one of the walls to avoid bringing shame on her family. It is said that guests have occasionally heard footsteps in the halls late at night, but that may just be a rumor.

Scheelsminde

Scheelsminde
Peter Jensen, manager
Scheelsmindevej 35
DK-9100 Aalborg
Telephone: 98 18 32 33; **FAX:** 98 18 33 34
Rates: Single, 680 kr.; Double, 980 kr.; Suite, 1,280 kr.; Extra bed, 140 kr. **Restaurants:** Breakfast, lunch, and dinner are served in the dining room. There is a Hans Christian Andersen lounge and library bar. This manor house is a member of Danish Heritage Castle and Manor Houses.

Scheelsminde Manor House, surrounded by a lovely park and grounds, is really just outside the city of Aalborg rather than far out in the countryside. The original manor house built by military surgeon and Counsellor Christian Paul Scheel in 1808 has been modernized and built on to so that it now has 70 guest rooms, all with private baths, cable television with videocassettte players, hair dryers, and all the modern amenities. After a succession of owners from the early nineteenth century, the estate was taken over in 1929 by De Danske Spritfabrikker, the famous maker of Danish snaps. The makers of snaps used the complex of buildings as their experimental laboratory for more than 30 years. Because the hotel is now often used as a conference center for Danes, the owners have made every effort to provide all types of activities for guests after a day of seminars and meetings. An indoor swimming pool, together with a sauna, solarium, and Jacuzzi, comprises the hotel's OASIS section, where the guests can help themselves to free snacks, food, beer and wine, or coffee and tea. The restaurant, a member of the French gastronomical association

Confrerie de la Chaine des Rotisseurs, allows the diner a lovely view over the estate's park. For those who would like to visit Aalborg, one of Denmark's largest cities, there is much to see. A visit to Jens Bangs Stenhus, a superbly preserved private house from the seventeenth century, or North Jutland's Art Museum with its collection of modern Danish art, are well worth it. Aalborg is also an excellent place for shopping.

Store Restrup Herregaard

Store Restrup Herregaard
Ann Vibeke and Gorm Lokdam
Restrup Kærvej 10, P.O. Box 320
9100 Aalborg
Telephone: 98 34 18 88
Rates: Single, 650 kr.; Double, 775 to 975 kr.; special weekend and half-board rates from 635 to 735 per person, per night. **Restaurant:** Breakfast and dinner are served in the manor house's dining room. This manor house is a member of Danish Heritage Castles and Manor Houses.

The Viking named Ref is said to have sailed up the Hasseris River and taken this property for his farm. The earliest written documents mentioning Store Restrup Herregaard are from 1314 when the Gyldenstierne family lived here. Another early estate owner, Jørgen Marsvin, is said to have been able to lift himself and his horse off the ground simply by holding onto the iron ring on the house's large door. In 1685 one of King Frederik IV's general majors, Hans Friedrich Leventzow, became owner of the estate and bought up much of the land around the Lim Fjord. One of Leventzow's sons, Christian von Levetzau, who was an officer during the Great Nordic War, in 1723 built the existing manor house in the baroque style popular in Jutland during that time. By then he had become one of the richest men in Denmark and went on to build one of the wings of Amalienborg, the residence of the royal family today in Copenhagen. He had a reputation of being especially cruel to the local peasants in Jutland and became known as "the evil count." They were convinced that he was taking orders from the devil and there is a story that says he can still be seen on dark nights riding his black horses followed by vicious dogs. Leventzow's nephew, Iver Rosenkrantz, inherited the estate and was known as a clever and progressive landowner. His life ended tragicially when he drank poison after an unsuccessful attempt on the life of Christian VII. Again, it was a nephew, Siegfred Raben, who inherited Store Restrup Herregaard and the family became known as Raben-Levetzau. The nephew bought a series of 200-year-old French tapestries with English hunting and fanciful Italian scenes that have now been restored by the National Museum in Copenhagen and hang in the manor house's salon.

There are now 21 guest rooms in the old manor house, each with canopied bed and private bath. After crossing over the moat, one enters a main hall that, up until 100 years old, also served as an entrance for carriages during rainy weather. The elegant dining room serves wild berries from the woods and fresh vegetables from the garden.

DRONNINGLUND

Dronninglund Slot

Dronninglund Slot
Inger and Peder Normann Jepsen
Slotsgade 8
DK-9330 Dronninglund
Telephone: 98 84 33 00; **FAX:** 98 84 34 13
Rates: Single, 485 to 550 kr.; Double, 570 to 750 kr.; Children, one to six years of age in their parents' room, are free; children, six to twelve years of age, are half price; meals for children are half price. **Restaurant:** Breakfast, lunch, and dinner are served in the dining room. Lunch and dinner are served only from June 24 to August 10.

The Benedictine Order of nuns were the first residents of Dronninglund Castle. They had come to this beautiful piece of nature in the early twelfth century and built their Hundslund Cloister, as it was then named. It had been founded in the eleventh century by Odinkar the Younger, a bishop of northern Jutland who lived in the southern Jutland town of Ribe. The cloister is believed to have been Denmark's oldest. By the middle of the thirteenth century it was growing and prospering, due primarily to the generous gifts of women such as Queen Margrethe I, who gave more than 100 farms to the convent in 1394. After the Reformation, all of the documents and papers from the cloister were thrown out and we know that it came under the crown at that time. By the end of the sixteenth century, the estate was owned by Hans Johansen Lindenow, who added the two corner towers to the building. From 1690 to 1729, the church, the castle, and the estate were owned by King Christian V's wife, Charlotte Amalie, who gave it its present name of Dronninglund. After the queen's death it was willed to her son, Frederik IV, who in turn gave it to his sister, Princess Sophie Hedevig. She generously restored the church and made a school in the castle. In the following years, many well-known people owned the estate. Among them were Count Adam Gottlob Moltke, who was responsible for the design and execution of the estate's gardens, and Brigadier General William Halling, who built the old, established Hotel Phønix in Aalborg.

Dronninglund Castle is located north of Aalborg in an area rich in forests and close to good beaches. The large white castle with the bright yellow trim welcomes the guest through wrought-iron gates that form an imposing entrance. The main staircase with its decorative garlands leads one from the main reception hall up to the high-ceilinged landing where the door openings are surrounded by stucco carvings. The building's interior has a medieval look with its rounded arches and thick walls. One of the castle's truly interesting endeavors is its Educational Center for the Deaf and Blind, which holds regular conferences for participants from throughout Norden. Its seminars, library, and experts serve as a resource center for those who come to learn and contribute within the setting of this wonderful castle.

EBELTOFT

Molskroen

Molskroen

Dorte Mette Jensen and Arne Fremmich, owners; Arne Fremmich, manager
Hovedgaden 16
Femmøller Strand
8400 Ebeltoft
Telephone: 86 36 22 00; **FAX:** 86 36 23 00
Rates: Double, 1,480 kr.; Double (family) room in new wing, 1,890 kr.; Suite, 3,200 kr. **Restaurant:** Breakfast, lunch, and dinner are served in the dining room. Terrace dining is offered in the summer months. There is a bar.

At times when Dorte Mette Jensen and her husband have traveled with their children, they have had difficulty finding rooms that were big enough to accommodate two adults and two small children. When they bought Molskroen in 1996 and were planning its renovation and expansion, they decided that it would be a great idea to design rooms large enough for couples traveling with little ones. The result will be 10, two-level rooms with fireplaces that will sleep a family of four comfortably. The half-timbered hotel was built during the early years of this century, although it looks much older because of its almost medieval style. The architect was Egil Fischer, known as the planner of Denmark's first groups of "summer houses." He felt that the best setting for these summer houses was a well-planned village setting. This was the idea behind Femmøller Strand, where Molskroen is located. Fischer, in speaking about the new hotel said, "There has to be an inn if you want a place where people can gather." The inn was to be an essential part of the overall summer colony on the coast. There had been a very old inn on the same spot, but a bigger hotel was needed that would retain the old qualities of the Danish inn.

Ebeltoft is one of the most charming places in Denmark that one can visit if one's interests include exploring old buildings. An old merchant town, it contains a wonderful old town hall from 1789 and the Ebeltoft Museum, which includes the Old Dyeworks and the Helgenæs Vicarage. The Fregatten Jylland (The Frigate Jutland) and the Glass Museum are also close by and worth seeing. You can also follow the watchmen around on their nightly rounds and listen to their wonderful old stories. The Mols Bjerge (Mols Hills) provide a great location for hiking along the coast; and it is possible to stop to visit the old Iron Age Settlement, Toggerbo or Trehøje, where King Dyrenborg and his two sons are said to be buried in the large burial mounds.

Molskroen is located on the Bay of Ebeltoft and the hotel guest can just walk through the garden and across the road to get to the sandy beach. There are lovely views of the bay from the hotel. The restaurant is light and airy and has two large fireplaces to provide just the right atmosphere. The old tables and chairs from the original hotel have been combined with modern Italian lamps. There are three different menus in the dining room, one for fish, another for meat, and a special one for vegetarians. Only the freshest produce and other ingredients from neighboring farms and gardens, as well as the fresh fish that comes into Ebeltoft, will be used.

FANØ

Sønderho Kro

Sønderho Kro

Birgit and Niels Steen Sørensen
Kropladsen 11, Sønderho
DK-6720 Fanø
Telephone: 75 16 40 09; **FAX:** 75 16 43 85
Rates: Single, 645 to 980 kr.; Double, 780 to 1,190 kr. **Restaurant:**
Breakfast, lunch, and dinner are served in the dining room. This inn
is a member of Relais and Chateaux.

One of my favorite places in Denmark is the island of Fanø. I am
fascinated with its history, the windswept dunes and beaches, and
the winding streets with old fishermen's houses. Even the old folk
costumes with turbans and face masks once worn by the women of
the island to protect their faces from the whipping sand and cold air
are intriguing. On the southern end of the island, in the cozy grouping
of thatched-roofed buildings that make up the village of Sønderho,
one finds Sønderho Kro, tucked in behind the dunes just next to the
sea and looking as though it has been there forever. I agree with an
author from Belgium who once wrote: "Fanø is a world, Sønderho is
its capital, and Sønderho Inn is its heart." Since 1722 this is where
the fishermen have gathered while in port. Surrounded by natural
beauty, it is easy to understand why artists such as Jakob Agersnap, who
had a summer studio here for 35 years, were attracted to this special
place. In the inn's early days, not only could you and your horse eat

and rest here, but you could also find a bakery, post office, and small general store all under the same roof. Peter Hansen Brinch, who began the inn at the beginning of the eighteenth century, was the great-great-grandfather of the present owner, Birgit Sørensen. The food served at the inn has become so well known that Mrs. Sørensen has written a wonderful cookbook with the recipes for dishes served in the inn.

I have visited the inn twice and both times it was a delightful experience. When I entered the front door for the first time, it was difficult to just sit down and wait to be served. It is like walking into a wonderful museum with so much to see. I wandered from room to room and enjoyed the paintings, blue-and-white tiles on the wall, and the traditional antique furniture.

I am quite sure that this is as close as the traveler can come to actually experiencing what it must have been like to eat in an early eighteenth-century inn on Denmark's west coast. I chose to order an old Fanø specialty called Bakskuld, a salted, dried, and smoked fish that used to be served together with a cup of coffee and snaps for breakfast in the island's early days. I was a bit skeptical at first, but after the first bite, I became a devoted fan of this old Danish dish. The guest rooms in the inn are wonderfully charming, some with slanted ceilings and all with exposed wooden beams.

FREDERICIA

Kryb-I-Ly Kro

Kryb-I-Ly Kro
Sven Kristiansen
Taulov
DK-7000 Fredericia
Telephone: 75 56 25 55; **FAX:** 75 56 45 14
Rates: Single, 725 kr.; Double, 925 kr. **Restaurant:** Breakfast, lunch, and dinner are served. There is a bar and cozy library where the guest can have a drink or coffee. This inn is a member of Dansk Kroferie.

There was an inn by the name of Søholme Kro on this location in the year 1610. It was named after the large estate of Søholm. As the story goes, the present inn got its unusual name in 1737 from King Christian VI, who passed by a group of farmers bringing in the harvest nearby. They were suddenly caught in a violent downpour and the king was supposed to have told them in Old Danish to "krybe-i-ly," or "creep into a shelter," referring to the inn. The inn was given the royal privilege by the king. Today it is known as such a perfect example of the old royal inn culture that it has been nicknamed "the inn of inns."

Since 1973, when fire demolished part of the old inn, it has become a combination of a thatched-roof building, restored to its old glory, and rooms with the modern amenities that today's travelers expect. Overlooking the Kolding Fjord, the inn is set amidst the lovely scenery of Jutland. It is also close to Vejle and Kolding (home of Koldinghus Castle), two towns worthy of a visit. The guest rooms are furnished in what the inn describes as "manor house" style and all have private baths, televisions, minibars, videocassette players, and hair dryers. A large indoor swimming pool, as well as sauna, solarium, billiards, and jogging paths, are available.

GRINDSTED

Filskov Kro

Filskov Kro
Ole Østergaard
Amtsvejen 34, Filskov
DK-7200 Grindsted
Telephone: 75 34 81 11
Rates: Single, 450 kr.; Double, 650 kr. **Restaurant:** Breakfast, lunch, and dinner are served in the dining room. This inn is a member of Dansk Kroferie.

If you are in the middle of Jutland and plan to visit Legoland, this is a great place to stay since it is only 17 kilometers from Billund, where Legoland is located. This part of Jutland is lovely with rolling farmland and the Skjern and Gudenåen rivers nearby for excellent trout fishing.

The story of this inn began in the first half of the nineteenth century when two brothers, Christian and Anders, were repairing the straw roof of their parents' farm. Hidden away high up in the roof they found a bag of money amounting to 400 rigsdaler, not a small sum in those days. Christian took his share of the find and built his own farm, including a stall for horses so that he could also take in overnight guests and run a business as an innkeeper. The inn was given a royal privilege by the king in 1853, which lasted until 1967. The original inn was actually built a mile or so away and the new inn was relocated on this spot in 1903.

An interesting incident happened just before the owner's death in 1939. His wife had died three years earlier and there were seven children to care for. He knew that he was dying and, on his deathbed, married the longtime waitress from the inn so that his children would not be orphans. The inn is now owned and managed by the fifth generation of the Østergaard family.

A new wing expanded accommodations to a total of 35 guest rooms, all in a basic, modern style with private baths. The lovely dining room is decorated with paintings by the Danish artist Sven Saabye. The specialty of the house is fried trout, fresh from the nearby river. A heated outdoor swimming pool and a tennis court are part of the inn complex, as are a private runway and heliport. There is also a golf course only 9 kilometers away.

HENNE

Henne Kirkeby Kro

Henne Kirkeby Kro
Hans Beck Thomsen, owner and chef
Strandvejen 234
6854 Henne
Telephone: 75 25 54 00; **FAX:** 75 25 54 99
Rates: Single, 495 kr.; Double, 695 kr. **Restaurant:** Breakfast, lunch, and dinner are served in the dining room.

I admit that western Jutland is my favorite part of Denmark. Its windswept North Sea beaches, small villages, and typical Danish farms hold a special fascination for me. But it also happens to be the home of one of Denmark's most acclaimed inns, Henne Kirkeby Kro. I was sitting in the hair stylist's salon one day in Copenhagen when I found an article about the inn's owner, Hans Beck Thomsen, in a magazine. I was so intrigued by what I read that I asked for permission to take the magazine with me.

The story of the inn is one of three generations who have turned innkeeping into an exercise in excellence. Hans Thomsen grew up watching the day-to-day operation of this inn during the many years his mother ran it and prepared the marvelous meals served there. After an education as a chef in Denmark and other countries, he returned to take charge of the inn and combine his knowledge of traditional Danish "kro food" with the creative ideas he had developed through his training and travels. Thomsen's kitchen uses only the freshest ingredients—vegetables and fruits from the inn's garden, herbs from his carefully tended herb garden, fresh fish from the nearby west coast harbors, and fresh lamb from the inn's own herd of sheep. He is even known to pick his own wild mushrooms. During the winter months, Thomsen's life is a combination of weekdays spent in Copenhagen with his wife and sons and weekends spent in Jutland where the whole family works in the inn. During the summer, the family moves to Jutland to stay there for the busy time of the year. The cuisine at Henne Kirkeby Kro has become so well known that a new cookbook, filled with marvelous photographs of the inn and its food, has been written. The English edition is entitled *From the Kitchen in Henne.* Danish food critics have so consistently given this inn's restaurant five stars that it is worth a trip here just to have the privilege of sampling its cuisine.

The building that houses the inn is a typical Frisian house from 150 years ago. Its simple red-brick exterior with thatched roof is inviting and warm. The dining room is quaint yet dignified, with gray wooden ceiling beams and moldings and original landscape paintings of Jutland's west coast. The guest rooms, with large, multipaned windows, are decorated with Laura Ashley-type fabrics and wicker furniture.

HOBRO

Bramslev Gaard

Bramslev Gaard
Lene Bedstrup
Bramslev Bakker 4
Valsgaard, 9500 Hobro
Telephone: 98 51 20 30; **FAX:** 98 51 21 30
Rates: Single, 425 to 475 kr.; Double, 525 to 575 kr.; an apartment for
two, 500 kr. plus 60 kr. for each child. **Restaurant:** Breakfast, lunch,
and dinner are served in the manor house's dining room. Special
meal of the day is available.

   This old manor house prides itself on being the perfect place for
families to vacation today. With beautiful forests and the Mariager
Fjord just 200 meters away, it provides a safe, natural environment for
children who like to explore. With the hills and woods surrounding the
estate, it is a walker's paradise for those who wish to enjoy this special
part of Denmark called Himmerland, while the peaceful park in back
of the main building provides comfortable furniture on the lawns
where the guest can simply relax. There are also farm animals (since
the estate is also a working farm) and pets that the children can enjoy.
There are 15 guest rooms, of which 5 are family apartments, each with
a kitchenette.
   The history of this area is evident in the prehistoric monuments still
found on the estate. The name Bramslevgaard goes back to between
A.D. 300 and 500, although the estate was known as Havnø as early as
the sixteenth century. The current manor house was built 130 years
ago, after a long line of noble owners. For those interested in history,
the nearby town of Hobro is a wonderful place to explore, particularly
for those fascinated by Viking history. Fyrkat is a restored Viking

settlement/fortress from A.D. 980 where one of the sixteen "long houses" has been reconstructed. The visitor can walk inside and imagine what life was like for the Viking families who lived there. A lovely old mill next to the settlement has also been renovated and can be explored. In the town of Hobro, there is a lovely little local history museum and an unusual church built from two different colors of brick that have been used to create an interesting pattern on the exterior. Hobro is also very close to Rebild and would be a convenient place to stay while attending the famous Fourth of July celebration.

HOLSTEBRO

Hotel Schaumburg

Hotel Schaumburg
The Taulbjerg family
26 Nørregade
7500 Holstebro
Telephone: 97 42 31 11; **FAX:** 97 42 72 82
Rates: Single, 702 to 780 kr.; Double, 845 to 980 kr.; Junior suites, 880 to 1,080 kr.; Suites, 1,080 to 1,280 kr.; Extra bed, 150 kr.; Two adults and two children in one room, 995 kr.; Room rates include a ticket to Holstebro Badland. **Restaurants:** Neptun Restaurant serves breakfast, lunch, and dinner, including a three-course "menu of the day" at a reasonable price; Fox and Hounds Scottish Pub serves light meals and specializes in a number of different kinds of beer and whiskey from around the world. This hotel is a member of Best Western.

Hotel Schaumburg's yellow-and-white neoclassical facade overlooks Holstebro's main square, with a view toward the old town hall, the walking street (one of the oldest in Denmark), and a wonderful sculpture by the Italian artist Giacometti. Holstebro is located in western Jutland and is a very old trading town, a reputation it has kept up with its 200 shops that line the walking street. It is also a town that takes its cultural side seriously, with a historical and an art museum, the Odin Theater, the Holstebro Cultural Center, and a well-known school of music. The hotel property started out in 1771 as one of the largest farms in Holstebro. At a later time, it became a large place of business for a grocer who carried all types of goods. The main building, as it exists today, was built by a painter named Heinrich Schaumburg in 1852, after which he opened the largest inn next to the newly built town hall. Schaumburg had come to Holstebro from Odense in order to paint the old church's pulpit and altar. He met a young woman named Sophie and decided to stay, inheriting his mother-in-law's farm and continuing his artistic career in the area. One of Denmark's more famous sons, Hans Christian Andersen, stayed in the inn in 1859, as well as the author Meir Goldschmidt, whose letter to the inn is now a part of the Royal Library's collection.

Although the exterior of the hotel has maintained its historical integrity, the interior has been modernized. In the lobby one finds a large replica of the *Little Mermaid*, perhaps in honor of the hotel's earlier guest who wrote the fairy tale. The guest rooms are simple, modern, and comfortable, with 20 rooms set aside for nonsmokers and 6 with hardwood floors where special attention has been paid to visitors with allergies. Just down the street from the hotel is one of Denmark's nicest "subtropical" *badeland*, an indoor swimming pool environment with all kinds of activities for the family.

HORSENS

Jørgensens Hotel

Jørgensens Hotel
Anne Kathrine Koed Jørgensen, manager
Søndergade 17-19
DK-8700 Horsens
Telephone: 75 62 16 00; **FAX:** 75 62 85 85
Rates: Single, 675 kr.; Double, 800 to 1,450 kr. **Restaurant:** Breakfast, lunch, and dinner are served in the hotel's dining room. Outdoor dining is available during the summer months.

In the middle of Horsens, located in the center of Jutland on the eastern coast, is Jørgensens Hotel, also known as "the Lichtenbergske Mansion." When you first see it, you know immediately that it must be the most beautiful building in town. In fact, it is exactly for that reason that it received an award in 1994. Its perfectly balanced facade, imposing carved doorway, and unusual details give this baroque-style building its special character.

It was originally built as the private residence of Gerhard de Lichtenberg in 1744. Horsens was a trading city in the eighteenth century and both sides of Gerhard de Lichtenberg's family had been wealthy businessmen. He studied in Germany and took the family name of his uncle there. When his uncle died, he inherited both his father's and uncle's companies. He began to buy properties throughout Jutland and became Horsens' most prominent citizen. He bought a half-timbered house that he then built into a mansion.

The interior is rococo with stucco ceilings and wooden doors and woodwork in keeping with the elaborate style. The hotel lobby's grand staircase is from that time, as is the sandstone entrance with the de Lichtenberg coat of arms and the inscription *"Was Gott beschert uns niemand wehrt, anno 1744.*" When King Frederik V came to visit him at his home, a special wooden throne was constructed for the occasion. The throne is today part of the furnishings in the King's Suite. Gerhard de Lichtenberg died in 1794 and is buried in the Klosterkirken (Cloister Church) in Horsens. In 1813 the mansion became an inn and it has remained so until today.

Situated in the heart of Horsens, the location is perfect and there is easy access to parking spaces. The 41 guest rooms are really very lovely. All are light and airy with attractive fabrics and traditional furnishings that work well in the historic setting. The marble bathrooms are very modern and the rooms have trouser presses, minibars, hair dryers, and color cable televisions. In the elegant dining room you may sit at a table beneath the portrait of Gerhard de Lichtenberg and enjoy traditional Danish cuisine with an international flair.

Serridslevgaard
Dorthe Nissen
Serridslevgaardvej 25
DK 8700 Horsens
Telephone: 75 66 73 75; **FAX:** 75 66 72 57
Rates: Single, 800 kr.; Double, 1,000 kr. per person; Half and full board available. **Restaurant:** Breakfast, lunch, and dinner are available. There is a cafe in the manor's cellar, where light lunches, pastries, wine, and coffee or tea are served. This manor house is a member of Danish Heritage Castles and Manor Houses.

One Christmas while I was watching Danish television, I saw the most wonderful program called "Christmas at the Manor House" broadcast from Serridslevgaard. I cannot imagine a more perfect setting for a Christmas celebration than this beautifully decorated house where the hospitable owner, Dorthe Nissen, puts up garlands, lights, bows, and Christmas trees to give it the look of the traditional Christmas we all dream of. Mrs. Nissen took over the estate in 1980 from her grandmother. Since then she has been the sole proprietor of the 75-room manor house, a farming operation with a large pork production, as well as Artiskokken (the Artichoke), where visitors can buy fabulous decorative art objects and things for the home. Although the hours are long and hard for her, Dorthe Nissen is the consummate hostess who simply loves to have guests in her historic home.

The history of the estate goes back to 1424 when Katrine Clausdatter Krumpen gave the property to the Maribo Cloister on the island of

Funen. A series of families owned the estate until 1749 when the Councillor of State, Gerhard de Lichtenberg, who was born in Horsens, bought Serridslevgaard. When he died in 1764, his widow deeded the property to her son-in-law, Maj. Frederik L. Beenfeldt, who gave the house the look it has today. The main wing, neoclassical in style, underwent a major reconstruction in 1777, making the middle section higher and more impressive. This main wing has an entrance chamber facing the court. Its original Louis XVI-style decorations have carefully been restored by Ms. Nissen, whose family has owned the estate since 1919. The manor house's garden was designed and executed in 1768 and now includes a temple, a labyrinth, and a philosopher's corner where one can sit amid flowers and benches. The garden is said to be one of the oldest of this type in Denmark. Among the distinctive features of the park are the many bells hanging in the trees, which give a walk through this area a feeling of being in a fairy-tale. The landscape stretches from a river into beech forests.

The guest rooms at Serridslevgaard are a special treat. Beautiful fabrics and carpets, appropriate to the house, are featured together with creatively used works of art and wooden paneling. Everything at Serridslevgaard reflects a commitment to the historic integrity of the building and the aesthetic enjoyment and material comfort of each guest. If you wish to have a guided tour of the estate between 10:00 A.M. and 4:00 P.M., you may telephone ahead of time and make a reservation.

HOVBORG

Hovborg Kro

Hovborg Kro
Lund Petersen
Holmeåvej 2
DK 6682 Hovborg
Telephone: 75 39 60 33; **FAX:** 75 39 60 13
Rates: Single, 315 kr.; Double, 335 to 450 kr.; Extra bed, 90 kr.; Children under 12 in their parents' bed, free; Half board available; Golf package, 1,150 kr. per person; Fishing trip package, 770 kr. per person; Weekend package with dancing, 535 kr. per person. This inn is a member of Dansk Kroferie.

If you have plans to take your family to Legoland (a 20-minute drive by car) or if you like to fish for trout (the river Holme goes through the inn's garden), this would be a great place to stay. The surrounding countryside is lovely, and the inn can arrange a horse and carriage to take you for a four-hour trip through the forests and villages. Along the way, you can stop to eat your specially made picnic lunch with beer, snaps, and homemade pastries, all for only 160 kr. per person.

The whitewashed, thatched-roof building with its low ceilings and small windows began 200 years ago as a stopping place for men herding cattle from Denmark to the German market. Up to 1,000 cows and 30 herders could be housed here overnight at one time. In the inn's public rooms these men drank punch, played cards, and told stories. Vibekke, one of the best known of the innkeepers, ran the inn from 1822 to 1860. Her first two husbands died, so she decided to marry a very young farm manager, hoping for a longer-lasting marriage. The third husband, Johan Kristoffer Sørensen, did much of the planting around the inn and the neighboring farms and is known as the founder of the Hovborg Plantage (Hovborg Orchard). Another innkeeper, Nikolaj Poulsen, built the first mill in 1868 for grinding grain and later built the first dairy.

There is a story attached to Hovborg Inn about a man many years ago who would walk a long distance to Hovborg Church, rather than attend services closer to home. After knowing this man for a long time, the pastor finally asked him why he would pass his own village church and walk to Hovborg each Sunday. After a long pause, he answered, "I must say, Pastor, it is because you have such a good inn here in town." There are still many reasons to stop at Hovborg Inn, including the inn's reputation for good, old-fashioned Danish cooking with butter and cream. Two of the specialties of the house are the fresh trout from the river and wild game.

HØJER

Rudbøl Grænsekro

Rudbøl Grænsekro

Anette and Paul Wendicke
Rudbølvej 36
6280 Højer
Telephone: 74 73 82 63; **FAX:** 74 73 86 86
Rates: Single, 448 kr.; Double, 598 kr. **Restaurant:** Breakfast, lunch, and dinner are served in the inn's dining room.

Dating from 1711, this inn sits on the Danish-German border. The inn's name means "Border Inn," obviously so named because of its location. In fact, the boundary separating the two countries at this point has been called "the world's strangest border" because it actually goes down the middle of the street! When a decision had to be made in 1920 about where the border should be located, an international commission came up with this solution. Today the town is considered Danish.

The town of Højer and its inn are also interesting because of their association with the famous artist Emil Nolde. Close to the inn, next to a bridge, is the house that Nolde lived in during the summers of 1909 and 1910. The artist, whose original name was Hansen, had taken his new name from a country village 10 kilometers east of Tønder in Denmark. In his autobiography he wrote about the west coast and the "wind that blows free and sharp over the flat countryside." During the summers that he was in Højer he took long walks along the dikes next to the sea and used a small boat for trips. It was also a very productive time in his career as he painted two Biblical works, *The Last Supper* and *Pentecost*, both of which are now in the permanent collection of the National Gallery in Copenhagen.

The inn has been expanded to include guest rooms and small apartments. The oldest part of the inn, which faces the road, is a cozy red-brick structure with a white picket fence enclosing an outdoor cafe during the summer months. There is also an indoor swimming pool, billiard and Ping-Pong room, sauna, solarium, and tennis court. The marshes and countryside are a delight for walkers and the town has many picturesque old buildings to explore.

KOLDING

Hotel Koldingfjord

Hotel Koldingfjord
Fjordvej 154, Strandhuse
DK-6000 Kolding
Telephone: 75 51 00 00; **FAX:** 75 51 00 51
Rates: Single, 925 kr.; Double, 1,225 kr.; Junior suites, 1,225 to 1,525 kr.;
Extra bed for children, 100 to 160 kr.; Special holiday and weekend
packages. **Restaurant:** Breakfast, lunch, and dinner are served in the
hotel dining room. There is a cafe.

Hotel Koldingfjord seems to have been dropped down in the middle
of the 50 acres of forest sloping down to the fjord. Little of the surrounding area has been disturbed. The building is quite large, with
115 guest rooms, and reminds me of the famous old resort hotels of
the southern United States. The hotel is rather unique in Denmark
because, unlike the cozy little inns that are so prevalent in the country,
this hotel is imposing and has a presence that will dazzle the visitor at
first sight. Its facade is an impressive example of neoclassical design
balanced on each side by a two-story, columned porch with carved
tympanum. Topping the middle section with engaged columns is a
small tower. Across the entire front is a sweeping arched columnade
with a balcony above. The result is stunning.

The history of the building goes back to 1903 when Postmaster
Holbøll came up with the idea of issuing a special edition of Christmas
Seals in order to establish a sanitorium for children with tuberculosis.
The fresh air in this part of the country on the fjord seemed like the
perfect location for those in need of recuperation. The building
already there was purchased and an architect was hired in 1906 to add
on to the estate. The sanitorium was opened in 1911 and existed until
1960 when it became an institution for children with physical handicaps.
In 1990 the hotel opened its doors.

The hotel today is first class. The modern guest rooms have private
baths, televisions, videocassette players, and minibars, not to mention

the wonderful views of the fjord. There are wonderful opportunities for walking and jogging on a network of paths near the hotel. An indoor swimming pool, sauna, solarium, tennis court, and billiards room provide many types of recreation. For those interested in history and culture, the recently restored Koldinghus Castle and the new Trapholt Museum of Art (contemporary art) are in town. The hotel even offers a package with one of these museums included.

Saxildhus Hotel

Saxildhus Hotel
Per Elkjær, manager
Banegårdspladsen
DK-6000 Kolding
Telephone: 75 52 12 00; **FAX:** 75 53 53 10
Rates: Single, 395 to 645 kr.; Double, 495 to 745 kr. **Restaurant:** Breakfast, lunch, and dinner are served in Bertram's Kælder (Bertram's Cellar). Bertrum's Pub offers a light lunch, drinks, coffee, and cake, or a beer.

Saxildhus Hotel, built in 1905, is one of those large, established hotels that has become a name that everyone in Denmark has heard of. I have stayed there three times through the years and have always been aware that I was staying in a place with tradition and atmosphere. Its distinctive five-story facade with its pointed gables, copper tower, and Art Deco script occupies an imposing position on the street next to the train station. My trips to Kolding have always been to visit the historic, and newly renovated, Koldinghus Castle, just a short walk away from the hotel. The castle is located in a large park next to a charming lake and there is more than enough to occupy the tourist in Kolding for at least a day. The 93 guest rooms have been modernized and all have private baths, televisions, hair dryers, minibars, and trouser presses. There are special rooms set aside for nonsmokers and "green rooms" for those with allergies.

LÅSBY/RY

Hotel Laasby Kro

Hotel Laasby Kro
Lena and Niels Poulsen
Hovedgaden 49
DK-8670 Låsby/Ry
Telephone: 86 95 17 66; **FAX:** 86 95 10 92
Rates: With a Danish Kro check: Double, 585 kr.; Family room for two adults and one child, 665 kr.; Family room for two adults and two children, 745 kr.; Children to age four are free; there are special weekend packages. **Restaurant:** The Hotel serves breakfast, lunch, and dinner in dining room. This inn is a member of Danish Kroferie.

At the foot of Denmark's famous "mountain" Himmelbjerget (most would call it a large hill) lies Laasby Kro. This part of Jutland, near the larger town of Silkeborg, has a relaxing and lovely landscape of forests and lakes. The antique steamboat trip from Silkeborg to Himmelbjerget is lots of fun, as are the canoe trips on the lakes. Silkeborg is a wonderful shopping town and the Silkeborg Museum has in its collection one of Denmark's most famous "Bog People," one of the best preserved cadavers from the Iron Age.

The farm on which this inn was built goes back to the Middle Ages when it was part of Øm Monastery, a Cistercian order of monks. In 1737 Christian Knudsen Gyberg was given the royal privilege of running an inn here. It quickly became an important meeting place for those buying and selling horses, sheep, and pigs. From here, the herds were sent to southern Jutland, where they were fattened more before being sold in Slesvig and Holsten in what is now Germany. The large stalls associated with the inn often housed large numbers of horses in the 1860s on their way to market in Randers, Anbæk, and other large markets. At that time, each guest room in the inn had four double beds, each occupied by two people! The innkeeper, Rasmus Sørensen, would collect the money each man had in his possession and take it to his own bedroom, where he would make sure that it was safe during the night.

The famous Danish author Steen Steensen Blicher wrote about his stays at Laasby Kro in his work *Eventyr på Himmelbjerget i 1843 (Adventure on Himmelbjerget in 1843)*. When he stayed at the inn, he always told the innkeeper to make sure that no one else staying there knew who he was. The Blicher Salon today has memorabilia relating to Blicher as well as the painting collection of A. Brændgård Andersen. One of the reception rooms is from 1867 and has maintained the old atmosphere. The inn has now been run by three generations of the same family.

There are modern guest rooms, although there are still some of the older rooms with antiques available if you request them. The dining room serves Danish specialties, and there is also dancing. The inn arranges an extremely full program of Saturday night musical performances each year, primarily with Danish singers and musicians. There is a playground for children and an outdoor swimming pool, sauna, solarium, and dart and billiard room.

MALLING

Norsminde Gammel Kro

Norsminde Gammel Kro
Sneborg Alrøe
Gl. Krovej 2
8340 Malling
Telephone: 86 93 24 44; **FAX:** 86 93 14 24
Rates: Single, 390 to 430 kr.; Double, 590 to 640 kr.; Family room for two adults and two children, 595 kr.; Special weekend and vacation rates. **Restaurant:** Breakfast, lunch, and dinner are served in the dining room. There is a bar. This inn is a member of Marguerit Hoteller.

In the small town of Odder (which is Danish for "otter") just 23 kilometers from Denmark's second largest city, Århus, is the home of Norsminde Gammel Kro. The oldest section of the inn, built in 1693, is now the location of the restaurant and bar. In the eighteenth century, the owner of this royal privileged inn was given the responsibility of collecting the toll from those crossing the bridge nearby. Six skillings were to be collected for a carriage, two skillings for a mail wagon, one for a horse, one for a person on foot, and even one skilling for a pig being conveyed to the other side. There was an arrangement whereby people automatically dropped their tolls into a slot in a long table in the inn. This original table is still used in the inn today.

Today's traveler can't help but notice that there are elephants (not real ones, of course) everywhere in the inn and everyone wants to know why. They are the mascot and are on the inn's logo because of an earlier owner, H. W. Alrøe, who in 1913 wanted to build a lasting monument in his garden that would serve to commemorate his 25 years as a machine maker. As he looked across his garden he saw that some flowers were dying because they were getting either too much sun or too little. He poured a huge concrete flower pot (made from his own secret formula) and then decided that there should be a ring of elephants holding the heavy structure off the ground. He then took a motor from a Model T Ford and used to it mechanize the planter so that it would rotate in a circle. That way, all the flowers would get an even distribution of sun and shade. The elephant planter still stands today but the elephants have multiplied around the grounds and buildings of the inn. As you drive up to the front of the half-timbered, green-and-yellow building, an elephant even holds up the Danish flag. The newly renovated guest rooms are simple yet tastfully decorated and comfortable. All have private baths and cable television.

MARIAGER

Hotel Postgaarden

Hotel Postgaarden
Kurt Clausen
Torvet
9550 Mariager
Telephone: 98 54 10 12; **FAX:** 98 54 24 64
Rates: Single, 425 kr.; Double, 600 kr. **Restaurant:** The hotel serves breakfast, lunch, and dinner.

If you are driving through northeastern Jutland, a visit to the picturesque, rose-filled town of Mariager (Maria's Field) will give you the opportunity to see some of the best-preserved buildings in Denmark. Located on the Mariager Fjord, it was once a small fishing village and ferryboat stop on the way between Randers and Aalborg. It was in 1410 that the Brigettine Nuns built a convent and the village suddenly became a place for nobles to come to worship in their beautiful church. When the Reformation came to Denmark, the church became a sanctuary for the Protestants and the convent eventually closed its doors. Today, however, the beautiful church and convent still stand and are a short walk from Hotel Postgaarden, located on the main square of the town. It is also only a few minutes' walk down to the fjord where you can take a trip on the old steamboat *The Swan*. There is also an vintage steam-engine train that will take you between Mariager and Handest.

Hotel Postgaarden, a colorful yellow and brown, half-timbered structure, is located on the cobblestoned street going through the middle of town. It was built in 1710, but it was fully restored to its original condition in 1982. The dining rooms are filled with antiques, some of which have been a part of the hotel for years. The windows are small and the doors are low, giving the visitor a sense of a time gone by. When sitting in the dining rooms, you can't help but notice the slanting walls and uneven windows, a product of the settling of the inn over the years. An addition was added to provide rooms for overnight guests. As we walked down the hall to our room, we noticed that one wall was actually the original exterior of the building. Although the rooms are new, ours had an atmosphere compatible with the age of the inn and it looked out over a small pond where the geese served as our alarm clock in the morning. All the rooms have television and modern baths, although there is only a pay telephone in the hall.

RANDERS

Hvidsten Kro

Hvidsten Kro
Gudrun Fiil and C. A. Paetch
Mariagervej 450
DK-8981 Spentrup
Telephone: 86 47 70 22
Rates: Single, 180 kr.; Double, 280 kr. **Restaurant:** Breakfast, lunch, and dinner are available in the inn's restaurant.

The story of this inn is so well known and significant that it is included in many of the history textbooks read by Danish school-children. It is the heroic story of the Fiil family and their involvement in the Danish Resistance Movement during World War II. Today the inn is owned by a descendent of the Fiil family, Gudrun, but the beginning of the story goes back to 1884, when the Fiil family first owned the inn. Four of the local farms had burned down and Peder Fiil, a skilled carpenter, came to the area to help rebuild. He fell in love with one of the farmers' daughters and they were married by Blicher, a local pastor who later went on to become one of Denmark's most famous poets. They bought Hvidsten Kro for their son Niels, who ran the inn with his wife. Their son Marius moved into the inn with his wife, Gudrun, and continued the family tradition of innkeeping, although he had to work as the local mailman in order to bring in some needed extra income. Even with a limited income, he began to collect antiques of all kinds to furnish the inn. One of the best known pieces, a village drum with the Hornbæk coat-of-arms, is still installed in one of the rooms.

The inn prospered under Marius's management and, even in the 1930s, there could be 1,000 guests on a Sunday afternoon. But in 1943 the Resistance Movement was in need of some dedicated members and the local mayor asked Marius to participate. Together with his son and son-in-law, they brought even more men together into a brave group of fighters. They completed a number of successful operations but, on March 11, 1944, the inn was surrounded by the Gestapo and all the male members of the family were shot to death. The two daughters were sent off to German concentration camps and Gudrun, the mother of the family, was left with great grief to bear. She did not give up the inn and continued to attend to the daily running of her business. On her sixtieth birthday, she said, "I certainly lost much, but I still think that those who lost their men and their means of subsistence were harder afflicted than I. I still have my job and enjoy every day." One of the guests at the inn later wrote, "Strong were those who fought, but stronger even the ones who suffered." As I sat in the dining room of this wonderful old inn and listened to the German tourists around me, I couldn't help but be grateful that that tragic time has passed and hope that the world has learned from its lessons.

The thatched-roof, half-timbered building still stands next to the road, halfway between Mariager and Randers, where travelers used to rest on their way to the larger commercial town of Randers. Originally built in Hald in 1634, it was moved to Hvidsten in 1790 as a result of an argument between the innkeeper and the local pastor. Today, the inn is a cozy, welcoming place where "Gudrun's Recipe" is still available on the menu. It is the traditional Danish type of meal that the old inns know best how to prepare. When I visited the inn, we were served the most wonderful pastry, which, I am sure, was right from the oven. You will even receive an invitation from the owners to visit their kitchen and, in their own words, give them the opportunity to "learn whether or not you have enjoyed your meal." The guest rooms all have a sink, but guests must use the toilet and bath down the hall.

RIBE

Hotel Dagmar

Hotel Dagmar
Lene and Leif Petersen
Torvet
DK-6760 Ribe
Telephone: 75 42 00 33; **FAX:** 75 42 36 52
Rates: Single, 675 to 945 kr.; Double, 875 to 1,145 kr. **Restaurants:**
Restaurant Dagmar, Vægterkælderen

When you are in Ribe, Denmark's oldest town, the country's oldest hotel seems like the logical choice for lodging and food, and Hotel Dagmar is a splendid place. From your window you can look across the street to the cathedral and its lovely chimes will greet you in the morning. It is an ideal place to stay in an ideal setting. Ribe is a place of history with more than enough to keep you entertained for several days as you explore its cobblestoned streets and its old half-timbered houses.

The new Viking Centre here is related to the town's Viking roots and there are a number of other museums, cloisters, and churches that are ready for you to explore. Something that is especially fun to do is to follow the town's watchman at 10:00 P.M. as he goes about his evening rounds through the streets, making sure that all is peaceful and in good order. Dressed in his traditional uniform, he tells stories about Ribe's history and points out places of interest. If you are staying at Hotel Dagmar on a Sunday night, there is a special 11:00 P.M. tour just for hotel guests.

Hotel Dagmar has not always been a hotel. The building was originally built by the town's mayor, Laurids Thøgersen, in 1581. After that, the wealthy Baggesen family lived there for part of the hotel's history. In the eighteenth century it became a residence for Ribe's grand mayors during the town's most prosperous economic period. From 1800 the house became known as Grejsen's Hotel. It wasn't until 1912, during a period of restoration, that it became the Hotel Dagmar.

From the moment you enter the hotel, you are aware of the sense of history that has been preserved in this building. Lovely paintings on the walls of the lobby and antique furniture provide the perfect atmosphere. The rooms have small windows and have managed to retain the feeling of "oldness" while still providing modern amenities such as hair dryers, televisions, and comfortable baths. I can recommend the two restaurants that are in the Hotel Dagmar. The main dining room is first class in every way. Just seeing it is a visual treat with its paintings, porcelain, small-paned windows, and large wooden liturgical sculpture. The kitchen is obviously run by very talented and experienced chefs. The traditional Danish food that I had the pleasure of enjoying was superb. The Vægterkælderen, in the hotel's cellar, is a more informal place where one can order from a children's menu.

Weis Stue

Weis Stue
Knud Nielsen
Torvet 2
DK-6760, Ribe
Telephone: 75 42 07 00
Rates: Single, 200 kr.; Double, 400 kr. **Restaurant:** Breakfast, lunch, and dinner are served in the inn's dining room.

Should the traveler to Ribe, one of Denmark's most charming and historical towns, want to stay within the shadow of the country's oldest cathedral in an inn from the sixteenth century at a bargain rate, then Weis Stue is an experience that you don't want to miss. It is simply a wonderful place to stay. Its half-timbered red facade slopes with age and inside one finds a 400-year-old grandfather clock, Dutch faience tiles, and a 700-year-old baptismal font. The wooden wall panels are decorated with various biblical motifs.

On the first floor you will find a typical Danish inn restaurant where you may have to duck down to enter the doors. The plaice fish we enjoyed there was superb, fresh from the waters of the west coast. You will be seated at a table where the chairs and benches, as well as a cupboard in one room that may be one of the oldest in the country (c. 1500), take you back to 1704 when the interior was almost exactly the way it is today. The name of the inn comes from one of the eighteenth-century owners, Anders Andersen Weis, who originally came from

Slesvig. In one way or another, it has existed as a place of lodging continuously since it was built in the sixteenth century.

There are only five guest rooms in Weis Stue, which only serves to contribute to its sense of original coziness. To get to the second floor where the rooms are located, one has to climb a rather steep ladder-type staircase that is known as the "chicken stairs." With the help of a rope attached to the wall, it is possible to experience what it was like for travelers several hundred years ago. There is one double room facing the square where the cathedral is located that I recommend. Its low ceiling, wood paneling, small windows, and antique beds take the guest to another era. There is one large bath shared by the guests, but the inn is so charming that a private bath is hardly missed. In fact, one might even feel less a part of the historic atmosphere if it were any other way.

The rooms on the opposite side look down on a courtyard at the back of the building. In any room, however, you will be able to enjoy the glorious bells coming from the cathedral's tower. When one considers that the cathedral was the center of town life when it was built in the twelfth century, then the location of Weis Stue could not be more authentic. Ribe is a town to be explored on foot while visiting the fine museum collections and the medieval cloister of St. Katharinæ and its church. You should climb to the top of the tower of the cathedral to see the breathtaking view of Jutland's west coast, or just look for the storks who return to Ribe in the summer and build their nests atop the many old buildings. Weis Stue gives you the luxury of being a participant in this old town's history.

SEVEL

Sevel Kro

Sevel Kro
Ruth and Hans Kurt Nielsen
Sevel
7830 Vinderup
Telephone: 97 44 80 11
Rates: Single, 200 kr.; Double, 400 kr. **Restaurant:** Breakfast, lunch, and dinner are served in the dining room. Breakfast is 40 kr. extra.

As with so many of the traditional Danish inns, Sevel Kro is located between the village church and the old grocery store, a remnant of the days when this was the center of all local activity. The surrounding area is very ancient with reminders of the prehistoric period in the form of Bronze Age burial mounds. There was originally a medieval cloister for Benedictine nuns nearby that served as the first place here to take in overnight guests. The history of the inn goes back to a building, Bakkehuset, known to have been on the same site and first mentioned in 1662. It sat next to an important road that connected Holstebro to Skive in the area of Lim Fjord in northern Jutland. It was already a royal privileged inn in 1771, although the oldest official privilege was awarded to judge and prefect Niels Sehested in 1801. This royal privilege allowed him to brew beer and serve it to travelers, an activity carefully guarded by the crown.

The inn burned to the ground in 1838 but was rebuilt under the name of Sevel Kro. The most famous of the inn's owners, Mads Christian Hansen, took over in 1927. His hospitality and reputation as an innkeeper were so well known that the inn now maintains the *Mads Hansens Stue* (Mads Hansen's Room), where the guest can read about that particular part of the inn's history and the host who made that period so significant. He was known to go out onto the front step of the inn in his wooden shoes to greet the guests personally. He always insisted upon peeling the potatoes himself and it was only when there were more than 100 guests that his daughter was called in to help. Eight years ago the inn experienced another major fire, but it was rebuilt in its original style. There are now 10 guest rooms in a lovely, simple country style, all with private baths. Ruth and Hans Kurt Nielsen have worked hard to keep up the old inn tradition of fine food, using, for example, old recipes such as the one for beer spareribs. Only the best ingredients are used, including a special beef from Limousin cattle.

SILKEBORG

Kongensbro Kro
Hanne and Ole Andersen
Gl. Kongevej 70, Kongensbro
8643 Ans By
Telephone: 86 87 01 77; **FAX:** 86 87 92 17
Rates: Single, 450 to 590 kr.; Double, 575 to 740 kr.; Half and full board available. **Restaurants:** Breakfast, lunch, and dinner are served; Danish and Continental cuisine are offered. This inn is a member of Dansk Kroferie.

My cousin's husband, who is quite a gourmet, told us that this inn was known for its wonderful food. What we discovered was not only some of the best cuisine around Silkeborg (they serve fresh pike caught in the river 100 feet away) but also one of the loveliest locations and some of the friendliest people. Their slogan, "Peace . . . nice cooking and the atmosphere of come again," is very apropos. Although the inn is located in Ans, it is only a 15-minute drive from Silkeborg and we recommend it as an ideal location if you want to explore the many wonderful things to see and do in Silkeborg.

The name Kongensbro, or King's Bridge, reportedly came about when the king's carriage was trying to ford the Gudenåen River (Jutland's longest) and overturned, giving His Majesty a royal dunking. As a result, he commissioned the building of a bridge, now located right next to the inn. The history of the inn goes back to 1663, when King Frederik III gave a member of the local nobility, Ebbe Gyldenstierne, royal permission to offer refreshments and rooms to travelers.

During the nineteeenth century and up until 1920, barges traveled up and down the Gudenåen River, with freight such as the bricks made in Silkeborg. The inn provided a place where the barge workers could eat and spend the night. In the beginning, men actually pulled the barges and, later, horses took over the hard labor. The path worn by the horses next to the river still exists today and the hiker can follow it from the inn all the way to Silkeborg. We took a shorter walk during twilight and were rewarded with views of the peaceful river, winter woods, and pleasant farms. A boat is available from the inn if you should choose to explore by water. There is also a playground for children, a fact that pleased my daughter.

The original eighteenth-century inn almost completely burned down and was rebuilt with the help of the Marshall Plan after World War II. After the inn was restored, the Tourist Association of Jutland decided that an old inn should be created that would serve as a model for other innkeepers wishing to study the "old inn culture." To accomplish this, Else and Hans Andersen were asked to serve as the managers. They did this for 40 years, eventually owning it. Since 1984 their son and daughter-in-law, Hanne and Ole Andersen, have been the second generation to run this fine inn. Ole is the very talented head chef who is responsible for the inn becoming a member of the Confrerie de la Chaine des Rotisseurs.

Svostrup Kro

Svostrup Kro
Niels Løgager Nielsen
Svostrup, DK-8600 Silkeborg
Telephone: 86 87 70 04; **FAX:** 86 87 70 47
Rates: Single without bath, 320 kr.; Single with Bath, 520 kr.; Double without bath, 420 kr.; Double with bath, 680 kr.; Bridal Suite, 780 kr.;

Suites, 680 to 1,800 kr.; Special weekend rates. **Restaurant:** Breakfast, lunch, and dinner are served in the dining room.

Svostrup Kro is situated next to the Gudenå River where the old barges, pulled by men, traveled on their way to and from Silkeborg. These traders used the inn for meals and lodging as they traveled along. The still-existing towpath provides a wonderful walk along the river with the Gjern Hills in the background. Even before the inn received its royal privilege in 1834, there was mention of a small farm on this spot as far back as 1784. Although it was not officially an inn, the establishment served snaps to travelers stopping there. In 1809 the inn was sold by Capt. Erik Muller, owner of two estates, Grauballegaard and Mollerup. According to the royal privilege, "In 1834 the inn is given its first license, in which Søren Bull is allowed to keep an inn and provide the travellers with food, drink, and necessary lodgings for a reasonable payment against paying to the king an annual fee of three 'rigsdaler in silver.'" This was at the same time that the ferry received permission to travel here. For that reason, a two-story warehouse and a grocery store were built. Today you can still see the decorations painted on the ceiling of the grocery that were done in exchange for a night's lodging and food.

You now enter the inn's cobblestoned courtyard through a gate connected to the quadrangular, thatched-roof white buildings. Outside the inn is a large garden with a playground for children, always a consideration in Denmark. The inside looks exactly as you would imagine an eighteenth-century inn to appear. Low-beamed ceilings and half-timbered walls are filled with wonderful antiques and paintings. It is as cozy and welcoming as it must have been one hundred years ago. The specialty of the house is fresh fish, as well as traditional Danish inn fare. An excellent wine cellar is available.

SKAGEN

Brøndums Hotel

Brøndums Hotel
Knud Voss
Anchersvej 3
DK-9990 Skagen
Telephone: 98 44 15 55; **FAX:** 98 45 15 20
Rates: Single, 410 to 500 kr.; Double, 695 to 895 kr.; Extra bed, 150
kr. **Restaurant:** Breakfast, lunch, and dinner are served in the hotel
dining room. There is a wine cellar.

The first hotel on this spot was built by Erik Brøndum, a merchant
and landlord, in 1840. It was a well-known destination for famous
guests such as Hans Christian Andersen. It unfortunately burned to the
ground 30 years later and a new building of gray bricks was constructed.
In 1890 the Danish architect Ulrik Plesner came to Skagen to inspect the
lighthouse and was persuaded to design an extension to the hotel. As
the hotel grew, Plesner continued as the architect, giving a consistency
to the overall design. In 1906 a very well known architect, Thorvald
Bindesbøll, was asked to design a dining room that would feature the
family's collection of paintings. Skagen was home to a very special
group of painters in the nineteenth century who came to this place
because of the special light. The Brøndum family was connected to
these painters and a picture gallery of their works was spotlighted by the
hotel in Bindesbøll's unique display. At one point, the Skagen Museum
and the hotel were run as one entity. Today the museum is separate
but you can still see the paintings, which have now been removed from
the hotel and are part of the museum's permanent collection.

Skagen is a unique place where the waters of the Skagerak and the Kattegat meet at the point land ends. There is also a famous church that is almost completely covered with sand. Only the tower remains above ground despite repeated efforts to dig it out. The winds of northern Jutland can be harsh and the sand has remained the constant enemy of this deserted church. On a sunny summer day, it is a pleasure to sit outside the hotel under an umbrella for an alfresco meal at the hotel. The hotel's kitchen prepares classic Danish dishes, some of which have been named after the Skagen painters. Cuisine with a French touch is also available.

SKANDERBORG

Sophiendal Gods

Sophiendal Gods
Ann Vibeke and Gorm Lokdam
Låsbyvej 82, Veng
DK-8660 Skanderborg
Telephone: 86 94 47 88; **FAX:** 86 94 48 10
Rates: Single, 650 kr; Double, 775 to 975 kr.; Special weekend and castle packages. **Restaurant:** The manor house dining room serves breakfast and dinner. This manor house is a member of Danish Heritage Castles and Manor Houses.

In Danish, the word "gods" means a large estate that consists of a manor house as well as working land that is farmed or has forests. This is also true of Sophiendal Gods, which has 750 hectares of land to raise Angus beef cattle and various crops. Located between Veng Sø and the Knudå River, one can actually see Himmelbjerget, the highest hill in the country, from the manor house's tower.

This particular place has a history going back to the eleventh century when a Benedictine monastery, Veng Abbey, was built. The monks from there also built other monasteries and also produced the famous *munkesten* (monk bricks) that were also used to build the cellar of Sophiendal Gods.

Baron Col. Gottlob Rosenkrantz, who is also associated with Rosenholm Castle, built the Renaissance-style house in the 1870s. The architect was the Dane H. B. Storck. In the beginning, it was divided into three sections, each for a different family. With two wings stretching out on each side of the main entrance to embrace the visitor, the red-brick building has a quiet dignity. There are now 23 rooms, each with a canopied bed, and the Baron's Bedroom is worthy of the most distinguished guest. The a la carte restaurant uses the freshest ingredients available with each season and serves the Angus beef raised on the estate. Each Saturday, the wine cellar is open from noon to 4:00 P.M. to taste special Rumanian wine. There is also a boutique that sells the wine and other crafts and decorative art objects.

THYHOLM

Tambohus Kro

Tambohus Kro
Inger-Lisse and Steen Rysgaard
7790 Thyholm
Telephone: 97 87 53 00; **FAX:** 97 87 51 55
Rates: Single, 465 kr.; Double, 650 kr. **Restaurant:** Breakfast, lunch, and dinner are served in the dining room.

As the legend goes, the island of Jegindø was created when some trolls began to throw rocks and earth at the Søndbjerg Church. They must have thrown quite a few because the island, located in the western part of the Lim Fjord, is now 6 kilometers long and 3 kilometers wide. It is a peaceful place with only 540 inhabitants, most of whom are involved in either agriculture or fishing. Tambohus Kro sits on the mainland and looks over the fjord toward the island of Jegindø and it is because of the island that the inn exists.

Chresten Pedersen was a fisherman who had been a drummer in the army. Because of this, he became known as Chresten Tambour, Chresten the Drummer. In 1830 he rescued a woman from drowning and, as a reward, was given a license by the king to run the ferryboat over to the island. This was not the end of his acts of heroism. In order to capture a gang of local criminals, he became an undercover member of the gang and helped to trap them for the authorities. Again he was rewarded by the crown, this time with permission to open an inn in 1842 under the name Tambohus. Niels Lund Pedersen and his wife, Ane, took over at the end of the nineteenth century and Mrs. Pedersen continued to run the inn even after she became a widow. The local grocer, Håkon Rysgaard, bought the inn in 1947 and it is his son and daughter-in-law, Inger-Lisse and Steen Rysgaard, who own the inn today. There is no longer a necessity to take a ferry to the island since a causeway was built in 1915.

Thyholm, where the inn is located, is a beautiful peninsula two hours by car from Aalborg. The train stops just five minutes from the inn. For walking and bicycling or swimming and windsurfing, it is a paradise, and the inn can help by loaning the guest a bicycle, fishing rod, or rowboat. The beauty of Jegendø Island is that there is almost nothing there, just a church, a couple of shops, a bank, and some houses. The beauty of the winter months with their storms rivals the wonderful summer with its beaches and meadows filled with wildflowers and birds. The modern guest rooms are in a newer annex to the original inn and all have private baths, telephones, and radios.

TYLSTRUP

Gammel Vraa Slot

Gammel Vraa Slot
Tylstrup, 9382 Tylstrup
Telephone: 98 26 13 77
Rates: Overnight accommodation, afternoon coffee with pastry, a three-course dinner with aperitif and hors d'oeuvre, and breakfast, 700 kr. per person; Weekend stay with the same meals, 645 kr. per person. **Restaurant:** Breakfast and dinner are served in the castle's dining room. This castle is a member of Danish Heritage Castles and Manor Houses.

Situated in northern Jutland just 17 kilometers north of Aalborg is Gammel Vraa Slott (Old Vraa Castle). The white main building with the red-tile roof is flanked on both sides by two half-timbered wings and is reached by crossing a moat. Set amid forests and fields, it traces its history back to the fifteenth century. At that time it was just a poor cottage, lived in by a widow. It did actually become a castle and was lived in first by Predbjørn Gyldenstjerne from 1500 to 1524. Count Rodsten and generations of his family that followed produced the family crest that can still be seen in the throne room of the castle.

Inscriptions from the same family can also be seen on the pulpit and altar of the local church, Aistrup Church. Count Holck built the wings of the castle as we see them today. In the main building, under the ceiling, there is inscribed the names of Count Holck and his wife, Marianne Trappauds, and the year 1779. The bridal suite is named after Count Holck and the original fireplace in that room is still in working order.

A legend concerning a naval officer, Jørgen Bille, tells of how his ghost came galloping into the castle each night in a carriage pulled by headless horses. They tried everything they could to get rid of the ghost but to no avail. The story says that he was looking for a red jacket that he had loved to wear. In order to calm the ghost down, the jacket was placed on his grave one night and he was never heard from again. Of course, you may be brave enough to spend the night in the "Ghost's Room" with its canopied bed.

The oldest part of the castle that still exists is the cellar, used today as a small dining room. The castle has been beautifully restored and stands in perfect condition with elegant rooms and furnishings. The dining and reception rooms look exactly as one would imagine a castle should look. High ceilings, surface carving and moldings on the walls, porcelain stoves, and chandeliers are but some of the details that delight the eye. One may use the indoor or outdoor swimming pools, sauna, solarium, or billiards room, or enjoy a round of golf at a nearby course. The surrounding countryside is perfect for riding or walking. The head chef is a member of the prestigious EURO-TOQUES, an association of European chefs.

ØSTBIRK

Sandvad Kro

Sandvad Kro
Kongevej 25
8752 Østbirk
Telephone: 75 78 17 50
Restaurant: This old inn is now only a restaurant. The more informal bar and "inn room" opens at 4:00 P.M. and the restaurant with more formal dining opens for dinner at 5:00 P.M.

Placed in the middle of some of Jutland's loveliest scenery, near the Gudenå River with its wonderful fishing opportunities, is this typically Danish inn where the locals go for their special meals and parties. The cheerful yellow building that is now Sandvad Kro was originally built by Ivar and Birthe Hansen in 1865. Their initials are still clearly visible on the middle portion of the facade, right next to the year of its origin. Unfortunately, it was only a year after its construction that the inn burned and had to be rebuilt, this time on the other side of the road. It was King Frederik II who planned this road through the Mattrup Forest and gave an earlier inn on this spot its royal privilege in 1730. The main dining room has its original dark-wood beams and an open fireplace. During the summer months, the inn also serves meals on its outdoor terrace. The food is typical Danish inn fare with main dishes such as roast pork with caramelized potatoes, soups, smoked trout, and homemade ice cream. The prices are very reasonable.

ÅRHUS

Hotel Royal

Hotel Royal
Niels Heede, manager
Store Torv 4
DK-8100 Århus
Telephone: 86 12 00 11; **FAX:** 86 76 04 04
Rates: Single, 1,145 kr.; Double, 1,295 kr. **Restaurant:** Buffet breakfast, lunch, and dinner are served in the Queens Garden Restaurant.

Royal was the first hotel to open in Århus 153 years ago, the result of better roads and ferry and railroad service bringing more travelers to this east Jutland city. Two neighboring buildings, one called the "King's Manor," were purchased by Niels Larsen with the intention of catering to the "well-to-do visitors." By the time the hotel was put up for sale in 1846, it had an inventory that included a stable for 40 horses and 34 cows, as well as a carriagehouse. But, instead of its being sold, the Larsen family expanded the hotel into three stories with room for "major social gatherings." Just a short two years later, in 1849, the Germans invaded the hotel and used it as their headquarters. The same thing happened again in 1864 and from 1940 to 1945. An early guest in the hotel, Johanne Heiberg (1812-90) described how her night's stay was disturbed by "street peddlers, the smith, cursings and screamings, carriages, poultry, and mice behind the wallpaper," although she had to admit that the food was extremely good.

The hotel as it appears today is from 1903 and 1913. It is a large hotel with 106 rooms, all with private baths, televisions, videos, and minibars. The rooms in the "Royal de Luxe" category all overlook the town squares and are elegantly furnished with lovely furniture, fabrics, and original artworks, not to mention fax machines for the business traveler. The stately white facade with its pilasters, tiled roof with balustrade, and twin towers presents an impressive exterior.

The hotel has also had a long tradition of providing good entertainment. Danmarks Radio (the Danish Broadcasting Corporation) brought weekly programs from the Hotel Royal with performances of its jazz orchestra. There were also floor shows with every type of entertainment from ballet and magicians to floor-show revues and dance music. Today the Hotel Royal continues to provide its guests and other visitors with entertainment in one of the most beautiful casinos in Europe. Sixteen artists from different European countries were commissioned for the paintings and interior of the casino, creating a special atmosphere where formal attire is required.

NORWAY

Oslo

NORWAY

Oslo

Oslo

Frogner House Hotel

Frogner House Hotel
Skovveien 8
0257 Oslo
Telephone: 22 56 00 56; **FAX:** 22 56 05 00
Rates: Single, 680 to 1,080 kr.; Double, 880 to 1,380; Demi-suites, 1,300 to 1,595 kr.; Extra Bed, 220 kr.; Children under age 10 staying in their parents' room are free. **Restaurant:** Breakfast only is served in the hotel's breakfast room. Room service is available.

Frogner House Hotel is located in Oslo's West End, just behind the Royal Palace. It's an easy ten-minute walk to the center of town (the main street of Karl Johansgate and the harbor) and the hotel itself is in an area of galleries and nice shops. Although the hotel only serves breakfast, there are a number of fine restaurants in the immediate vicinity, including the elegant restaurant Bagatelle. Only a few minutes away is Aker Brygge, a complex of popular restaurants and wine bars.

Run entirely by women (except for a few night porters, as pointed out by the female staff), this hotel caters to those who want a smaller, more intimate hotel. The friendly and personal service has gained its owners an excellent reputation for providing a homey, helpful atmosphere. Although the hotel is a handsome corner building from Oslo's past, with ornamented windows, some with balconies, it has functioned as a hotel only since 1992. An elegant art nouveau staircase

179

leads the guest up to the second floor. Furnishings are traditional from the lobby to the guest rooms, all of which have private baths with heated floors, televisions with cable channels, minibars, trouser presses, and hair dryers. High ceilings and tall floor-to-ceiling windows give the rooms an old-world elegance.

Grand Hotel

Grand Hotel
Jan E. Rivelsrud, managing director
Karl Johansgate 31
Postboks 346 Sentrum
N-0101 Oslo
Telephone: 22 42 93 90; **FAX:** 22 42 12 25
Rates: Single, 850 to 1,520 kr.; Double, 1,090 to 1,670 kr.; Suites, 2,050 to 5,900 kr., Extra bed, 250 kr. **Restaurant:** There are three restaurants serving breakfast, lunch, and dinner with Norwegian and International cuisine. The Grand Cafe serves Norway's largest buffet; the Julius Fritzner Restaurant is an intimate restaurant from 1874; and Palmen Restaurant serves meals or just a cup of afternoon tea. There are two bars: Limelight is off the lobby and Etoile Bar serves sandwiches, pastries, and drinks and offers a wonderful view of Oslo. The Bonanza Nightclub offers live music on weekends.

When I was a university student in Oslo, one of my favorite places to go was the Grand Cafe on the street level of the Grand Hotel. I would always make a special point of sitting at the table that was once the spot where the famous Norwegian playwright Henrik Ibsen sat. Even today, his chair with the sign saying "reserved for Dr. Ibsen" stands in the cafe. One of Edvard Munch's 1902 lithographs, entitled *Henrik Ibsen in Grand Café*, shows the playwright seated at a table behind a dark curtain while people walk in the rain outside the window. During my own many visits to the hotel I often looked across the room toward the massive mural by Per Krohg that occupies the entire wall. I tried to imagine what it would have been like to have seen Oslo's well-known personalities from the 1890s parading in and out of the restaurant. The painting depicts many of those who frequented the cafe and were famous in the cultural and literary circles of Oslo. Among those in the painting are poet and playwright Bjørnstjerne Bjørnson; artists Fritz Thaulow, Christian Krohg, and Edvard Munch; and actors Milly and Ludvig Bergh. The painter Edvard Munch was poor in those days and often exchanged paintings for meals. It was in the Grand Cafe that Edvard Munch spent time with author Hans Jæger the day before he was sent to prison.

Even today, all of Oslo seems to pass by outside on Oslo's major boulevard, Karl Johansgate, but it is the atmosphere inside the Grand Cafe that is so unique. The wood paneling, high ceilings, and famous caryatids all contribute to a wonderful atmosphere of nineteenth-century Oslo. In my student days I could not afford the sumptuous buffet lunches offered to diners here but they must certainly be an experience. The table of culinary delights seems to go on forever and the hotel's own bakery is responsible for the extravagant desserts.

The Grand Hotel is an institution in Oslo. It is where the Nobel Peace Prize celebration is held each year and there is a special Nobel Suite where the recipient stays, stepping out onto the balcony to receive his or her congratulations. The location of the hotel is superb, right on the main street leading up to the royal residence and near the Parliament, Royal Theater, University of Oslo, National Gallery, and many of the great shops and restaurants in the capital. Almost everything in downtown Oslo is within walking distance of the hotel and the subway station is almost just across the street. The hotel opened in 1874 during the time when Oslo was called Kristiania. A baker of fine pastries, Julius Fritzner, bought the former private residence of Professor Christian Heiberg and turned the building into this wonderful hotel. The Grand Hotel underwent a major restoration just a couple of years ago but the guest rooms have maintained their traditional comfort and atmosphere. In this full-service hotel, guests can take advantage of a swimming pool, fitness center, sauna, solarium, and massage.

Holmenkollen Park Hotel Rica

Holmenkollen Park Hotel Rica
The Høegh family
Kongeveien 26
N-0390 Oslo
Telephone: 22 92 20 00; **FAX:** 22 14 61 92
Rates: Single, 845 to 1,745 kr.; Double, 990 to 1,845 kr.; Suites, 2,500 to 10,000 kr. **Restaurants:** There are two restaurants, including *De Fem Stuer* (the Five Rooms) serving Norwegian and French cuisine. There is a coffee shop, bar, and lounge.

Dr. I. C. Holm, a physician in Oslo who treated tuberculosis patients, started this hotel in the last half of the nineteenth century. He hired architect Baltazar Lange in 1894 to design a sanitorium where one could recuperate in a restful environment where clean air and water were in abundance. It was built in the then-popular "dragon style" with its gingerbread carvings, balconies, and towers. Although much of this original building burned in 1904, part of it has been preserved and is the location of the hotel's restaurant. The new Holmenkollen Turisthotell was occupied by the Germans during World War II and was renovated at the end of the war. When the World Skiing Championship was held in Oslo in 1982, an expansion of the hotel that included 4 new wings was built to accommodate the visiting athletes. During all of the building, the original stylistic integrity has been maintained.

The walls of part of the public areas are made of logs and the open wooden staircase is a masterpiece in carving. Throughout the large hall are carved wooden panels depicting the Norse saga of Sigurd the Dragon Killer. There are also 100-year-old tapestries from the designs of Gerhard Munthe, ceramic reliefs, and paintings of traditional Norwegian life from the nineteenth century. The intertwining dragon tails so prevalent in Viking art seem to be everywhere, including unexpected places such as mirror frames. Many large windows allow the guests a good view of the breathtaking scenery surrounding the hotel.

Situated 350 meters above Oslo, the hotel must certainly be the best location for enjoying nature around the city and yet still have the convenience of being only 15 minutes from the center of town or the Fornebu Airport. Just in back of the hotel is the famous Holmenkollen Ski Jump (where you will also find the Ski Museum), which seems to have inspired the theme for many of the rooms; the guest rooms are named after famous Norwegian skiers. Other famous Norwegians such as Sonia Heine the skater, Roald Amundsen the explorer, and Gustav Vigeland the sculptor have also given their names to guest rooms. You will find historic photographs of them in the rooms.

It is easy to get from the hotel to downtown via the free shuttle service. The hotel has a Swim and Trim department with swimming pool, sauna, and Jacuzzi. If you prefer walking, there are numerous hiking and skiing paths all around the area. Different types of sports and entertainment can be arranged by the hotel, including an evening on a medieval farm, sledding and canoeing, and shopping tours. Each guest room has cable television with video and in-house movies, fax and computer outlets, air conditioning, and hair dryers. There are also nonsmoking rooms available.

Hotel Bristol

Hotel Bristol
Øivind Larstorp, manager
Kristian IV's gate 7, P.O. Box 6764
St. Olavplsss, 0130 Oslo
Telephone: 22 82 60 00; **FAX:** 22 82 60 01; **E-mail:** bristol@sn.no
Rates: Single, 675 to 1,450 kr.; Double, 890 to 1,675 kr.; Chldren from
ages 5 to 15 may stay in a parent's room for 50 kr. per child; Special
Easter, Christmas, and summer rates. **Restaurants:** Breakfast, lunch,
and dinner are served in various hotel dining rooms. Winter Garden
serves coffee, tea, and pastries. There are also the Bristol Lounge,
library bar, and Bristol Night Spot. Bristol Grill is the hotel's main
restaurant. This hotel is a member of Nordisk Hotellpass and Inter
Nor Hotels.

The president of Norway's Parliament and his wife lived in a suite
on the fifth floor of Hotel Bristol for 18 years. Another frequent guest
during the years was Prince Axel of Denmark. The bridal suite, with
one of the most beautiful antique beds I have ever seen, is named after
Josephine Baker, another resident. The hotel opened its doors in 1920
and soon became the meeting place for Oslo's high society. The more
well-to-do matrons of the city liked to meet here for their afternoon
pastries and tea. Now one is more apt to meet Norwegian business-
people, politicians, and members of Norway's contemporary cultural
and artistic world.

The wood-paneled, book-lined library bar with leather furniture is one of the cozier spots, while the impressive high-ceilinged lobby with its chandeliers, grand arches, live piano music, and palm trees is appropriate for any meeting. The location of the hotel, just one block off of Karl Johansgate, is perfect. You can get to almost any place in downtown Oslo on foot, and the National Gallery is almost right next door. With only 141 rooms, the Bristol is not one of Oslo's really large hotels, a fact that is to its advantage. There is a more intimate atmosphere to the hotel, giving the guest a more comfortable feeling. The rooms are traditional in design and there are 62 smokefree rooms you can request. All have minibars, private baths, cable television with videocassette players, and hair dryers. There is free valet parking; you can just leave your keys at the reception desk and decide when you will need your car brought to the front of the hotel.

Hotel Continental

Hotel Continental
Ellen Brochmann, owner; Lars Christian Krog, director of operations
Stortingsgaten 24/26, Postboks 1510 Vika
0117 Oslo
Telephone: 22 82 40 00; **FAX:** 22 42 96 89
Rates: Single, 820 to 1,585 kr.; Double, 1,090 to 1,730 kr.; Deluxe
room, 1,300 to 1,985 kr.; Suites, 2,250 to 7,000 kr.; Extra bed, 175 kr., a
cot is free of charge. **Restaurants:** Theatercafeen (Theater Cafe),
Dagligstuen (Lobby Bar), Steamen (Jazz Bar), and LIPP Bar. This
hotel is a member of Leading Hotels of the World.

The Hotel Continental has always been tied by tradition to the
National Theater—located across the street—to the point that it has
been said, "First came the theatre and then the inn." The hotel's Theater
Cafe, has always been a traditional stop for those coming to the city to
attend the theater. It is a particularly elegant crowd that I remember
seeing when I was a diner in the cafe.

The hotel's history began in 1860 when Caroline Bowman
migrated from Sweden to Oslo. She had come from an extremely
poor background and had vowed: "I just will not die poor or in a
hospital or in an old people's home." Her fear of living her life out
in poverty seems to have been the motivating factor behind her rise
to success in the hotel business. She began as a cook at the Grand
Hotel, where she met her husband, then a waiter. Together, they
rented a building owned by a brewery and started Hotel Continental.
Three years later, they bought the building and were well on their way

to establishing the extraordinary hotel that is here today. Her husband died and Caroline continued to run the Hotel Continental.

Problems arose when her waiters formed a union and she felt compelled to ask her son, Arne, to return to Norway from the United States, where he had completed his education at Harvard. Arne returned to Norway with his American wife and daughter and took over the management of the hotel, expanding it into the two neighboring buildings. When Arne died, his daughter Ellen and her husband took over the hotel and continued its expansion, which now occupies one city block in downtown Oslo.

Although the hotel is located on the busy street leading one way to the Parliament and the other to the Royal Palace, it is an oasis of elegance and sophistication. The style of the hotel was best described by a patron who said, "The Continental, although making allowance for modern trends, still caters especially to guests who luxuriate among leather and velvet and oil paintings." From its sedate, English-style lobby to its large, private collection of lithographs by Edvard Munch, it is first class all the way.

The guest rooms are beautifully decorated with dark-wood furniture in traditional English styles, rich fabrics, and lovely artwork. The baths have an old-fashioned look while, at the same time, being modern in their facilities.

The Theater Cafe looks like a Viennese restaurant from the turn of the century. The ceiling is painted with garlands on either side of the chandeliers and the wood paneling is painted a warm green accented with gold. It is definitely a place out of another era, one perfect for an elegant dinner before the play at the theater begins.

Lysebu

Lysebu
Lysebuveien 12
Postboks 109 Holmenkollen
N-0324 Oslo
Telephone: 22 14 23 90; **FAX:** 22 49 43 06
Rates: Single, 800 to 1,300 kr.; Double, 500 to 1,050 kr. per person;
Breakfast, 70 kr. extra. **Restaurant:** Breakfast, lunch, and dinner are
served in the dining room.

Lysebu, a remarkable place, was organized by *Fondet for dansk-norsk samarbeid* (Foundation for Danish-Norwegian Cooperation). It was built as a center where Danes and Norwegians could come together to meet, get to know each other, and learn more about each other's countries. The whole foundation was started because the Danes had done so much to help the Norwegians during World War II. This conference and course center/hotel was begun as a meeting place where friendships and understanding between the two countries could develop. Even the hotel dining room serves both Danish and Norwegian dishes. For those travelers who just want a beautiful place to stay in Oslo, Lysebu provides a perfect alternative to the downtown hotel.

Lysebu, originally built as a private residence in 1918, is situated just 8 kilometers from the middle of Oslo. From its dark-wood buildings in traditional Norwegian style, one can see far over the surrounding forests and hills. The original building, occupied by the Nazis in the 1940s and then bought by Carl and Borghild Hammerich who began the foundation, was expanded according to the designs of architect Magnus Poulsson. Later in the 1960s, Poulsson's son, Anton, also an architect, was called in to design yet another wing. Keeping with tradition, a third generation of the Poulsson architects was invited to design a further addition in the 1980s. It is now a friendly and welcoming place where one is just as apt to encounter a bridal couple at their wedding dinner as one is to meet participants in a conference. The interior is decorated in a traditional manner with many original works of art such as the three Lysebu Tapestries designed by Kristin Lindberg.

Trugstad Gård

Trugstad Gård

Tove and Martin Haga
2034 Holter
Telephone: 63 99 58 90; **FAX:** 63 99 50 87
Rates: Single, 350 to 430 kr.; Double, 700 kr.; Suite, 1,100 kr.
Restaurant: Breakfast is an additional 55 to 95 kr. Lunch and dinner are served in the inn's dining room. The inn is open to overnight guests from May to October.

When you arrive at Trugstad Gård, Tove and her husband, Martin, will greet you at the door, an indication of the owners' personal approach to their guests. They must be doing something very right because more than five thousand guests from 25 countries have come to this hotel just 40 minutes from Oslo. The fact that Tove has been the recipient for the past three years of the coveted "Wild Game Cook of the Year" award in Norway is an indication of the quality of cuisine served in the dining room. All of the inn's food is prepared solely by Tove and everything is made from scratch using the freshest ingredients possible. Dishes of wild reindeer and duck are always found on the menu and luscious, calorie-ridden cakes are another of Tove's specialties. Her cooking is so famous that she has written a gorgeous cookbook, *Smaksopplevelser fra Trugstad Gård (Taste Experiences from Trugstad Farm),* and her cooking courses at the inn are very popular. The inn is also a participant in the European Society of Happy Cooking, which offers courses around Europe.

The kitchen in which Tove prepares the meals is more than 250 years old. Guests are always welcome there. The only thing she will not prepare is chicken. This may be due to the fact that she has a collection of more than 135 of the little critters in porcelain, glass, and other materials displayed all around the inn. After dinner, another type of collection, that of 150 liquor glasses, including one 400 years old, is used for the guests. The cabinet is opened and the guest may choose any glass he or she would like to use for a cognac or liquor. Documents show that this property was lived on and farmed 1,000 years ago. By the fifteenth century, the cathedral in Oslo owned the land and it later became the home of the Head Master of Oslo Cathedral School. In 1536 it was once again a farm. Eventually it was bought by Martin's great-grandfather in 1850. The main building still has a portion of the structure from the eighteenth century. This building has old pine walls and a fireplace, which are in the old country style of this region. Two *stabbur* (farm storage buildings built off the ground) house guest rooms for up to 10 people, with modern baths and a little kitchen. Many bridal couples have rented the whole stabbur as a bridal suite. The inn also has a boutique where typical Norwegian crafts, together with baked goods, are available for sale. This working farm—not too far from Gardermoen Airport—is close enough to Oslo to offer easy access to the city and yet provide a typical rural Norwegian experience in a beautiful natural setting.

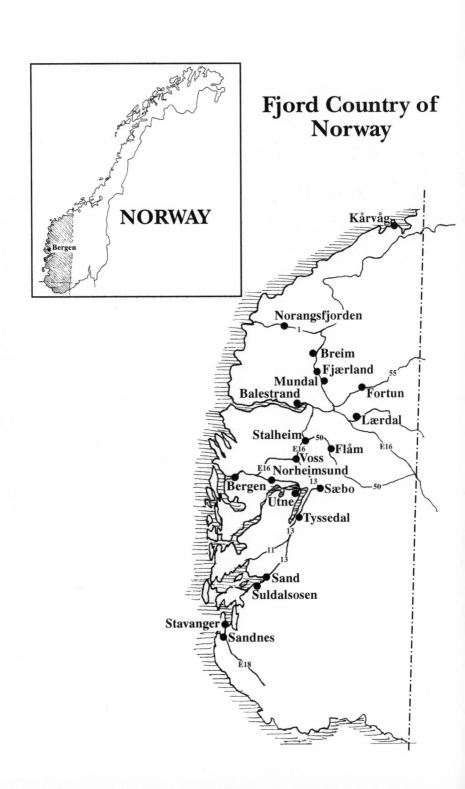

Fjord Country of
Norway

NORWAY

Bergen

Kårvåg

Norangsfjorden
1

Breim
Fjærland
55
Mundal
Balestrand
Fortun

Lærdal

Stalheim 50
E16 Flåm E16
Voss
E16 Norheimsund
13
Bergen Sæbo 50
Utne
Tyssedal
13

11
13

Sand
Suldalsosen

Stavanger
Sandnes

E18

Fjord Country of Norway

BALESTRAND

Kvikne's Hotel

Kvikne's Hotel
Mulla Kvikne
Balholm
N-5850 Balestrand
Telephone: 57 69 11 01; **FAX:** 57 69 15 02
Rates: Double, per person, 349 to 495 kr.; Half board per person, 510 to 665 kr.; Single supplement, 170 kr.; there is an extra supplement for fjord view. **Restaurant:** The hotel dining room serves breakfast, lunch, and dinner. This hotel is a member of De Historiske Hotel.

The history of Kvikne's Hotel goes all the way back to 1752, when a small place of lodging and a grocery were known to have existed at Balholm. In 1867 an 18-year-old boy, Ole Andersen Kvigne, came looking for a job. Since the transportation on the fjord was helping to bring more visitors to the town and the business was improving, the innkeeper agreed to educate Ole in the art of innkeeping. He eventually bought the business and he wanted to expand it to meet the increasing demand for a good hotel, but he did not have the capital to do so. At about the same time, a letter arrived from his brother, Knut, in America. Knut had saved quite a lot of money and was willing to return to Norway to become a partner with his brother. By this time, his name had been changed from Kvigne to Kvikne, on the theory that Americans could pronounce the latter more easily. This is how the current hotel's name came about.

After several successful years, the architect Franz Wilhelm Schiertz, a student of the famous Norwegian painter J. C. Dahl, was commissioned to design a large hotel building. At the turn of the century, German Kaiser Wilhelm II developed a fondness for Kvikne's Hotel. When he visited the area, he was escorted down the fjord by a German naval flotilla. On one visit, he actually saved the hotel when a disastrous fire broke out in a nearby shop. He was standing on the other side of the fjord and was one of the first to see it. He boarded one of his boats and quickly instructed the crew to use the ship's hoses to put out the blaze. The largest part of the Swiss-style hotel building you see today, with decorated balconies and turrets, was, for the most part, constructed in 1912. It is now the largest fjord hotel in Norway.

The interior of the hotel houses a number of beautiful antiques and paintings by Norwegian artists. One room, Høiviksalen, is completely decorated with wooden furniture and wall-surface ornamentation carved in the dragon style, which originated from the patterns found in the Viking art of the Middle Ages. Together with tapestries and paintings in this room, it gives the visitor an exceptional glimpse into the rich decorating tradition of the early part of this century. There are two sections of guest rooms, one in the original part of the building and one in a newer addition. If you want to experience the more traditional atmosphere of the hotel, you may want to request one of the older rooms.

BERGEN

Grand Hotel Terminus

Grand Hotel Terminus
Narve Johansen, manager
Zander Kaaesgate 6
5001 Bergen
Telephone: 55 31 16 55; **FAX:** 55 31 85 76
Rates: Single, 895 kr.; Double, 1,080 kr. **Restaurant:** Terminus Cafe
and Restaurant serves breakfast, lunch, and dinner. There is a bar. The
hotel is a member of De Historiske Hotel.

The summer that I graduated from high school, my parents took me
to Bergen on vacation. We stayed at this hotel and I can still remember
the high-ceilinged main hall and the impressive wood paneling. But the
Grand Hotel Terminus of the 1970s and the building of today cannot be
compared. While doing everything possible to retain the original
architectural integrity of the building, the owner poured 35 million
kroner into the restoration of the hotel to bring it back to its original
grandeur. It is appropriate that the hotel received the Hansa Kulturpokal
award for superb restoration in 1994, complementing the A. H. Houens
Fond award in 1929 for excellence in architecture.

When the hotel opened in 1928, it was called the most "luxurious"
in Bergen. It was in the elegant "Hall," as it is called, that the famous
explorer Roald Amudsen, together with his chosen team, planned
their polar expedition. In the 1920s, guests put their shoes outside the
door of their room and found them nicely polished the next morning.
A Dane was hired to walk back and forth across the floor of the
reception area with steel wool attached to the bottoms of his shoes in

order to grate the surface. Those guests arriving from Oslo by train were met in Voss by some of the hotel's staff so that keys to the rooms could be given out and registration accomplished before coming to the hotel. That way, the guests could go straight to their rooms without delay. A guest could arrange to have a private maid just to take care of him. Service was provided in abundance to all guests. It was also a popular destination for Americans arriving by ship, and trucks transported luggage back and forth between the hotel and the harbor.

During the occupation of Norway in World War II, the Germans took over the hotel as their headquarters, and where the "Hall" stands today was the head office. The German officers lived in luxury at Bergen's best hotel and, as the war drew to a close, a fire was set in part of the building in order to burn secret papers.

The hotel is located right in the middle of Bergen and could not be more convenient. Almost right outside the door is a lovely park with a lake and the train station is just 200 meters away. It is extremely easy to get from here to almost anywhere in Bergen and many places are within walking distance. The 131 guest rooms are each of a different decor and size. The upper floor has been transformed into a fitness center with sauna, solarium, and Jacuzzi. The restaurant and cafe area, in a room of high wooden columns and brass chandeliers, has a balcony where an orchestra plays. The chocolate cake is especially famous and the chef will give you the recipe if you ask.

Solstrand Fjord Hotel

Solstrand Fjord Hotel
Børrea Schau-Larsen
Osøyro
N-5200 Bergen
Telephone: 56 57 11 00; **FAX:** 56 57 11 20
Rates: Single, 850 kr.; Double, 1,000 kr. **Restaurant:** Dining room in
the hotel serves all meals.

In 1903 the English travel writer Charles Wood wrote the following
passage to describe the fjord and scenery near Solstrand: "Presently from
the summit there suddenly lay spread before us one of the loveliest, most
wonderful of views. An immense landlocked bay slept and shimmered in
the sunshine. We stood spellbound. The view had come upon us so
suddenly that it affected us like magic, dazzling sight and sense." This
is an apt description of a part of Norway that must be seen to be truly
appreciated. If the visitor does come to the fjord country near Bergen,
Solstrand is the place to stay. Like the landscape, it is beautiful. A
brightly colored Swiss-style building from the turn of the century looks
across sloping green lawns to the blue waters of the fjord. Beautifully
decorated interiors of creatively used colors, fabrics, and antiques,
combined with a breathtaking view from every window, present an
experience worthy of its location.

In 1895 Christian Michelsen, the first prime minister of independent
Norway, bought the property where the hotel is now located. It had
originally belonged to Lysekloster, a Cistercian convent founded in
1146 as a daughter house of Fountains Abbey in Yorkshire, England.
With property holdings of over 200 farms, it was one of the richest
abbeys in Norway. Michelsen completed the hotel in 1896. Built

for vacationing families of Bergen's merchant aristocracy as well as foreign visitors, it was a hotel reserved for the upper crust. It was to the hotel's advantage that the railway had just been completed two years before, making the trip from Bergen much easier. Os, the nearest town, had also begun to be served by steamship service, resulting in rapid growth. Interestingly enough, Michelsen also built a number of summer houses along the fjord for his various girlfriends. In 1926 a restaurateur, Ludvig Larsen, and his wife, Marie Schau, bought the hotel. Since that time, it has remained in the Schau-Larsen family. Today, it is a family-run business that prides itself in its tradition.

BREIM

Gordon Gjestetun

Gordon Gjestetun

Liv Nakken Førde
Reed, 6865 Breim
Telephone: 57 86 81 01; **FAX:** 57 86 83 76
Rates: Single, 380 kr.; Double, 245 to 280 kr. per person; Family
rooms, 170 to 190 kr. per person; Half board available; Children in
parents' room, 70 kr.; Apartments, 600 to 800 kr. per day; 2,700 to
4,000 kr. per week. **Restaurant:** Breakfast and dinner served in dining
room. During the summer months, an a la carte menu is available and
a three-course dinner is served during the winter months. This hotel
is a member of De Norske Gjestehus.

Gordon Gjestetun has been in continuous operation as a hotel for
the last 180 years. Not only that, but it has been run by the same family.
Now in the ownership of the seventh generation, it is probably a record
in Norwegian innkeeping. It was in 1817, during the time of King
Oscar I, that Lars Redbakken received permission to manage an inn
together with his business as a grocer. In 1884 a new building was
constructed on the same site. It was called Gordon because a visitor
from Scotland who happened to be passing by recommended the
name. The little town of Breim on the water was an isolated place until
the end of the nineteenth century when the railroad built a station
here for the mail train traveling from Oslo (then called Christiania) to

Trondheim. At the turn of the century a steamboat began its routes. From then on, more and more visitors began to come to this ideal place in the mountains. The interior of the hotel looks more like a cozy home than a hotel. Everything is warm and inviting, from the needlepoint chairs to an inviting fireplace. One room has artifacts and antiques from the last century, producing a small museum-like setting, together with a large collection of books. Staying at Gordon Gjestetun is convenient for travelers who would like to visit the Briksdal Glacier, the Glacier Museum at Fjærland, Geiranger, the Coastal Museum at Florø, or the Stryn Summer Ski Center. Trout fishing in Breim Lake is excellent, as are the swimming and boating. If you want to explore the mountains, the hotel can arrange walking or hiking trips, as well as excursions on horseback. During the winter months, cross-country and downhill skiing are available nearby.

FJÆRLAND

Hotel Mundal

Hotel Mundal
Marit Orheim Mauritzen
5855 Fjærland
Telephone: 57 69 31 01; **FAX:** 57 69 31 79
Rates (per person): Single, 375 to 615 kr.; Double, 470 to 685 kr.; Half board available. **Restaurant:** Hotel's dining room serves breakfast, lunch, and dinner.

Hotel Mundal has always been a center for glacier crossings and hiking since its opening in 1891. Even before that year, Fjærland was visited by those adventurers who wanted to be guided across the glacier, including King Oscar II, who came here in 1879. Mikkel S. Mundal, who together with his brother built the hotel, was an experienced glacier guide whose expertise and image were a part of Hotel Mundal for many years. The two brothers hired Peter A. Blix, a well-known architect who also designed Fleischer's Hotel (see the listing in this chapter) as well as the church in Vik. The hotel design became so elaborate that the future owners were accused of "throwing their money away." In the early years, the mostly upper class from western Norway arrived by boat on the fjord. After World War II, the hotel became a popular vacation spot for British tourists. Norwegian royalty have stayed at the hotel while on hiking trips. Another famous guest was former United States vice president Walter Mondale. His great-grandparents immigrated to the U.S. from Fjærland in 1858. A family reunion was held at the Hotel Mundal in 1973.

The building has changed little through the more than 100 years the hotel has been in existence. In what was originally the music and billiard rooms, for example, much of the original furniture can still be seen. One of the early owners, Brita Dahl, won a gold medal award for her weaving in the Bergen Exhibition of 1928. One of her tapestries still hangs in the hotel entrance hall. Hotel Mundal continues to be owned and operated by the same family, now in its third generation. It is located on the Sognefjord, only 10 kilometers from the Jostedal Glacier and 2.5 kilometers from the Norsk Bremuseum (the Glacier Experience Museum).

FLÅM

Fretheim Hotel A/S

Fretheim Hotel A/S
Hans P. Thorrud, manager
57 43 Flåm
Sognefjorden
Telephone: 57 63 22 00
Rates: 420 to 495 kr. per person with a 200 kr. single room supplement; Half board available. **Restaurant:** Breakfast, lunch, and dinner served in dining room. The hotel is a member of De Historiske Hotel.

The Flåm Railroad, which runs down the Flåm valley from Myrdal to the Sognefjord, opened this part of Norway to tourists wanting to experience the incredible beauty of its mountains, fjords, and waterfalls. Before it opened in 1909, Flåm was a remote area that only a few travelers could enjoy. In 1870 Lord Wigram from England actually rented the river for his own salmon fishing. It was then rented by a succession of fishermen, including an American, who relished the exclusivity of their right and the ability to catch 10 salmon on a good day. The area's richest man, Christen Fretheim, took over a large farm in 1879. By 1880 a boat began coming to Flåm once a week and Mr. Fretheim, seeing the future potential of his beautiful surroundings, built a dock and a post office and began to organize boat trips on the river. As more and more tourists began to arrive, he was ready with a hotel. In 1902 he added a livery stable with 14 horses. He married, but

204 SCANDINAVIAN HISTORIC INNS

his wife died in 1903. Needing someone to run the hotel, Fretheim invited his sister, Marta, to come and help out. She became the best known of the hotel's owners and was responsible for the lovely gardens that have continued to thrive. She was so caring of her guests that she followed each to their rooms with a candle each night to make sure that they arrived there safely. In 1908, 79 ships docked in the area, bringing 10,202 passengers. As with many Norwegian hotels, Fretheim was taken over by the Germans during World War II. After the war, it became a popular winter sports destination for tourists from Bergen.

Today, with scenery as breathtaking as any to be found in Norway, the hotel attracts tourists from around the world whose cruise ships dock there. Salmon fishing is also another attraction, and the hotel has fishing rights to 1.5 kilometers along the river. The long, white building in traditional Norwegian style is framed by the mountains on all sides, with the fjord in front. All rooms have a private bath and balcony. Rowboats may be borrowed from the hotel for short trips on the fjord. The visitor to Flåm will certainly agree with the Catholic bishop who visited in 1895 and commented, "Never before in my life have I seen such a wild and romantic landscape."

FORTUN

Turtagrø

Turtagrø
Ole Berge Brægni
5834 Fortun
Telephone: 57 68 61 16 and 57 68 61 43; **FAX:** 57 68 61 07
Rates: Double, 630 kr.; Full board for three nights or more, 520 kr. per person in a double room; 620 per person in a single room. Full board includes breakfast, lunch packet and thermos to take along on hikes and sightseeing, and a three-course dinner with coffee in the evening. **Restaurant:** Breakfast and dinner served in dining room. **Open:** From May 1 to mid-October, approximately the same time the Sognefjell Mountain Road is open to traffic.

If you are into mountaineering, fishing, or skiing, or just someone who enjoys spectacular scenery, this hotel is an excellent choice. Situated 884 meters above sea level on the northwest border of the Jotunheimen National Park, it is on the Sognefjell Mountain Road, the highest mountain crossing north of the Alps. The road has been opened to car traffic since 1939. It took 200 young workers two years to complete the 20-kilometer section, often working in snowstorms and under difficult conditions. Before the road was built, travel was perilous because of thieves who preyed on those who had to cross the mountains. One notable site is now called Galgeberg, or Gallows Rock, so named because irate citizens finally got fed up and hanged several robbers here before throwing them off the mountain. As you cross Sognefjellet today there are fjords, valleys, mountains, and glaciers to see, as well as reindeer and a number of species of birds and plants. Henrik Ibsen, during a trip here in 1862, is believed to have been inspired to write his wonderful works *Peer Gynt* and *Brand*, as well as his poems *On the Plains* and *High Mountain Life*.

A farm is known to have been here in the early part of the nineteenth century. Ola Berge built a hotel on the property in 1888 and became almost a legend as a mountain guide with remarkable abilities to climb the high peaks. From that time to today, the hotel has been known as a haven for mountaineers in the Luster area. For climbing in July and August, it is possible to take either a rock and ice climbing course or use one of the hotel's professional guides to help you find your way. A range of easy or advanced trails can be found by consulting the hotel's hiking map of marked trails. Telemark and cross-country skiing is possible in April and May, and it is possible to hire a professional instructor or guide through the hotel during the month of May. Turtagrø Hotel is now being managed by the fourth generation of the Brægni family. The red wooden hotel, built in old Norwegian style, enjoys the luxury of being alone in its spectacular setting with the snow-capped mountains as a backdrop. The hotel has undergone a number of renovations recently but prides itself in maintaining its special, relaxed atmosphere and homemade food.

KÅRVÅG

Håholmen Havstuer

Håholmen Havstuer
Kari and Ragnar Thorseth
Postboks 9
N-6433 Kårvåg
Telephone: 71 51 24 12; **FAX:** 71 51 25 02
Rates: Half board, including breakfast and large lunch, 995 kr.; Special package tours with Braathens SAFE Airline are available and include the flight to Kristiansund or Molde. **Restaurant:** Breakfast, lunch, and dinner served. Restaurant in Ytterbrygga is from the nineteenth century. The Silver Bell is in one of the inn buildings from the same period. The intimate Bakeriet/Peisestua dates from the seventeenth century and has places for 20 people. Fresh fish is a specialty in the dining rooms. There is dancing in the bar, which features wooden beams and old tools hanging on the walls. **Open:** From the middle of March to the middle of December. This hotel is a member of Kultur Hotel.

Ragnar Thorseth calls Håholmen Havstuer his "dream island," which it would be for anyone wanting to experience a Norwegian coastal island where fishermen have been coming for the past 300 years. On this isolated spot, Ragnar Thorseth's grandfather settled in 1898. Many of the red and white wooden buildings are from the eighteenth and nineteenth century, grouped together on one side of the island next to the harbor and its docks. Although the coastal area is windswept and often experiences harsh weather, the buildings with their white picket fences are cozy and inviting, giving the island an appealing intimacy. At one time there was a farm with cows, pigs, and chickens here. A bakery supplied bread to several hundred people along the coast, salmon was smoked, and butter and cheese were made here. Perhaps one of the most interesting things about the island is the collection of reproduction Viking ships moored in the harbor. A small museum has been created to show the visitor what has been learned through ten years of sailing these ships. Owner Ragnar Thorseth has taken a number of trips in these sailing vessels. Visitors can see a film about his expeditions in the museum's theater. The ships themselves are works of art and worthy of study. The guest rooms are all unique. Some have a built-in cabinet bed, others a sleeping loft. Many of the rooms have bunk beds, allowing room for a separate sitting area. Some have fireplaces. The generous use of natural wood on walls, ceilings, and floors gives a coziness and natural appeal to all of the interior spaces. The bathrooms are all modern. There are also boats that may be rented, and fishing trips can be arranged. This is an island and coastal culture to be experienced by those who value peace and the beauty of nature. There is a regular boat service from Geitøya, Atlanterhavsvegen, during the summer months.

LÆRDAL

Lindstrøm Hotell

Lindstrøm Hotell
The Lindstrøm family, owners; Knut Lindstrøm, manager
N-5890 Lærdal
Telephone: 57 66 62 02; **FAX:** 57 66 66 81
Rates: Single, 670 kr.; Double, 900 kr. **Restaurant:** Breakfast, lunch, and dinner served. Coffee, pastry, and sandwiches are available in the hotel garden.

This dragon-style wooden hotel sits facing a garden so lush and green that its beauty rivals that of the surrounding scenery of Sognefjord, known as the "King of All Fjords." The Lærdalselven (Lærdals River), famous among fishermen, is known as the "Queen of Salmon Rivers." To travel the road between Lærdal and Aurland is an experience not to be missed. The trip offers a stunning view of the fjord and the Jotunheimen plateau. A half-hour drive will take the traveler to 1,400 meters above sea level. Lærdal is an agricultural community with only 2,200 people and is situated in the long and narrow Lærdals Valley. Until the middle of the twentieth century, it was the only route open all year between eastern and western Norway. Tunnels now being built will extend for more than 20 kilometers, enhancing transportation through these mountains. One of the most beautiful churches in Norway, Borgund Stave Church, a wooden building from the year 1150, can be found a half-hour's drive from Lærdal. If you are interested in a bicycle or fishing trip, equipment can be checked out at the hotel's reception desk.

Lindstrøm Hotel has been owned and managed by the Lindstrøm family since 1845. The hotel was originally built as a coastal stop and consists of five buildings—each in a different style-around a common courtyard. The Prince Cottage was built by Prince Axel of Denmark in 1936 for fishing trips. The hotel is located in a preserved part of town called Gamle Lærdalsøyri. It was inhabited as early as 1600. Approximately 160 wooden buildings built in the local style in the eighteenth and nineteenth centuries have been perfectly preserved. Until 1965 the Linstrøm family ran the local ferryboat service. Today they are also the proprietors of a grocery and a bookstore located in one of the buildings.

NOEHEIMSUND

Sandven Hotel

Sandven Hotel
Trond Bach
N-5801 Norheimsund
Telephone: 56 55 20 88; **FAX:** 56 55 26 88
Rates: Single, 600 kr.; Double, 850 to 900 kr. **Restaurant:** Breakfast, lunch, and dinner served in dining room.

When Trend Bach took over as new owner of Sandven Hotel in 1994, instead of throwing out all the old things from the hotel's earlier era that he found in the basement, he began to polish them up and utilize them in the renovation of the building. A pair of handsome etched-glass swinging doors turned out to be the original doors from the dining room. They were carefully restored and installed in their proper place. Careful attention was also paid to match the colors of the original facade and decor. The story of this hotel began in 1845 when ship captain Skutlaberg Sandven built the house and opened a store. In 1887 he was given permission to run a hotel. Thirty years later the hotel opened its first restaurant. In its early years, Ole Bull, Norway's famous violinist and national figure, performed here. By 1896 the tourist traffic was increasing because of the more frequent routes of the steamships. Nils Sandven, then the owner, felt that it was time to add more rooms to the hotel. He was an innovator in many ways, establishing a private electricity plant in 1914, buying the first car in town, and seeing that telephone service was extended to Norheimsund.

The architecture of Sandven Hotel is what Norwegians call the dragon style, reflecting the country's Viking heritage, with motifs seemingly taken directly from the prows of medieval ships. The building's twin-gabled facade looks out over the fjord, with a lovely mountain as a backdrop. The look of warm wood pervades the hotel, especially the lobby and dining rooms. In the area around Norheimsund, the scenery is breathtaking. Thirty minutes away is the Steinsdalsfossen, a spectacular waterfall that one can walk behind. Over the fjord is Folgefonn, a superb place for cross-country skiing in the winter. If you choose to have a driving tour, what could be more fun than a trip in the hotel's 1927 Cadillac convertible?

NORANGSFJORDEN

Hotel Union Øye

Hotel Union Øye
Christina and Lars Aanes, managers
N-6196 Norangsfjorden
Telephone: 70 06 21 00; **FAX:** 70 06 21 16
Rates: Not available. **Restaurant:** Breakfast, lunch, and dinner
served in the hotel dining room. Bar. The hotel is a member of De
Historiske Hotel.

Where else can one bathe in Kaiser Wilhelm's original bath tub
(Room #12) or spend the night with a ghost named Linda (the Blue
Room)? Both of these experiences can be yours at Hotel Union Øye,
one of the "fjord castles" built at the end of the nineteenth century.
It was intended to accommodate the many members of high society
and aristocracy who began to seek out unique destinations and hotels
where all their expectations could be met. Other famous guests, whose
names can still be seen on guest books dating to the hotel's beginning
in 1891, include King Haakon VII and Queen Maud of Norway, Queen
Willemina of Holland, King Oscar II, and the present King Harald,
and his wife, Queen Sonja, when they celebrated their silver wedding
anniversary here in 1993. In 1996 Hotel Union Øye was chosen as
one of the 12 most exciting hotels in the world.

The white Swiss-style wooden building has recently been restored,
although great attention has been paid to maintaining the original
details and, in the words of the management, giving the visitor "a voyage

back in time." Charming four-poster beds in beautifully painted guest rooms with stenciling, stucco-decorated ceilings in salons with antique furniture, and a delicately decorated blue-and-white dining room from the turn of the century are but a few of the accommodations you will find in their renewed state. Television sets and telephones are purposely absent from the guest rooms, allowing the visitor an experience closer to that of one hundred years ago. A British mountaineer, William Cecil Slingsby, wrote that the view from Slogen, one of the mountain peaks next to the hotel, was "the proudest view in Europe." If you are interested in hiking, Hotel Union Øye is a wonderful base, and the hotel will arrange trips with an experienced guide or simply provide a map and expert directions if one wants to go it alone. For the fisherman, a lake, river, and fjord are all filled with salmon and boats can be rented from the hotel. A scenic route runs from the hotel to the Geirangerfjord, providing the best bicycling in this part of the country. From the hotel it is a short distance to Ålesund and the bird island of Runde, as well as Geiranger.

SAND

Mo Laksegard

Bjørn Moe, manager
N-4230 Sand
Telephone: 52 79 76 90; **FAX:** 52 79 73 03
Rates: From January 1 to July 1: Single, 485 kr.; Double, 385 kr. per person; Full board from 685 to 785 kr. per person. From July 1 to December 31: Single, 420 kr.; Double, 520 kr. per person. **Restaurant:** Breakfast, lunch, and dinner are served in the dining room. The hotel is a member of Kultur Hotel.

Mo Laksegard, located in the Suldal region in the middle of the southern fjords of western Norway, is an ideal place for the whole family to unwind and enjoy nature. A grouping of buildings comprises a working farm where children can enjoy the farm animals. Relaxation and quiet are the two ingredients, combined with beautiful scenery, that bring many guests to this special place each year. It is a four-season location where special activities are available all the months of the calendar. In summer and fall, there is superb fishing, especially for salmon as the name Laksegard implies, in nearby Suldalslågen River. Mo Laksegard has fishing rights to large areas along the banks of this river. Guests may also choose to fish from a boat on the fjord or on one of the mountain lakes. Boats and canoes can be rented from the hotel. Guests may place their daily catch in one of the large freezers to keep until their departure. There is also a heated swimming pool for guests, miles of marked trails for hiking and berry picking—a national sport in Norway—as well as horseback riding, canoeing, and bicycling. The fall is hunting season for stag, roe deer, and snow grouse in the gorgeous autumn foliage of the woods. Suldal claims to have a greater chance of long-term snow than almost anywhere else in Norway. This opens up wonderful possibilities for both cross-country and downhill skiing for guests who choose to come during the winter.

Mo Laksegard is a collection of rustic buildings, one of which is more than 200 years old. As in so many farms in Scandinavia during that time period, one house was provided for the older couple whose offspring had married and taken over the running of the farm. The couple remained on the farm until the end of their lives, although they lived in a separate house. That was the original purpose of this particular building. Individual cabins built of solid wood can be rented (complete with modern kitchen and separate bedrooms for the parents) or regular guest rooms can be reserved. A laundry room is available.

SANDNES

Kronen Gaard

Kronen Gaard
Vatne, 4300 Sandnes
Telephone: 51 62 14 00; **FAX:** 51 62 20 23
Rates: Single, 585 to 845 kr.; Double, 740 to 995 kr.; Suite, 880 to 1,295 kr.; child in his or her own bed, 125 kr., including breakfast; child in the parent's bed is free but breakfast not included. **Restaurant:** Kronestuene is the hotel's dining room and serves breakfast, lunch, and dinner. Gaardshuset Pub is the hotel's bar in what was the stable. The hotel is a member of De Historiske Hotel.

Kronen Gaard was built originally as a summer residence for its owner, Gunnar Block Watne, a timber merchant. He must have been quite wealthy since the house included 60 acres of land, a large estate for the time. Many guests and family members visited the summer house through the years, just as visitors come today to this intimate hotel. With only 34 rooms, this is not a large hotel, and guests enjoy its coziness. The white wooden buildings were built at the turn of the century and are surrounded by mountains. The weeping beech tree on the south side of the property is thought to be the oldest in Rogaland. The buildings and grounds may remind visitors of the older large estates in North Carolina. The rooms, all with private baths and televisions, are more modern in design, with dark wood furniture. From April to September, the hotel hosts special luncheons and evening barbecues outdoors in Gaardstunet. Sunday dinners are also special meals at the hotel, and the chef takes pride in the fresh ingredients.

STALHEIM

Stalheim Hotel

Stalheim Hotel
Ingrid Thomassen
5715 Stalheim
Telephone: May to October: 56 52 01 22, November to April: 55 96 13 03; **FAX:** May to October: 56 52 00 56, November to April: 55 96 01 50 **Rates:** Single, 700 kr.; Double, 990 kr., Family room, 1,250 kr.; Suite, 1,800 kr.; Half board available, Single, 850 kr. per person; Double, 640 kr. per person; Family room, 1,635 kr. per person. **Restaurant:** Two hotel restaurants serve a traditional Scandinavian buffet breakfast, a large Scandinavian smørgåsbord lunch, and a three-course dinner. An a la carte menu is also available. Traditional Norwegian dishes are a specialty. There is a bar. The coffee shop offers lighter meals. **Open:** May 15 to September 15. The hotel is a member of De Historiske Hotel.

The view from the guest rooms and terrace of this hotel is more than reason enough to stay here. The Nærøy, Brekke, and Jordal valleys and several spectacular waterfalls provide a backdrop so unbelievably beautiful that a written description could never do it justice. In 1902 a British tourist's reaction in her travel diary was, "Simply sublime." The hotel is built on the edge of a 250-meter cliff from which one can view the 935-meter mountain Jordalsnuten (Sugar Lump). This fjord region of the west coast is simply the most breathtaking scenery to be found in the country, and this hotel has it all right outside its doorstep. Located two hours by car from Bergen and five hours from Oslo, it can also be reached by train to Voss, which is only 35 kilometers away. From Bergen a bus continues on to Stalheim.

The first hotel in Stalheim was built in 1885 to accommodate the postal carriers and horses who needed to rest on their mail route between Bergen and Christiania (Oslo). The world's first travel agent, Thomas Cook in London, began to organize tours to Stalheim the same year. In 1887 the owner of the hotel bought Stalheimskleiva and its two waterfalls and built a pipeline, creating the first privately owned electric plant in Norway. Stalheim Hotel became one of the first hotels in Europe to have water closets in each guest room. In 1890 the hotel burned down but was immediately rebuilt. It burned again in 1902. In 1906 Meinhardt's Hotel was moved from Voss and, a few years later, the hotel was relocated 37 meters closer to the cliff. A set of logs was used to roll the entire building. At this time, two Viking burial mounds were discovered. They can be seen today in the hotel's garden. At the outbreak of the Russian Revolution in 1917, many refugees from Russia came through Finland and Sweden to Bergen, where they were to take a ship to England. The wing in which they stayed is still called the "Russian Attic." In 1927 the Rønneberg family took over the ownership of the hotel and it is now being managed by Ingrid Thomassen, the third generation of the family.

When World War II broke out, many people were evacuated from Bergen to the smaller villages, Stalheim included. With 160 beds in the hotel, up to 600 people were accommodated at times to help out with the housing shortage. During the war the Germans occupied the hotel. They built trenches along the top of the plateau. From there they could control the entire Nærøy Valley. One of the German bunkers still exists in the hotel's garden. In addition to being used as a recreation facility for the German officers, the hotel was also a nursery for Hitler's *Lebensborn* program. The legs on all the hotel's tables and chairs were shortened to accommodate the children, and scenes from *Grimm's Fairy Tales* were painted on the dining room walls. In 1959 the hotel burned down once again. The hotel you see today was built in 1960.

Next to the hotel is Stalheim Folk Museum, founded by Kaare Tønneberg, an owner of the hotel for 50 years. He assembled a collection of buildings and objects, from the Middle Ages to the nineteenth century, that gives visitors an overview of Norwegian farm life in times past. It is now one of the largest private museums in Norway. The hotel is also an excellent starting point for walking tours along the famous Stalheimskleivene, Northern Europe's steepest road. Several trout lakes are situated in the mountains near the hotel. The river and fjord provide other great fishing locations.

STAVANGER

Victoria Hotel

Victoria Hotel
Rolf S. Hodne, manager
Skansegt. 1, P. O. Box 279
N-4001 Stavanger
Telephone: 51 86 70 00; **FAX:** 51 86 70 10
Rates: From 550 to 1,445 kr. **Restaurant:** Cafe Leopold offers a grill with Norwegian and International dishes. Churchill's Bar is a cozy, wood-paneled place with quiet corners.

Victoria Hotel is located right next to the harbor where all manner of boats, from old tall ships to cruise liners, find a place to dock. With a location in the middle of Stavanger, it is close by the Old Town, Fish Market, and Stavanger Cathedral, as well as shopping and the theater. As the hotel prepares for its 100th anniversary, it can look back on a long history as an imposing, dignified lodging for important dignitaries. Built in 1900 by an architect from Bergen who preferred the English style, it was the first building in the region to have an electric elevator, although the toilets remained in the backyard near the stables. This did not keep the King of Siam from visiting in 1907 as he traveled to the North Cape. All of Norway's twentieth-century kings have been guests. During the sadder part of its history, it was occupied by the Gestapo during World War II. Upon their departure in April 1945, the Germans set fire to the hotel. For many years afterward, the building was a combination hotel and office headquarters for the canning industry, which has always played an important role in Stavanger's sardine and herring business. In fact, there is a museum devoted to this subject near the hotel. By the 1970s, oil drilling in the North Sea produced a boom in Stavanger's growth. For this reason, a new floor was added to the hotel. The guest rooms are tastefully decorated, all with coordinating fabrics for draperies, bedspreads, and upholstered furniture. Furniture is in a traditional English style, fitting in with the general design and atmosphere of the hotel.

SULDALSOSEN

Lakseslottet Lindum

Lakseslottet Lindum
Tove Sztanka, manager
N-4240 Suldalsosen
Telephone: 52 79 91 61; FAX: 52 79 94 95
Rates: Single, 400 kr.; Double, 600 kr. **Restaurant:** Breakfast, lunch, and dinner are served in the hotel dining room.

Lindum's Salmon Castle is the English name for this hotel and, as its name implies, it is a haven for those wanting to fish in the Suldalslågen River and the fjord. In fact, it was the salmon that were the center of some controversy in this region of Suldal. The farmers whose land bordered the river fought over who had the rights to the river. An Englishman, Walter Archer, saw to it that permanent fishing tackle was banned from the area. From 1885 to 1924, he controlled all fishing privileges. But it was one of Archer's friends, an aristocrat named Montagu Waldo Sibthorp, who fell so much in love with Suldal that he built the biggest and most elaborate Salmon Castle in 1885. Constructed of timber from the neighboring forest, it was called Lindum, the ancient Roman name for Lord Sibthorp's hometown of Lincoln. He spent every summer of his life there until 1914. Much of the house stands today exactly as it was during his lifetime. Visitors can even sleep in Lord Sibthorp's bed. In 1920 the Norwegian National Health Association took over the Salmon Castle. The purpose of the house was to provide a healthy environment for sickly young boys from Stavanger who were in danger of contracting tuberculosis. The idea was that country cooking and fresh mountain air would improve their health and enable them to resist the disease. It was not a resting period for them, though, and in the phrase of the time, they were put to work "for the good of body and soul." In 1950 the building became a convalescent home for women. Ten years later it was made a holiday home for retirees and those taking part in courses given by the Norwegian National Health Association. It has been a hotel since 1995.

Today the red wooden building in the typical nineteenth-century style welcomes the visitor against the backdrop of snow-covered mountains. The hotel has 22 rooms, but the visitor may also request one of the 17 cabins or may camp out in the hotel's campsite. In addition to fishing, activities at the hotel are almost unlimited. Marked hiking trails through the mountains are to be found in the summer and the Gulligen Alpine Center, where skiing is possible four or five months out of the year, is just a short drive away. There are special hunting areas for roe deer, stag, elk, reindeer, and grouse. Canoes, as well as horses and ponies, can be rented 2 kilometers away, and trips and picnics by horse and cart can also be arranged. On the grounds of the hotel itself, the guest can play cricket, boccia, badminton, volleyball, and table tennis.

SÆBØ

Viking Sagafjord Hotell

Viking Sagafjord Hotell
Andre Erni, manager
N-6180 Sæbø
Telephone: 70 04 02 60; **FAX:** 70 04 03 50
Rates: Double, 450 kr. per person per day for half board; Single, 150 kr. supplement; Full board, 100 kr. extra. **Restaurant:** Breakfast, lunch, and dinner served in the dining room. There is a bar. **Open:** Closed from January to April. The hotel is a member of Best Western, Viking Hotels A/S.

Where else can you find a hotel where goats are munching grass on the roof and salmon are jumping just 40 meters away? These are two of the unique aspects of Viking Sagafjord Hotell, cozily situated in a small harbor on the Hjørund Fjord amid the Sunnmør Mountains. The traveler can reach this west coast paradise by flying or driving into Ålesund and then taking the ferryboat, a one-and-a-half-hour trip along the fjord. The attractive complex is made up of brown and red wooden buildings, a mixture of old and new. The grass-turf roofs tie all of these buildings together in a very pleasant arrangement which, in the case of the dining room, literally extends out over the fjord. All of the 48 guest rooms and 2 suites have private baths, telephones, and cable television.

The location of the hotel amid some of Norway's most spectacular scenery provides endless opportunities for outdoor activities. Guests can rent one of the hotel's boats, as well as an experienced guide, for all types of fishing. For the boater, the hotel's small harbor provides everything needed, from gasoline and food to shower facilities and fresh water. If you want to have someone else take you out on the water, the hotel can arrange this on the *Øyskyss*, which can take 36 passengers. Hiking tours and hunting trips can also be arranged. In winter the Alpine Ski Center just 10 minutes from the hotel provides excellent skiing terrain.

TYSSEDAL

Tyssedal Hotel

Tyssedal Hotel
N-5770 Tyssedal
Telephone: 53 64 69 07; **FAX:** 53 64 69 55
Rates: Single, 695 kr.; Double, 880 kr. **Restaurant:** Breakfast, lunch, and
dinner are served in the hotel dining room. The hotel is a member of
Kultur Hotel.

Tyssedal is situated in the dramatic scenery of Skjeggedal, the site of
the Ringedal Dam, the largest of its kind in Norway. The Ringedal
waterfall plunges 160 meters from the mountain top. Only 4 miles from
the town of Odda, this location has much to offer. An old funicular
railroad takes the traveler 985 meters up the mountainside to the
Hardangervidda plateau. Lilletopp, or Little Peak, is not little at all,
and from here you can enjoy a spectacular view of Sørfjord and the
Folgefonna glacier. From this height, pipes carry water down to the
power plant below. Within the village of Tyssedal is the Western Norway
Industrial Museum, primarily devoted to Tyssedal's history as a pioneer
in the development of hydroelectric power.

Foreign travelers came here as early as the 1830s. By 1900 Tyssedal
had 10 hotels, one of them the second largest wooden building in
Norway. Leading architects of the time produced the designs for
everything from the Tyssedal Power Station (1906-1918) to the
Tyssedal Hotel, built in 1913 in the popular Jugend style. English and
French industrial pioneers once used this hotel for their business
meetings. The bright red exterior houses a small but exciting collection
of Norwegian paintings from the nineteenth century. Nils Bergslien

(1853-1928) painted his large work, *Åosgårdsreien,* directly on the walls of the main hall. Bergslien is known for his use of caricatures and humorous figures commenting on everyday life. This work will grab your attention. Bergslien traded this wall painting for room and board at the hotel and sold a number of his paintings to other travelers staying here. A very impressive work, *Fisherman Mending Nets* by Christian Krohg, was painted during the well-known Norwegian artist's stay in Skagen in Denmark. You are sure to enjoy the other delightful paintings, many of which depict life on the fjord during the last century, as well as the ugly trolls which are said to inhabit the nearby mountains.

UTNE

Hardanger Gjestegard

Hardanger Gjestegard
Torild and Per Mælen
Alsåker, 5797 Utne
Telephone: 53 66 67 10; **FAX:** 53 66 66 66; **Mobile Phone:** 90 16 76 32
Rates: Single, 350 to 600 kr.; Double, 500 to 800 kr. **Restaurant:** Guests prepare their own meals in their apartments, although meals for 10 people or more can be arranged. The hotel is a member of Kultur Hotel.

In 1898 this inn was built as a winery next to the fjord. Cider, soft drinks, and various jams and preserves were also produced here from fruit grown in nearby orchards until 1940 when the production stopped and the building was closed. For more than 50 years it sat vacant until it was saved and given loving restoration. The preservation efforts have resulted in the award of the Ullensvang District Council's Byggeskikk prize for the successful restoration of a historic building, as well as the 1995 Diploma of Honor from the Society for the Preservation of Historic Norwegian Monuments. The original wine press and production equipment are still there, along with several hundred of the original wine bottles in a room now used for receptions. In the cellar, large wine barrels still rest on huge carved beams where guests can sit in the candlelight atmosphere and sample the "cider of the house" made with the original equipment. Preserves were made in the nineteenth century in what is now the kitchen, reception area, and bar.

The hotel is located two hours from Bergen, a little more than one hour from Voss and an hour from Odda. Next to the fjord, the scenery is beautiful and can be enjoyed from the windows of the hotel. A boathouse has also been restored, as well as two old grain mills. One of the hotel's rowboats may be borrowed for a trip on the water. Each of the five apartments offers exciting and different details. In the room Valhall, for example, one finds a bed built against the slanted roof that has carvings elaborate enough to be considered a work of art. In Kontoret (the Office), there are bunk beds in a cabinet-like style unlike anything you have ever seen before. Small kitchenettes are tucked into the natural spaces of the rooms, never disturbing the original beams.

Utne Hotel

Utne Hotel
Anita Granum and Finn-Selmer Olsen
N-5797 Utne
Telephone: 53 66 69 83; **FAX:** 53 66 69 50
Rates: Single, 670 kr.; Double, 1,060 kr. **Restaurant:** Breakfast, lunch, and dinner are served in the dining room. The hotel is a member of De Historiske Hotel.

I first read about Utne Hotel in a 1996 edition of the newspaper *Hardanger Folkeblad.* In it was a picture of a happy couple, holding hands and dressed in the beautifully embroidered folk costumes of Hardanger. I learned from the article that not only were Anita Granum and Finn-Selmer Olsen the proud new owners of the hotel and were about to begin to celebrate the hotel's 275th year, but they were also going to be married on the first day of the hotel's anniversary celebration. The wedding was to be a traditional Hardanger wedding, once the subject of some very famous Norwegian paintings. The weddings in Hardanger are events that may last up to three days. But there is one big difference between the earlier weddings and this one. This wedding and the hotel's celebration were covered on the Internet!

Utne Hotel is a living museum and is actually a part of the collection of the Hardanger Folk Museum. The history of the hotel dates to 1722 when Officer Peder Larsson Børsen, returning from the Great Nordic War, was given a royal privilege to run the inn for the king instead of a salary. It turned out to be a rather lucrative business for Mr. Børsen, especially when Utne became a county seat with a *tingsted* (place where court cases were heard and certain issues were voted on). A project is currently under way to restore the *Ting* so that it can be a part of the hotel. The hotel was sold in 1785 and five generations of the same family ran it until modern times. It is said to be the oldest hotel in Norway still in operation. The white wooden building has traditional Norwegian interiors, with lots of painted wooden furniture and lovely paintings and decorative arts. Its gorgeous location, with Voss as the closest railway station and Bergen 138 kilometers away, is perfect for hiking and fishing. The glacier Folgefonna is very close by and a summer skiing center is a 35-kilometer drive from Utne. For those with a special interest in embroidery, the hotel can arrange a demonstration of Hardanger needlework and folk costumes.

VOSS

Fleischer's Hotel

Fleischer's Hotel
Gerd and Olaf Fleischer Tønjum
N-5700 Voss
Telephone: 56 51 11 55; **FAX:** 56 51 22 89; **E-mail:** fleischr@sn.no
Rates: Single, 895 kr.; Double, 595 kr. per person per day; Children
between 5 and 14 years of age receive a 50 percent reduction on half
board; Half board rates available; Apartment, 240 to 345 kr. per person
per day. **Restaurant:** Breakfast, lunch, and dinner are served in the
hotel dining room. Frederik's Bar has piano music. Terrace dining is
available in good weather. The hotel is a member of De Historiske Hotel.

Fleischer's Hotel has an interesting and well-documented history.
To record this fascinating story, a beautiful book has been published.
It is also the history of how a family persevered through fires (one at
which the King of Norway was present), wars (during World War II
Voss was attacked by Germany, and the bomb that landed next to the
hotel failed to explode), and threats of demolition. If you are fortunate
enough to stay at this hotel, ask about the English edition of this
marvelous publication.

Paul du Chaillu, an American travel writer visiting Voss in 1878,
wrote: "Fleischer's Hotel . . . was comfortable and of excellent standard.
It is the only civilized place a traveler can stay between Sogn and
Hardanger." The excellent recommendation given in the nineteenth
century still holds true today. Fleischer's may be the only hotel in the
world purchased with money made from the sale of a church. During
hard times in Norway, the state sold off some of its churches for
much-needed revenue. Voss church was sold to the Fleischer family in
1752, and they even had their own "Fleischer Lodge," or gallery, in
the church, where only their family could sit. Frederik Lyth Ørum

Fleischer, who had fought in the American Civil War, sold the church back to the state in 1864 and used the money to open the first Fleischer's Hotel. The style chosen was the popular Swiss style, with gables, verandas, towers, spires, and overhanging eaves. Tragically, the hotel burned to the ground the same month it opened and, thanks to the fact that Mrs. Fleischer had conscientiously taken out insurance, it was rebuilt right away using the same architect and design. By this time, the first steam train route had opened between Bergen and Voss, and the upper crust of Bergen became guests who returned year after year. Among other guests were the Swedish royal family, King Edward of England, Queen Wilhelmina of the Netherlands, and the King of Siam.

One manager of the hotel met his wife on a boat returning from one of his trips to America. While at sea the two discovered that their mothers were sisters. As soon as they got to Norway they were married, never to return to the U.S. At one point the hotel was sold and then purchased again by the Fleischer family. The current owner, Olaf Fleischer Tønjum, is the fourth generation of the hotel family. He has been responsible for bringing the hotel up to twentieth-century standards, with amenities such as an indoor swimming pool, modern baths, and an addition to the hotel that echoes the style of the original structure.

Southern Norway

NORWAY

Bergen

Oslo

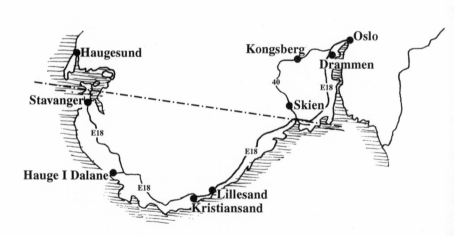

Haugesund

Kongsberg

Oslo

Drammen

Stavanger

40

E18

E18

Skien

Hauge I Dalane

E18

E18

Kristiansand

Lillesand

Southern Norway

HAUGE I DALANE

Sogndalstrand

Sogndalstrand
Eli Laupstad Omdal
Sogndalsstrand
4380 Hauge i Dalane
Telephone: 51 47 72 55; **FAX:** 51 47 60 84; **Mobile:** 94 13 55 10
Rates: Single, 590 kr.; Double, 590 to 760 kr. **Restaurant:** Breakfast and lunch are served in the hotel dining room; dinner can be ordered with advance notice. The hotel is a member of Kultur Hotel.

In a part of southern Norway where the rocky coastline rises sharply from the sea, 110 kilometers south of Stavanger, is a charming collection of four buildings clustered along the harbor of this small town of just over 3,000. This grouping of buildings from the eighteenth and nineteenth centuries was originally an important trade center connecting local sellers of fish and timber with buyers on the Continent. Snugly tucked in between golden-colored wooden buildings is a central building of white wood housing the guest rooms. The other buildings, apart from the hotel, include a fishery museum, cafe, and 65 old wooden houses, all of which are still residences of local citizens. A more picturesque area to explore within the peace and quiet of a small village would be difficult to find. The guest rooms have a traditional feel to them, with wooden floors, lace curtains, warm colors, and old-fashioned iron beds.

From the coast you can travel inland to the moors and mountains that rise 500 meters above the sea. There are many lakes for canoeing, skiing, and bicycling along quiet roads, as well as salmon fishing. If hiking or mountaineering is your sport, guides can be arranged. This area of Norway is ancient, and explorers will find many rock carvings, burial mounds, runic writing, and other traces of the distant past.

KRISTIANSAND

Villa Frobusdal Hotel

Villa Frobusdal Hotel
Galina Lind and Arne Herigstad
Frobusdalen 2
N-4613 Kristiansand
Telephone: 38 07 05 15; **FAX:** 38 07 01 15
Rates: Single, 490 kr.; Double, 315 to 375 kr. per person; Special weekend
rates. **Restaurant:** Breakfast only is served in the dining room. The hotel
is a member of Kultur Hotel.

Centrally located in Kristiansand, only three minutes from the
walking street and close to the train station, is this cozy, family-run
hotel that is very much like the country-inn type of bed and breakfast
establishments found in the U.S. The house was built in 1917 and is
considered one of the best examples of a "Bergensk" merchant's
house in this area called Sørland. The style of the two-story wooden
house is a combination of art deco, neo-rococo, and classical. The art
deco is most evident in the living area and dining room, with furniture
and mahogany panels carved with dragons and snakes in the typical
Viking style. An architect trained in Dresden designed the house for
a shipbuilder and merchant named Syversen. After the stock crash
of 1923, the bank took over the house. For several years it was the
residence of a master painter, then a grocer, and, until 1992, a head
physician. The name of the inn, however, comes from a Danish tax
collector named Hartvig Egertsen Froboes (1685-1741), who lived
on this property before the present house was built. At that time,
Kristiansand was a military town with a fortress built in 1641. Froboes

had been a soldier in the German-Danish War as well as in Denmark's war against Sweden.

In addition to retaining the hotel's atmosphere as a merchant's house from the turn of the century, the present owners have also preserved much of the feel from the 1920s. A large stained-glass window from 1917 hangs in the staircase. The kitchen has the lace curtains and colors from that time period, as do the guest rooms, all of which are simple and comfortably furnished. Each has floral wallpaper, English-made carpets, and lace curtains. All have television and private baths with under-the-floor heaters. Particularly impressive is the fact that the entire inn is smoke free.

LILLESAND

Hotel Norge

Hotel Norge
Torill Kjær and Nils Arne Taranger
Strandgaten 3
4790 Lillesand
Telephone: 37 27 01 44; **FAX:** 37 27 30 70
Rates: Single, 595 to 890 kr.; Double, 890 to 1,050 kr.; Suite, 1,350 kr.; Additional bed, 150 kr. **Restaurant:** Breakfast and dinner (from 3:00 P.M.) are served in the hotel dining room. Lunch and dinner are also served in The Garden, and light meals are served outdoors. A grill party is held here each Thursday evening. Coffee, tea, and light refreshments are served in The Library or main lounge. Skjenkestuen No. 1, the hotel's pub, is located next door. The hotel is a member of De Historiske Hotel.

In 1838 an Irish immigrant who had participated in the Irish Rebellion and later fled to Norway built two buildings at an angle to each other. They were to be used as a tannery, general store, and warehouse. In the back, a water mill was constructed as a part of the tanning process. The first hotel was opened on the current premises in 1873, and in 1890 a Dane known as "Jensen in Norway" built the two older sections of the current hotel. In addition to the guest rooms, there were also a billiard parlor, tennis courts, a bowling alley, and a theater. World War I was not kind to Lillesand, and Jensen was forced to sell the hotel to a shipmaster. During the 1930s, author Knut Hamsun was a regular visitor, always staying in the same room, today known as "Hamsun's Room." It has been said that he wrote part of his trilogy from 1927 to 1933 while occupying this room. It is a wonderful room with an old writing desk, Victorian furniture and lighting, a painted wooden floor, and Hansun's picture on the wall. In 1931 the abdicated King Alphonso XIII of Spain took a cruise to Norway. He checked into the Hotel Norge and while there scratched *Alfons Rex* into the mirror with his diamond ring.

When the hotel was renovated to form the wooden hotel that exists today, it was done in the Swiss style, with projecting roofs and ridges so popular in the 1860s. The hotel gradually lost its original architectural style through years of changes, but an extensive project was accomplished in the 1990s in order to bring it back to its 1890 style. Reproduction wallpaper was used and original beams were exposed. Antiques became a part of the interior redecoration to bring back the feel of the turn of the century. The discreet gray facade, with its balcony and peaked roof, sits back from the street behind a picket fence. The architecture seen in the charming town of Lillesand reflects its international flavor, a result of the comings and goings of the many sailing ships bringing sailors from all parts of Europe. There are still narrow streets to explore, as well as mansions once owned by the rich shipowners. The lovely harbor is filled with white swans and sailing boats, and there are wonderful islands to visit along this beautiful coast.

Snøringsmoen

Snøringsmoen
Else Rønnevig
Snøringsmoen, 4790 Lillesand
Telephone: 37 27 21 18; **FAX:** 37 27 28 51; **Mobile:** 92 01 64 66
Rates: Double room, 750 kr. **Restaurant:** Only breakfast is served. Other meals are available by special arrangement. **Open:** June 15 to August 15.

When Else Rønnevig bought Lillesand's oldest Swiss-style house in 1984, she knew she wanted to restore the badly deteriorated 1867 building that had stood empty for five years. But she didn't know exactly what she would do with it when it was finished. She had been familiar with the house from her childhood and remembers being deeply impressed by it when she was fourteen years old. At the time, she saw the old ship captain's house as a castle where there must surely be very fine people living. When she purchased the house on a cold, raw winter day, no one understood why she had done such a thing. But before and after photographs show that Mrs. Rønnevig's preservation efforts were well accomplished. Looking at the house now, it is difficult to believe that it could ever have been in such a sorry state. Its carefully restored gingerbread carvings are back in place. Careful attention was given to finding the original exterior colors. Tragically, one night in 1995 a fire started in the kitchen and the restored house went up in flames. Shocked but still determined that this house should once again be as it was, Else Rønnevig began the building's restoration a second time. Using both local and Oslo craftsmen, the determined lady completed the restoration and reopened it in the summer of 1997. The Victorian-style interior has more beautiful details than can be mentioned here. Hand-carved wooden door handles, a canopied bed, turn-of-the-century wallpaper, lace curtains, and a restored bread oven are but a few of the lovely things the guest will encounter here.

Else Rønnevig is a remarkable woman of many interests and talents. She has produced a Martha Stewart-type book entitled *Food and Home: A Cultural History Cookbook*. She combines traditional Norwegian recipes with a delightful exploration of regional food culture and architectural/interior design. Because of her special study of old wallpapers and the collection she has put together, she also includes a chapter on this subject. In the book Mrs. Rønnevig explains that the many women who have lived at Snøringsmoen "created an atmosphere, made people feel at home, made good food and showed care." This is also a good way to describe the current hostess and what she has accomplished for her guests.

Middle Norway

NORWAY

Tronheim

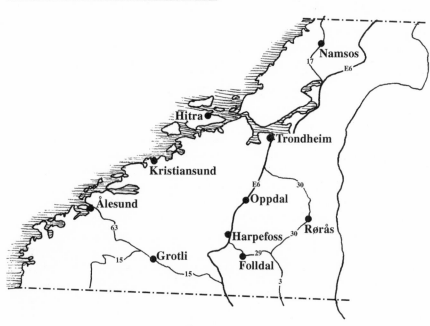

Namsos
17   E6
Hitra
Trondheim
Kristiansund
E6   30
Ålesund
Oppdal
63
Harpefoss   30   Rørås
15   Grotli   29
Folldal
15   3

Middle Norway

Hitra Herregård

Hitra Herregård
Ingrid and Erik Herje
7241 Ansnes
Telephone: 72 44 05 46
Rates: Single, 590 kr.; Double, 690 kr. **Restaurant:** Breakfast, lunch, and dinner are served in the dining room. This hotel is a member of Kultur Hotell.

This hotel, although only a little less than fifty years old, exemplifies the typical coastal home built in Norway in the years directly following World War II. Hitra Herregård was owned by Hjalmar Gøntvedt, who had a fleet of at least eight fishing boats and more than 100 men working for him. By the early 1970s, herring, which had been the fishermen's main catch, greatly decreased in the North Atlantic and the company ran into problems. Mrs. Gøntvedt opened a boarding house. After she died, her daughter Ingrid took over the house and turned it into a professionally run hotel. What makes the house so interesting is that it has original furnishings, paintings, and other decorative elements so the visitor can see how successful businessmen and their families lived in this coastal town during an earlier time. To stay here is like being in a private home with a cozy atmosphere from the past.

Hitra, on the western coast, can be reached via tunnel or by boat from Trondheim. Situated next to the water, the hotel is known for its excellent food, especially the seafood so abundant here. All of the 11 guest rooms now have private baths with showers and television.

FOLLDAL

Folldal Fjellstue

Folldal Fjellstue
Randi and Jens Hammer
2580 Folldal
Telephone and FAX: 47 624 90 186
Rates: Single, 370 kr.; Double, 250 to 300 kr. per person: Full board available; A *seterhus* (cabin) is available for group of 2 to 6 people, 200 to 350 kr.; Breakfast is 85 kr. but guests may take lunch ingredients from the breakfast buffet. **Restaurant:** Breakfast and dinner are served in the dining room. The hotel is a member of De Norske Gjestehus.

Folldal Fjellstue is located in Norway's highest agricultural district, 140 kilometers from Lillehammer and 120 kilometers from Røros, overlooking Rondane. From the hotel, it is 2.5 kilometers to the little town of Folldal. It was to this isolated area with its spectacular views that owners Randi and Jens Hammer came some years ago and discovered an abandoned *fjellstue*, a rustic lodge, that had been used by hikers in the days before roads were built into this area. The idea was to provide a *fjellstue* every so many miles so travelers would have a place to stop for lodging and food after a day of walking. As various types of transportation allowed easier and faster travel, many of the *fjellstue* fell into disrepair, as did this one. The Hammers could see the potential of this place, and they poured their energy into its restoration and furnishing. Today it is an inviting mountain lodge in some of the most incredible natural surroundings in Norway. Quite a few Americans have come here to experience their Norwegian roots. Aside from the breathtaking scenery, guests often come to this inn to enjoy an active outdoor life. The Norwegian Tourist Board has marked a number of paths that lead from the Fjellstue into the surrounding areas, although one can just as easily explore by horseback, bicycle, or, in winter, on skis (there are over 120 kilometers of cross-country ski trails). Fishing—including ice fishing—and small game hunting are particularly good here, and the water provides canoeing and rafting possibilities. For those who want to birdwatch or observe the abundant wildlife, there are beaver, musk ox, reindeer (among the very few wild reindeer left in Europe), and numerous species of birds. The mining industry was established in Folldal in the middle of the eighteenth century, and visitors can experience the Old Mine and its old tools, artifacts, and photographs.

HARPEFOSS

Sygard Grytting

Sygard Grytting
Hilde and Stig Grytting
N-2645 Harpefoss
Telephone and FAX: 61 29 85 88
Rates: Double, 495 kr. per person; Single, 225 additional kr.; Dinner, 250 kr. per person. **Restaurant:** Breakfast and dinner are served in the dining room. Lunch boxes can be prepared on request. **Open:** From June 15 to August 15. This hotel is a member of Kultur Hotell.

During the Middle Ages many pilgrims traveled from Oslo to the great cathedral of Nidaros, dedicated to St. Olav, in Trondheim. The road went through Gudbrandsdal. Gamleloftet (the Old Loft), one of the buildings at Sygard Grytting, was where many of these pilgrims spent the night. There is a parchment paper from 1343 that mentions Gamleloftet, although it is believed to have been built around 1300. This makes it the oldest surviving tourist stop in Gudbrandsdal, one at which King Magnus Magnusson spent the night in 1311. Today, this medieval lodging has been restored, as has the pilgrims' road between Oslo and Trondheim, and it is once again possible to spend the night here as others did 700 years ago. To travel the pilgrimage route and stay in one of the original hostelries along the way would be a most exciting travel program.

The old complex of 25 buildings, known as Sygard Grytting, is located 70 kilometers north of Lillehammer in Gudsbrandsdal Valley. From here one can see the snow-topped mountains of Sør Fron. This is an area rich in ancient archaeological finds, and Sygard Grytting's history goes all the way back to A.D. 300, when it may have been the most powerful place in the valley. What is so remarkable about Sygard Grytting is that it has been run by the same family since 1534, and the family may have owned it since 1300! That would make at least eighteen generations to call this home. Today the complex is one of the best-preserved farms in Gudbrandsdal and represents the best of the typical building style and notched-log construction unique to this area. Fourteen of the buildings form a double courtyard; the inner courtyard with its main building is from the end of the 1600s, and the lower courtyard is from the middle of the 1800s. For their owners'efforts in historic preservation, Sygard Grytting was awarded the Norwegian Heritage Foundation Conservation Prize in 1995. In the interior, for example, the Gryttings were very careful to reproduce the original wallpapers and, in other rooms, find the original colors of the wall glazes. The guest rooms all have antique furniture. Good, solid Norwegian food of the traditional kind is served here, including an authentic medieval soup. This is still a working farm, with sheep and fields of grain to give a strong feeling of authenticity to the whole experience of being here.

OPPDAL

Kongsvold Fjeldstue

Kongsvold Fjeldstue
Owned by the Norwegian government; Kari Mjøen Såstad, manager
7340 Oppdal
Telephone: 72 42 09 11; **FAX:** 72 42 09 80
Rates: Single, 450 to 550 kr.; Double, 300 to 550 kr. per person; Half
board available; Charge for extra bed, 275 kr.; Children under the age
of 12 pay half price. **Restaurant:** Breakfast and dinner are served in
the dining room. Lunch is served only during the summer months.
Coffee and cake is served in the evening. **Open:** May 18 to November
1 and February 5 to May 1. The hotel is a member of Kultur Hotell.

Kongsvold Fjeldstue is situated in the Dovrefjell National Park and
owned by the Norwegian Ministry of the Environment. If one is to
understand the history of this inn, it is necessary to go back to the
medieval sagas. Viking king Øystein (1103-1123) had shelters built on
Dovrefjell, which already had a road. The original inn, whose history
can be documented, called Hullet (the Hole) and built in 1670, was
actually a few kilometers away. King Frederik IV in 1704 gave the inn
a more appealing name, calling it Kongsvold (the King's Meadow).
This was during the Great Nordic War between Denmark–Norway,
then one kingdom, and Sweden. In order to impede the Swedish
army's invasion over the mountains, all of the inns in Dovrefjell
were burned so that the troops could not find food or shelter. The
unfortunate people from the inns had to leave all of their posses-
sions and retreat immediately; all they owned was lost. The
Kongsvold Fjeldstue was rebuild in 1720 and the first floor of

today's main inn building is from that time, as are the building called Nedre and another storehouse. The inn enjoyed flourishing prosperity in the 1800s because of its right to collect a "corn tax" during the winter months. The sled used to transport the tax collector is now on permanent display in the inn's cafeteria. By the time of the railroad at the end of the nineteenth century, people were no longer walking across Dovrefjell, and their need for safe shelter along the way was diminished. But with the advent of the postal system, the inn became an integral part of the tranportation of mail across the mountains. The Kongsvold family, who took their last name from the location, ran the inn for nine generations, from 1670 to 1973. Today the section of the government in charge of nature management owns the inn, and the University of Trondheim maintains a biological study station here.

Within the appealing grouping of the red and white wooden buildings of the inn is an aura of tradition and preservation. To step inside is to step into a piece of Norwegian mountain history, with many artifacts from the inn's past used as part of the decor. Some of the interior walls are made from logs, and others are of wooden planks, but everywhere is the warmth and coziness that earlier travelers enjoyed as they arrived weary and cold from their journey. An enormous wooden grandfather clock, painted green with a folk motif and unlike anything you have seen before, sits in the corner. An ancient iron stove provides warmth, and old photographs and antiques line the walls. Some famous artists have made paintings of the inn at various times in its history, including the great nineteenth-century Norwegian painter Gerhard Munthe. The latter's work can be seen in the National Gallery in Oslo. There are over 30 buildings at the inn, all with a wonderful history to tell. They range from the old washhouse, barn, and privy to the special building reserved for vagabonds with no place to stay. If you want to know more about the local flora and fauna before exploring the Dovrefjell on foot or horseback, the inn has an information center about the natural and cultural history of the area.

TRONDHEIM

Britannia Hotel

Britannia Hotel
Jon Einar Botten, owner; Frode Hofstad, manager
Dronningensgt. 5, Postboks 191
7001 Trondheim
Telephone: 73 53 53 53; **FAX:** 73 51 29 00
Rates: Single, 1,080 to 1,450 kr.; Double, 1,280 to 1,600 kr.; Suites
available. **Restaurants:** The hotel has three restaurants (Palmehaven,
Johnathan, and Hjørnet Bar and Brasserie) and two bars (Cocktail Bar
and Piano Bar).

In 1997, while Trondheim was celebrating its 1,000th year, Britannia
Hotel celebrated 100 years, although its history can be traced back to
1708, when a two-story wooden lodging was built on the same location.
By 1870 Norway's travel industry was booming, and it is known that
over 30,000 foreigners, mostly British who wanted to fish for salmon,
were registered visitors to the country. In 1888 a three-story brick
building was constructed. The structure still exists today. From the turn
of the century, the guest list at Britannia Hotel has been impressive, to
say the least. In 1906 Trondheim's cathedral was the location of the
crowning of King Haakon VII and Queen Maud. Because of the
coronation, the register listed princes, prime ministers, and even
Norway's famous explorer Fridtjof Nansen. Since that time, a lengthy
list of royalty, from Queen Elizabeth and Prince Phillip to Kong Olav,
have chosen this hotel as their living quarters while in Trondheim.
     Britannia Hotel recently underwent a total renovation program,
although the old traditional (neo-classical with a touch of baroque

thrown in) style has been perfectly preserved. It is an elegant hotel with warm wooden paneling, crystal chandeliers, and traditional furniture. The guestrooms are beautifully furnished with coordinating fabrics and wallcoverings. The hotel's restaurant, Palmehaven, is an institution in fine dining, going back to its opening in 1924. A well-known Norwegian once wrote that this restaurant "was the only civilized place north of Paris." This may or may not be true, but it was the first structure built of concrete in Norway. Built in the Moorish style, it has also been beautifully restored with skylight and palm trees.

Eastern Norway

Eastern Norway

EDLAND

Haukeliseter Fjellstue

Haukeliseter Fjellstue
Morten Robberstad, manager
3895 Edland
Telephone: 35 07 05 15; **FAX:** 35 07 05 19
Rates: Two types of accommodations are offered: guest rooms with private bath, or less luxurious rooms where you are in charge of your own bed linen, etc. There are also lower prices for those who have a membership; non-member rates are quoted here. Room with private bath, 370 kr.; Extra bed, 250 kr.; Children's bed, 100 kr.; Single room supplement, 200 kr.; Full board and family discounts available.
Restaurant: Breakfast and dinner are served in the dining room; lunch boxes are available.

If you are a ski enthusiast, Haukeliseter Fjellstue must be paradise. A book about the hotel even shows skiers jumping off the roof of one of the buildings. It is the sort of mountain inn placed in the type of nature and scenery where I know I could stay all year. In summer, the rocky landscape with its snow-capped mountains and many lakes is a hiker's dream. For those who care to bicycle, the old service roads in the area are perfect. The inn is located on the year-round route over Haukeli and is the middle point between Hardangervidda and the

Ryfylke/Setesdalheiene Hills. Here you will find Europe's largest reindeer herd and all types of flowers and plants. Because of the many lakes, it has been regarded for a long time as the perfect destination for fishermen, many of whom have come from England over the years. Boats can be rented from the hotel for fishing. Fossils and special minerals and rock formations are abundant in this area. In winter the skiing possibilities are endless. Here you will find the two highest peaks on Hardangervidda and the highest Rogaland peak. One of Norway's most southerly glaciers, Nupsfonn, is nearby. Ten kilometers away is a modern Alpine Ski Center. Even in May, there is still enough snow for skiing, although it is often done in shorts or bathing suits.

By 1867 the Norwegian government had purchased this 1,000-meter-high property for the purpose of establishing a mountain hotel. It became more and more popular. The Stavanger Tourist Organization took it over in 1963 and has continued to add onto the original buildings. There is now a network of mountain cabins for hikers. This hotel is the meeting point. The original dining room is from 1890 and is named after Norwegian explorer Fridjof Nansen, an avid fisherman and often a guest here. The main lobby, with its huge stone fireplace, wolf skin on the wall, and typical Norwegian wooden folk furniture, is exactly as it should be at a mountain lodge. The food is traditional Norwegian fare from this mountain area. From every window in the hotel the views are breathtaking. A small grass-roofed cottage, Ulevåbu, situated alone overlooking the lake and mountains, can be rented by a small family.

EGGEDAL

Eggedal Borgerstue

Eggedal Borgerstue
Henriette and Elizabeth Koren Bøle
3359 Eggedal
Telephone and FAX: 32 71 46 18; **Mobile:** 94 41 16 60
Rates: 550 kr. per person, includes breakfast, lunch, and dinner; Single,
645 kr. **Restaurant:** Breakfast, lunch, and dinner are served in the
dining room. Askeladden Bar. The hotel is a member of Kultur Hotell.

It is not difficult to figure out why several of Norway's most significant
painters of the nineteenth century chose this area for their homes. The
serenity and the lovely views over mountains and water provided
endless inspiration for artists such as Theodor Kittelsen and Christian
Skredsvig. Kittelsen's home, Lauvlia, and Skredsvig's residence,
Skredsvighagan, are both within a short distance of this cozy, family-run
hotel. Both are open to the public and provide interesting insight into
the lives of these giants of Norway's golden age of painting. Of special
interest is the *Stabbur*, or Store House, at Kittelsen's home, which has
been turned into an activity center for children. There youngsters
may take easels and paints outside. In this area of Norefjell are also
opportunities to ride the Krøderbanen, an antique railroad from
Vikersund to Krøderen; take a trip on the *Kryllingen* boat; or travel
through the mountains on horseback. One may also visit the nearby
Grøset Seter, a working dairy farm with herds of Telemark cows, goats,
and sheep. There authentic *seter* (a mountain farm where animals are
taken during the summer) food made from natural raw ingredients

such as mountain berries gives a true feel for the experience of this part of Norway.

Eggedal Borgerstue (the Townspeople's House) was built in the nineteenth century from funds earned by the farmers' corn collective. The building was for the use of all the residents as a kind of assembly hall and it quickly became too small, necessitating an enlargement in 1910. It was again extended in 1970, in keeping with the original style. The interior of the hotel has a country, farm-like feel that blends in well with the area. The walls are natural wood and the atmosphere is one of coziness, with warm colors and country furnishings. Great care is given to the food served here, and the kitchen specializes in Eggedal and Sigdal dishes such as lamb filled with herbs, and pancakes with ice cream and blueberry preserves. Bestemors Loft (Grandma's Attic) is the hotel's boutique, where country antiques, decorative arts, and textiles are sold. The hotel also has a permanent collection of paintings scattered throughout the building. The Koren Bøle family prides itself in personal service to guests and delicious homemade Norwegian food.

GEILO

Dr. Holms Hotel

Dr. Holms Hotel

Rasmus Sandnes, manager
N-35 80 Geilo
Telephone: 32 09 06 22; **FAX:** 32 09 16 20
Rates: High Season (January 1 to April 30): Double room for two nights with full board, 2,360 kr. per person; Low Season (May 5 to August 31): Double room for two nights with full board, 1,390 kr. per person. **Restaurants:** Dining room, Galleriet Restaurant, wine room, wine cellar, Ski Bar, Salon Bar, and Monarque Bar are available. The menu includes Norwegian specialties as well as Continental cuisine. The hotel is a member of the Historic Hotels.

Dr. Holms Hotel uses the slogan "the Specialist in Comfort and Well Being." It reflects a tradition well established by the hotel's founder, Dr. Ingebrikt Christian Holm. A respiratory specialist with a strong interest in nature and architecture, Dr. Holm started the hotel in 1909 as a place where asthma patients could find clean air and a sense of well being. He believed that the hotel should not only be a location for recovering good health but should also cater to the pleasure of all those who visited. While the hotel was being built, the railroad (Bergensbanen) also was constructing its first station in Geilo, connecting it with Oslo and Bergen. In fact, the little station received its name from a farm located just west of the hotel. With the train stopping just 200 meters away, the hotel soon became a favorite destination for vacationers from Christiania, as Oslo was then called, and Bergen. Guests such as Baron Rothschild, author Knut Hamsun, world-famous figure skater Sonja Henie, and two kings of Norway are listed on the registry. Dr. Holm sold the hotel in 1919. By that time it was a popular place to stay, with guests coming from Denmark and England for the fantastic skiing available just 50 meters away. In 1940 the hotel was temporarily closed by German troops, who occupied it for the rest of war.

Today the dignified white building, which seems to disappear into the landscape during the winter months, has 127 rooms, all with color television, minibar, trouser press, and hair dryer. A warm and inviting library has recently been added, providing a cozy place for a cup of coffee and a quiet moment. Unlike most hotel libraries, this one is stocked with the best that literature has to offer in beautifully bound volumes, together with lovely objects and furniture. The hotel also prides itself in its collection of Norwegian art by recognized artists, many of whom have chosen the Norwegian countryside and its culture as their subjects. In 1885 Dr. Holm published *Guide to the Use of Baths in Public Institutions and in the Home.* The hotel's early reputation as a place where one goes to "take the cure" has been continued with the establishment of a spa where one can receive a massage or skin care session, or use the sauna, swimming pool, Jacuzzi, or fitness center. These forms of relaxation can come in handy after a day of participating in the various sports available in the Geilo area. In summer, hiking in the mountains is a wonderful way to enjoy the spectacular scenery. Bicycling, trout fishing, rafting, glacier tours, and canoeing are also available. In winter, the skiing is best, with slopes of various levels of difficulty. Also offered are dog sledding, sleigh rides, and ice fishing. There are also special activities for the children, with a hotel playroom and game room. The hotel is located exactly midway between Bergen and Oslo. The trip from either city takes about three and a half hours by car.

GROTLI

Grotli Høyfjellshotel
Are Bergheim
N-2695 Grotli
Telephone: 61 21 39 12; **FAX:** 61 21 39 40
Rates: Single, 590 kr.; Double, 345 kr. per person; Family room, 425 kr. per person; Half board available; Children under six stay free, and children from seven to fourteen pay half price. **Restaurant:** Breakfast, lunch, and dinner are served in the dining room. The hotel is a member of De Historiske Hotel.

In 1869 the present owner's great-great-grandfather came to Grotli to build a *fjellstue*, or mountain hostelry, for the Norwegian government. The building in a mountain pass was to provide food and shelter for travelers and their horses. That building still exists, but the present hotel is in the building begun a generation later by the owner's great-grandfather, Andreas Grotli, who took for his last name the name of the area. It took him five years to build the three-story hotel from local timber, and it opened in 1905. At that time, it was possible to keep the hotel open only during the summer months because of the difficulty in clearing the road of snow. The walls of snow, reaching as high as 14 meters, had to be removed by hand. In the autumn, many of the family and staff moved down from the mountain and only 10 to 15 people remained behind. Grotli was strategically located on a peak between east and west, the road crossing on the way to Geiranger, Stryn, and Lom. For this reason, a post office (Grotli still has its own postal code) and telephone station were established here. The hotel was expanded in 1935 to the 52 rooms it has today.

Today the fifth generation of the family is involved in running the hotel, and three generations remain in Grotli during the sometimes hard winter months. The family goal is to provide good, homemade Norwegian food in an original country interior. The warm wooden walls, blue-painted beams and furniture, and hand-carved wooden columns make this a cozy place. In one corner, a fireplace is painted with scenes of mountain and fjord. A folk tapestry covers one wall, and handmade rag rugs add warmth. The doubledecker buffet table in the middle of the dining room is a sight to behold. There is skiing from March until May, with summer skiing in bathing suits possible in some places. Mountain hiking, water rafting, and biking are great in these mountains during the summer.

HØNEFOSS

Grand Hotel Hønefoss

Grand Hotel Hønefoss
Karl Erik Karlsen, manager
Stabellsgate 8
S-3500 Hønefoss
Telephone: 32 12 27 22; **FAX:** 32 12 27 88
Rates: Single, 550 to 650 kr.; Double, 750 to 850 kr. **Restaurant:** Breakfast, lunch, and dinner are served in the dining room. The hotel is a member of the Historic Hotels.

History records that an inn called Flattum Gjestgjveri was constructed on this spot in 1809. An addition was built onto the original inn in 1858 and was then renamed Jernbanehotellet (the Railroad Hotel). In 1912 the main section of the hotel was given a turn-of-the-century classic facade. By that time, it also had a stable of 14 horses, because visitors who came by stage or wagon needed to change horses. Also built were an ice house, a pig sty, and a carriage house. In 1920 the inn took the name Grand Hotel. For many years the hotel also served as a telephone and telegraph station. The salons on the main floor bear names such as the Rococo Lounge and the Cabinet and have red velvet, turn-of-the-century decor. With wood paneling and original paintings on the walls, the intimate atmosphere the hotel takes pride in is obvious. The 39 guest rooms have high windows and simple decor with a Victorian feel, and all have a private bath, television, radio, and telephone.

KROKLEIVA

Sundvolden Hotel
Bjørg and Arne Laeskogen
3531 Krokkleiva
Telephone: 32 15 91 40; **FAX:** 32 15 97 32
Rates: Single, 870 kr.; Double, 525 kr. per person. **Restaurant:** Breakfast,
lunch, and dinner are served in the hotel dining room.

One of the oldest inns in Norway, Sundvolden Hotel has provided
lodging to travelers for over 300 years, although one of the hotel's
buildings, the Stone House, dates from the Middle Ages. The first
recorded visitor to Sundvolden was Jens Nielssøn, Bishop of Oslo, in
1594. The Kroksund Farm, the first place to be inhabited in this area,
had stood vacant since the Black Death. The area was resettled in the
seventeenth century and ferryboat service was begun. The earliest
record of an inn owner here can be found in a letter of complaint in
1648: "The woman who owns the hostelry at the Stensjord crossing is an
accomplice of robbers, thieves, and vagrants. When she rows travelers
across she is usually excessively drunk, and she abuses her passengers."
Sundvolden Farm is listed in the registry for the first time in 1723. In
1809 a farmer opened a hotel there, and it became a popular tourist
destination. Guests included the Prince of Wales and the Duke of
Marlborough, who arrived by cariole, and, later on, the kings of Norway
and Sweden and Kaiser Wilhelm of Germany. The signature of King
Olav of Norway can still be seen in the hotel's registry. In 1840
steamship service was begun. There is still a wonderful boat trip that
one can take on Lake Tyrifjord. The original hotel garden was laid out
in the 1860s and Sundvolden was advertised as a bathing resort. The
100-year-old park surrounding the hotel is a perfect place for a walk.
Located about 30 minutes from Oslo and Drammen, the hotel is next
to the gorgeous Krogskogen Forest on the Nordmark plateau. The
Steinsfjord is close by and is an excellent spot for fishing, hiking, skiing,
and catching crawfish, a local specialty. To say that the hotel has a
very special atmosphere would not be sufficient to describe its beauty.
The decor, from the 900-year-old Gildehuset banquet hall with its
three-feet-thick stone walls to the 350-year-old dining room with low
ceilings and antique furniture and fireplace, is a feast for the eyes. A
collection of contemporary art also graces some of the lounges and bars.
Modern comforts, however, have not been ignored. For nonsmokers and
those who have allergies, special rooms are available, as are special

accommodations for the handicapped. The hotel orchestra plays in the Havesalongen (Garden Room) every night except Sunday. An indoor swimming pool, whirlpool, solarium, and sauna are available to guests.

LILLEHAMMER

Gjestehuset Ersgaard

Gjestehuset Ersgaard
Ragnhild Røsset Lande
2600 Lillehammer
Telephone: 61 25 06 84; **FAX:** 61 25 31 09
Rates: Double without private bath, 490 kr.; Double with private
bath, 650 kr. **Restaurant:** Breakfast and dinner (one set meal of the
day) are served in the dining room. The hotel is a member of De
Norske Gjestehus.

Although Ersgaard means Eirik's Farm in Norwegian, historical
documents show that Botolf Alvarsson owned this property in 1409,
as well as another farm called Bu. People have lived here since the
early Iron Age, and the farm was one of the few in the area to survive
the Black Death in 1349. Every fourth farm was affected by this plague,
and it took six generations for this part of Norway to regain its lost
population. It was recorded in 1642 that there was still a debt of "two
calfskins" on the farm property. In 1974 Ersgaard stopped operating as
an agricultural enterprise and became a full-time guest house. The
farm had accepted some summer guests as early as 1873, making it one
of the oldest farm-pensions in Gudbrandsdalen. Gjestehuset Ersgaard
is actually in Olympic Park, two kilometers above the center of
Lillehammer. It is just a short distance to the Olympic ski track and
only 300 meters from the ski jump. The drive to the mountains is only
an eight-mile trip. The famous Maihaugen Museum (a historic, open-air
exhibit) is only two kilometers away. The long white building with
the red roof sits on a hill overlooking Lillehammer and Lake Mjøsa,
although it really is in the countryside. Inside are cozy salons and
guest rooms, some with private baths and all with television. There is a
playground and plenty of open lawns for the children.

Lillehammer Hotel

Lillehammer Hotel
The Koppervik family; Dag O. Koppervik, director
Touristhotellveien 6, Postboks 153
N-2602 Lillehammer
Telephone: 61 28 60 00; **FAX:** 61 25 73 33
Rates: Single, 1,065 kr.; Double, 1,265 kr.; Half and full board available;
Nordic Hotelpass may be used on weekends and during the summer.
Restaurant: Breakfast, lunch, and dinner are available in the hotel
dining room.

Chosen as the host hotel for the International Olympic Winter
Games in 1994, Lillehammer Hotel is a luxurious, full-service hotel
that also has been the choice of royalty and other dignitaries over the
years. The hotel was formally opened in 1911 after a committee of 13
had spent 11 years planning how it should be designed. The idea was
that it should be a mecca for winter sports, as well as for those with
asthma who wanted the benefit of the fresh air Lillehammer had to
offer. During World War II, the German army, which had over 300,000
soldiers in Norway, took over the hotel as its headquarters. General
Bøhme's office was in what is now the White Salon. The hotel played
a central role in the country's wartime history, and many important
meetings took place here.
    Located 176 kilometers from Oslo, Lillehammer Hotel has much to
offer the traveler. Unbelievable buffet dinners; international bands
to provide dancing six nights a week; a park with sun terrace; minigolf;
an outdoor swimming pool; an indoor swimming pool plus sauna and
solarium; and a fitness room are but a few of the amenities available.

The hotel is a member is the French order Chaine des Rotisseurs and is known for its cuisine. It is also close to Maihaugen, a living museum of Norwegian culture and history, as well as Hunderfossen Family Park, one of the main attractions of the area. The Olympic alpine facilities still exist for the skier, and the cross-country skiing trails are excellent. In summer, hiking in the beautiful scenery is wonderful.

LOM

Fossheim Turisthotell

Fossheim Turisthotell
Svein Garmo and family
2686 Lom
Telephone: 61 21 10 05; **FAX:** 61 21 15 10
Rates: Single, 590 to 615 kr.; Double, 795 to 825 kr.; Extra bed, 170 kr.; Suites, 795 kr.; Half Board rates with a minimum three-day stay: Single room, 630 kr.; Double room, 530 kr. per person; Special weekend packages available. **Restaurant:** Breakfast, lunch, and dinner are served in the hotel dining room.

Located almost equidistant between Bergen, Oslo, and Trondheim in the Jotunheimen area, Lom is a national heritage center with a natural beauty unsurpassed anywhere in the world. It is here that the visitor finds the peaceful and tranquil refuge of Fossheim, where tradition and the care of historic surroundings have always come first. The Thorgeir Garmo family built the hotel as a coaching inn in 1897. Since that time, the family has collected old handcrafted timber houses as others collect art and has arranged them together with the original inn building. In the *tun*, or courtyard, one finds Gaukstadstugu, one of the best-preserved seventeenth-century timber houses in Norway. An evening spent among the antiques, brightly painted, carved windows, and warm, open fireplace is a unique experience. The hotel lobby and reception area also have the painted furniture and clocks so typical of the decorative arts of Norway.

Even the 30 rooms that were added in 1992 have the same warm country feeling, with plenty of windows to allow the outdoors to be a part of the interior. In addition to the main hotel, there is also Brimi Fjellstugu, a fishing and hunting lodge located in the mountains above the tree line. Three generations of the Brimi family are involved in the lodge, originally a timber dairy building the family rebuilt in 1947. The farm here is actually worked during the summer months. The area has been inhabited thousands of years, and one can find a number of Stone Age dwellings dating back 2,000 to 4,000 years. The trout-filled Tesse Lake is just outside the door, supplying the lodge restaurant with fresh fish. The mountains are ready for hikers who want to see some of the most beautiful scenery in Norway. There is a summer camp for children, and hiking and fishing trips are arranged by the lodge.

The Fossheim kitchen, called "Nature's Kitchen," is renowned, thanks to chef Arne Brimi, who in 1987 earned the honor of being the first Norwegian to participate in the World Championships of Cookery in Lyon, France. He was also given the Chef of the Year award, the highest distinction in the profession in Norway. In the chef's own words, "I obtain all my raw materials from farms, the fjords and rivers, the forests and the mountain plains. I find herb plants in pastures and gardens and on mountainsides and moors which blend in naturally with this concept." Organic produce is purchased from Aukrust Farm, where vegetables are still cultivated the same way they were during the time of St. Olaf of Norway when he was in Lom during the Middle Ages. Arne Brimi's products, such as jars of herbs, berries, and spices, are made in his kitchen and sold at the hotel. Cooking and wine courses are offered to guests.

Within the area of Lom, the traveler finds one of Norway's most beautiful stave churches, dating from 1170. There is also an open-air museum with 25 old buildings from Ottadalen, the Presthaugen Museum, and the Norwegian Mountain Museum. For the truly adventurous, glacier exploring can be tried in Jotunheimen National Park. Rafting on the Sjoa River and downhill skiing at the summer ski center on Galdhøpiggen are also available, as well as visits to Knut Hamsun's birthplace and other authors' homes. Lom is also known as a center for folk music and dancing, and performances can be seen during the summer months.

MOSS

Refsnes Gods

Refsnes Gods
A. Bjørn Christiansen, manager
Postboks 236, 1501 Moss
Telephone: 69 27 04 11; **FAX:** 69 27 25 42
Rates: Single, 650 to 960 kr.; Double, 800 to 1,080 kr.; Suites, 1,200 to
1,500 kr. **Restaurant:** Breakfast, lunch, and dinner are served in the hotel
dining room. There is a wine cellar and six bars and lounges. The hotel
is a member of Relais and Chateaux, Norwegian Inter Nor Hotels.

Refsnes Gods is located on the west side of Jeløy Island in the Oslo
Fjord. Beginning in the 1770s, it maintained a reputation as an elegant
private summer home where important members of Norwegian society
came for generous hospitality. It is known that the main building was
built in 1764. But David Chrystie, owner of a large timber company
and principal patron of the foundation of the Bank of Norway, took
over the estate and turned it into *the* place for high society to visit and
enjoy. It was he who built the famous linden tree avenue leading up
to the house that gave the house and gardens a patrician atmosphere
and style. One vistor's diary entry from the time tells of a masquerade
party for over 300 guests. Camilla Collete, a well-known Norwegian
painter of the nineteenth century, wrote, "This rich and handsomely
appointed family did everything to ensure our visit was pleasurable
and comfortable." After 50 years of spending his summers at Refsnes,
David Chrystie died in 1835, and Consul Lorentz Meyer bought the
estate for his summer residence. He had a great interest in gardens
and loved the many deciduous trees found at Refsnes.

The estate continued as a gathering place for society, a tradition maintained by Meyer's daughter, Sophie, who married a police doctor from one of Norway's most important families of science. The 1890s was a time when many notables visited Refsnes, including Hans Gude, one of Norway's most famous painters and friend of Henrik Ibsen, who was also invited to the estate but had to refuse because he was in the process of writing *Little Eyolf*. In 1898 Refsnes's most famous guest, King Oscar II, came to a dinner arranged in his honor. Refsnes was last used as a summer house in 1935, and it was then vacant for several years before it became a restaurant. It served as a respected restaurant until 1971, when it became a hotel. Two wings of newer rooms have been added onto the original white-columned, two-towered estate.

The well-appointed, traditionally decorated guest rooms have balconies looking out over the fjord. All have private baths, television, minibars, and radios. A heated outdoor swimming pool, private beach, sauna, solarium, and fitness room are available to guests. The hotel has arrangements with four 18-hole golf courses within 30 minutes of the hotel. Boats are available for hire from the hotel. The fjord, with its many islands, provides ideal waters for sailors. Alby Gård, one of Norway's most respected art galleries, is a five-minute drive by car from the hotel.

RINGEBU

Jønnhalt Gjesteseter
Astri and Anders A. Fretheim
2630 Ringebu
Telephone: 61 28 03 41; **FAX:** 61 28 02 55
Rates: The entire mountain farm may be rented by one group at a time. The group may be as few as 7 or as many as 25 people. The price depends on the size of the group. **Restaurant:** Breakfast, lunch, and dinner are served in one of the buildings. This hotel is a member of Kultur Hotell.

When you stay in this authentic Norwegian *seter* (a mountain farm where animals were usually taken during the summer months), you have the entire place to yourself. Your group will be the only one staying there as guests, and a hostess will come in to serve you meals and help you arrange whatever types of activities interest you and your group. Located in Gudbrandsdalen, 75 kilometers north from Lillehammer, this hotel is 2,500 feet above sea level and belongs to a farm further down the valley. The farm is run by Anders Fretheim (who once studied hotel administration in the U.S.), while his wife, Astri, is a school principal. But they dreamed of doing something with these 1870s buildings, which were built by Ole Steberg, famous for the red Norwegian cheese he made here. After four years of careful planning and precise restoration, and the addition of modern amenities, this historic place was completed.

The property overlooks the valley and the other farms and sits next to the edge of the mountain forest. Each 120-year-old building is used for a different purpose. Laven, which used to be the hay barn, is now a social/reception area on the first floor, with two bedrooms on the second. Selet was where the gudbrandsdalsost (Gudbrandsdal cheese) was made. It now contains the kitchen, the dining room, and a wonderful timbered area with a grand fireplace (the sofa was made from an antique bed). Fjøset was the original cow barn. Two houses on the lower end of the property, including the old goat house, each have bedrooms, a living room, and a kitchen. The *seter* is open all year and has miles of cross-country skiing paths.

SANDEFJORD

Hotel Atlantic

Hotel Atlantic
Arnt R. Mikalsen, manager
33, P.O. Box 144
Jernbanealleen 33, P.O. Box 144
N-3201 Sandefjord
Telephone: 33 46 80 00; **FAX:** 33 46 80 20
Rates: Single, 640 to 780 kr.; Double, 780 to 980 kr. **Restaurant:** Breakfast
and dinner buffet are served in the dining room. Wine bar is in the
cellar. Price of the room includes breakfast as well as coffee, tea, and
fruit available throughout the day, and waffles or cake served in the
afternoon. The hotel is a member of Choice Hotel Scandinavia.

Sandefjord has a long history as a whaling port, and the public
areas of the hotel reflect this tradition through an exhibition of pictures
illustrating this Norwegian industry of the past. Hotel Atlantic prides
itself in being a hotel for those who are accustomed to traveling often
and expecting first-class service. Located within walking distance of
both the harbor and the railroad station, it is a perfect base for the
tourist who wishes to explore the town on foot. It is only 100 meters
from the port where the ferryboat departs for Strømstad and is only 5
kilometers from the airport, which connects to all major cities in Norway
as well as Copenhagen. All of the 72 rooms have private baths, television,
radios, telephones, minibars, and trouser presses. There are 25 rooms
reserved for nonsmokers. The fifth floor is a spa area with Turkish
steam bath, Finnish sauna, solarium, and workout room.

Anders Skorge established himself in Sandefjord in 1898 and his
house, on the same location as the present hotel, was finished in 1900.
It became a type of boarding house, with the family living on the
second floor and the guests on the first. The teacher who taught in
Middelskole just across the street occupied the third floor. The grocer,

Schelbred, ran his store on the corner of the building facing the garden. A piano school and a goldsmith shop were also in this building. By 1914 plans were made by Anders Skorge and most of the town's more prominent citizens to build a regular hotel. The same architect who had designed Oslo's famous Grand Hotel, O. Sverre, was called in to put his creative abilities to work in Sandesjord.

A local newspaper reported at the time of the opening that the basement kitchen "must surely be the largest in the country" and described the dumb waiter, which lifted the food to the dining room. "Now the town has gotten a new hotel which can compare itself architecturally to the best that one can find in our country," the article concluded. Along with a billiards room and reading salons, a type of mercantile exchange operated in the public area of the new hotel. As a result of the booming whaling industry, the town needed a place where the prices for products such as whale oil could be discussed and sales concluded. After World War I the need for the exchange diminished, and it closed in 1932.

Hotel Kong Carl
Finn Andressen
Torggt. 9, Postboks 145
3201 Sandefjord
Telephone: 33 46 31 17; **FAX:** 33 46 31 19
Rates: Not available. **Restaurant:** Breakfast, lunch, and dinner are served in the hotel dining room. An outdoor restaurant is also available. The hotel is a member of De Historiske Hotel.

Hotel Kong Carl is the oldest hotel in the oldest building in Sandejord, an important town in whaling and shipping history. The building occupied by the hotel today was mentioned as early as 1690 in connection with a Danish merchant, Ole Simen Calundan. In 1741 the house was sold. Unfortunately, the owner went bankrupt, and it was again sold at an auction to a shipbuilder, Engvold Pedersen. When Pedersen died, his widow turned the property into an inn. For a while, it again became a private residence, this time of a sea captain and shipbuilder. By 1840 it was again an inn. It is now run by the third generation of the Andressen family. For the many years that Sandefjord was home to 6,000 whalers, Hotel Kong Carl was the place to which they returned for celebrating after their adventures at sea. In the late summer, after several months of parties, they would once again set out for the Antarctic and their dangerous life at sea. When the whaling industry diminished in importance, the hotel began to concentrate on attracting business travelers and tourists. The building itself has gone through a few changes. Where the side wing is located today was once the hotel's stables. The banquet hall was added at the turn of the century.

Authentic Norwegian cuisine is a specialty of the hotel, with special evenings devoted to cod and lutefisk dishes. The hotel was awarded the Prize of Landlordship, a distinction given by the Norwegian Hotel Union to hotels recognized for their excellent food and service. The guest rooms are attractively decorated, although with modern furniture. Sandefjord is a city of 36,000 that has maintained its traditional charm. It is centrally located, with access to ferryboats to Denmark and Sweden as well as flights to cities in Scandinavia.

STAVERN

Hotel Wassilioff

Hotel Wassilioff
Ann-Gerd and Gunnar Berseth
Havnegt. 1
N-3290 Stavern
Telephone: 33 19 83 11; **FAX:** 33 19 97 64
Rates: Single, 590 to 625 kr.; Double, 425 to 625 kr.; Half board available.
Restaurants: Excellensen (serves breakfast, lunch, and dinner) and Tatjanas kjeller (the hotel's intimate pub).

Until 1988 Stavern was considered Norway's smallest town, although it is now one of the country's most desirable summer vacation spots and home to an expanding community of artists. This is not surprising when one considers the fact that this lovely place on Oslo Fjord's western coast gets over 200 days of sunshine a year, unusual in Scandinavia. Stavern is an old garrison town with two forts to explore (Stavern Fort and Fredriksvern Verft). For those interested in a cultural experience, there is much to choose from. There is an art gallery on almost every corner, streets of charming wooden houses, and wonderful plays and festivals from the end of June until the end of July. It is no wonder that some of Norway's most famous artists and authors from the past found their inspiration in this town, nicknamed "Norway's Smile Hole."

In 1840 Michael Wassilioff, a refugee from the Russian Czar's Riga, was helped by a Norwegian sea captain to escape to Stavern. Four years later, Wassilioff married a local woman, Anne Marie, and together they started their first hotel. Their two children, Tatjana

Alexandrine and Ingebrigt, were later to take over as the second generation of innkeepers. Unfortunately, a large fire in 1883 destroyed the hotel and a large section of the town. A new hotel was then built by Wassilioff, this time closer to the coastline and overlooking the fort and citadel. Today the hotel reflects the close association Stavern has had with the fjord and its coastal life. The restaurant is named after *Exellensens*, a steamship known as "a boat that would go out in all kinds of weather." An 1889 painting by Reidar Thommesen, a yearly guest at the hotel, hangs in the restaurant. If you are a guest at the hotel, you may take a trip on the fjord in Hotel Wassilioff's own boat, *M/S Molly*. If you prefer a sailing vessel, a tour on the *Fritjof II* can also be arranged.

Hotel Wassilioff today is a bright, pleasant building with modern additions that blend in with the older parts of the hotel. The 47 guest rooms have private baths, television, and gorgeous views of the fjord and the island.

TRYSIL

Viking Trysil Hotel

Viking Trysil Hotel
Tove Grasaasen, manager
N-2420 Trysil
Telephone: 62 45 08 33; **FAX:** 62 45 12 90
Rates: Double, 330 kr. per person per night; Single room supplement,
150 kr.; 7-bed apartment, 430 kr. per person with additional charges
for maid service and sheets; 100 kr. per person for breakfast.
Restaurant: Breakfast, lunch, and dinner are served in the hotel's
two dining rooms. The eighteenth-century wine cellar also serves as an
intimate restaurant and can accommodate 8 guests. There is a bar
with dancing. Meals are also served outdoors during the summer
months. Breakfast is not included in the price of the room. The hotel
is a member of Viking Hotels, Best Western Hotel.

Located centrally in the town of Trysil, the hotel is approximately
210 kilometers from Oslo and 100 kilometers from Hamar, near the
Swedish border. There are two buildings, Løken and Torgalnup, each
with a different and interesting history. The Løken segment of the
hotel was built in 1897 and since 1902 has housed a number of
businesses, including a hat shop, bicycle and car repair shop, hair
dresser, and cafe. In 1932 it became Trysil's first hotel, called Innbygden
Hotel. In 1955 it was joined with Torgalnup to become the Trysil
Hotel. The Torgalnup part of the hotel was a farmhouse around 1660.
It remained so until 1877, when it became the local grocery. Over a
period of time it was a succession of various types of shops, a bakery,

and the local post office. It served as a cafe and guest house from 1900 until it was joined with Trysil Hotel. The two buildings have undergone extensive renovation, although one can still see the original stone walls from 1660 in the wine cellar, and the log walls from 1880 are still a part of the banquet room.

A new wing with 32 rooms and some apartments with 3 bedrooms was added during the recent renovation. All rooms have private baths with heated floors, cable television, and telephones. There are also two saunas, a solarium, and a special playroom with games and other activities for children. The Trysilelva River is only 15 meters from the hotel and provides wonderful fishing from traditional log boats. During the summer months the ski lift takes you up the mountain, a good starting point for either hiking or renting a mountain bike to get around. Wildlife safaris are a specialty here, with the opportunity to see bear, moose, and beaver. In the winter time, guests can use some of the 70 kilometers of cross-country ski tracks through forests and mountain terrain, or take a ski lift for alpine skiing down the longest continuous run of 5,400 meters. Special safe runs and lifts, as well as a special skiing school and après ski activities, are offered for children. Siberian Huskies are available for dog sledding. If you want to take it a bit easier, you can hire a horse and sled for a calmer trip through the countryside.

Northern Norway

NORWAY

Tromsø

Hammerfest

E6

Kirkenes

E6

Tromsø

E6

RUSSIA

FINLAND

Narvik

Bognas

SWEDEN

Bodø

Fauske

Myken

E6

Mo I Rana

Mosjøen

E6

Rørvik

Northern Norway

MOSJØEN

Fru Haugans Hotel

Fru Haugans Hotel
Bjørg Jurgensen Johannessen
Strandgt. 39, Postboks 81
8651 Mosjøen
Telephone: 75 17 04 77; **FAX:** 75 17 05 34
Rates: Single, 550 to 1,000 kr.; Double, 700 to 1,150 kr.; nonsmoking
rooms available. **Restaurant:** Haugestuen serves breakfast, lunch, and
dinner with Norwegian and Continental specialties. Møteplassen Pub.

Three generations of women have owned and managed Fru Haugans
Hotel. In fact, its name comes from the original owner, Fru (Mrs.)
Ellen Haugan, a mother of three young daughters with a husband
too ill to provide for the family. Because of her desperate need to
become the breadwinner, she bought the hotel sight unseen with the
idea of turning it into a productive business. Constructed in 1794 by
a skipper who used the building as a hotel and trade school, it did

not even have a stove or floor in the kitchen when Fru Haugan began her adventure in hotel management. By the time she died in 1914, the hotel was a booming success and her youngest daughter, Eli Jensen-Hals, took over. When she died in 1962, her niece, Bjørg Jurgensen Johannessen, became the owner and continues to manage the hotel today.

As the oldest hotel in northern Norway, the property received great care in maintaining the traditional atmosphere of the guest rooms during a recent renovation. Although the furniture is new, it has the lovely rustic look of old Norwegian country style. Beautiful fabrics have been chosen to blend nicely with the blond wood used in the rooms. In the bar, for example, the original timber walls add to the warm feeling of coziness. Located on the Norland railroad line, Mosjøen is easily accessible by train or plane. The hotel, with wonderful gardens that lead down to the Vefsna River, is a short walk from Sjøgata, the old part of the city with many buildings from the eighteenth and nineteenth century. Here you will find northern Norway's longest continuously listed wooden building, as well as old warehouses and boathouses. Wharves line the waterfront, and a local museum has an exhibition showing life in Nordland 200 years ago. Since salmon and trout fishing are so wonderful in the river, fishing tackle can be rented from the reception desk in the hotel. Marked hiking and skiing trails may be found in the Mosåsen Recreation Area near Mosjøen.

MYKEN

Myken Fyr

Myken Fyr

Helge Eriksen, owner; Ulf Skauge, manager
8199 Myken
Telephone: 750 960 30
Rates: The hotel is rented as a complete unit, based on a minimum of 4 guests. The hotel accommodates a maximum of 8 guests at a time. After the first 4 guests, a 50 percent discount is given. **Sample rates:** One week per person, 1,600 kr.; Two nights per person, 650 kr.; Children under the age of 4 are free. **Restaurant:** Breakfast, lunch, and dinner are served in the lighthouse.

Have you ever wondered what it would be like to live in a lighthouse on a small island? This hotel provides some of the flavor of life as the lighthouse keeper lived it at the turn of the century in this white wooden house near the Arctic Circle. During World War I, huge fleets of vessels with up to 1,500 men fished for herring in these waters. In the winter months, they fished at night but did not dare travel too far out to sea because of the lack of a lighthouse to guide them. As early as 1887, the fishermen began to petition for a lighthouse. Steamships were beginning to come to these northern islands at the end of the nineteenth century, and there was a greater demand for safe and improved harbors. If shipping and fishing were to continue to grow, a lighthouse was needed. In 1917 the Storting (Norwegian Parliament) voted to construct the lighthouse, the 189th of 200 lighthouses built in Norway. Six third-order lenses allowed the beams of the lighthouse to be seen up to 30 kilometers away. A lighthouse keeper was in residence only until 1974, but the lighthouse is still in operation.

Today the town of Myken has only 45 residents and is situated among a small group of little islands and skerries. The island on which the lighthouse is located is separated from the mainland by a sheltered harbor. As a guest, you will have the whole island to yourself. Living on Myken during the long, light summer days is an experience close to nature. Located on the highest point on the island, the lighthouse is a two-story wooden building atypical of those lighthouses found in the United States. Unlike so many other Norwegian lighthouses, this one survived because it is so high up on the rocky terrain that the waves were never able to reach it. You can get to Myken by boat from Tonnes and Vågaholmen or, by prior arrangement, the fishing boat *Josephine* will pick you up. While at the lighthouse, guests have free use of the 18-foot rowboat with an outboard engine, a sailing board, fishing equipment, lifejackets, and warm outerwear.

TROMSØ

Skipperhuset Pensjonat

Skipperhuset Pensjonat
Vibeke Jensen, manager
Storgata 112
9008 Tromsø
Telephone: 77 68 16 60
Rates: Single, 398 kr.; Double, 498 kr.; Triple, 598 kr. **Restaurant:** Only breakfast and light meals are available.

If you are looking for a historic hotel with reasonable rates, Skipperhuset Pensjonat is a good choice in this northerly town. The building was constructed in 1860 as a private residence for Hillebert Pettersen, the owner of a herring plant. From 1886 until 1907 it was run as a private hospital by Johannes Holmboe, a doctor. In 1907 it became St. Elisabet's Hospital and remained so until 1920. The Tromsø Ladies Association sold the hotel in 1920, and it became the Tromsø Sjømanshjem, a place where sailors on leave could spend the night. Old photographs from this era show a well-kept wooden building with a neat and clean interior. In 1986 the hotel was opened to all travelers.

Tromsø, known as Norden's Paris because of its many restaurants, cafes, and nightclubs, is in the area called Troms. It is located only one day's journey from the Polar Circle and the North Cape. The summer Midnight Sun illuminates deep valleys, fjords, and mountains, giving the region the appearance of a huge national park and nature preserve. Fishing abounds and fishing expeditions are a specialty. There is even a Fishing Festival each year in Harstad.

SWEDEN

Stockholm

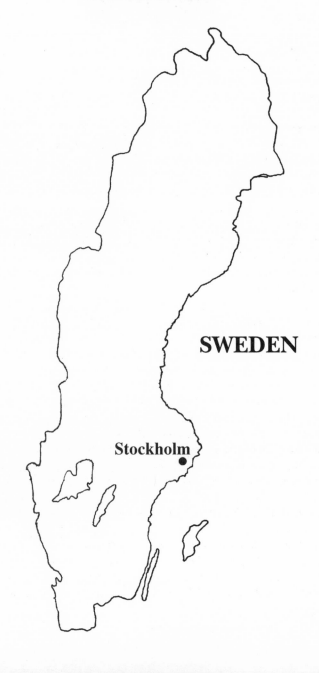

SWEDEN

Stockholm ●

Stockholm

Grand Hotel
Peter Wallenberg, Jr., manager
S. Blasieholmshamnen 8
Box 16424
SE-103 27 Stockholm
Telephone: (0) 8-679 35 00; **FAX:** (0) 8-611 86 86;
E-mail: vlinse@grandhotel.se; **Toll-free reservations:** (800) 223-6800
Rates: Single, 985 to 1,832 kr.; Double, 1,490 to 2,621 kr. **Restaurants:**
Grand Veranda serves a Scandinavian breakfast buffet, as well as lunch
and dinner menus specializing in traditional Swedish food and popular
Swedish Smorgådsbord. The French Dining Room provides gourmet
dining with a view of Stockholm. The Cadier Bar, called by *Newsweek*
"one of the world's best watering holes," also serves light meals. The
wine cellar, with over 25,000 bottles of wine, is the largest in Sweden. This
hotel is a member of Leading Hotels of the World and Steigenberger
Reservation Service.

Grand is an appropriate name for this hotel. Where else can you
get a buffet breakfast served in an almost life-size Viking ship or have
a meeting in an exact copy of Versailles' Hall of Mirrors? With 307
guest rooms, 21 suites, and 19 conference and banquet rooms, the
Grand has dominated the Strømmen waterfront of Stockholm since
1874. It is a deluxe hotel of international standing with an old-world
elegance that has elevated it to the prestigious National Heritage
Building list. With its gigantic chandeliers, gold-gilded columns, and a
magnificence almost beyond description, it has been home to celebrities,
political figures, and royalty, as well as Nobel Prize winners and their
families. It was awarded the title of "Third Best Hotel in the World"
by *Euromoney Magazine* for the past two years, and its French Dining
Room was named "Sweden's Best Restaurant" by the Swedish trade
magazine *Gourmet*.

Grand Hotel was founded in 1874 by Regis Cadier, a Frenchman
and King Oscar II's personal chef. He created a Continental atmosphere
so spectacular that merely entering the lobby was a dazzling experience.
The lobby was dominated by a gigantic birdcage, from which the

287

chirping created constant music. Live bear cubs roamed the lobby, often surprising unsuspecting guests. In 1902 Wilhelmina Skogh, who began her career as a dishwasher at age 13 in a Stockholm hotel, became the manager of the Grand. She is credited with the creation of one of the hotel's most distinctive features, the Winter Garden. It is a 20-meter-high room that has been the setting for a number of parties and meetings with unusual special effects. When the World Congress of Firefighters met here, the keynote speech was delivered to 600 people from the top of a skylift. Carl Larsson, the famous nineteenth-century artist noted for Swedish country scenes, painted the ceiling in what is now known as the Carl Larsson Room when he was still a young student at the Swedish Academy of Fine Arts. The guest rooms in the Grand Hotel are a luxurious treat for the traveler. All of the front rooms have a beautiful view of the Stockholm Stream. They are decorated in a regal, classic style with modern baths of green and gray marble.

Källhagens Wärdshus

Kallhagens Wardhus
Djurgårdsbrunnsvagen 10
S-115 27 Stockholm
Telephone: 665 03 00; **FAX:** 665 03 99
Rates: Single, 750 to 1,420 kr.; Double, 975 to 1,630 kr.; Suites, 1,175 to 1,900 kr. **Restaurant:** Breakfast, lunch, and dinner are served in the dining room. Dining on the outdoor terrace during the summer months. There is 24-hour room service. This hotel is a member of Countryside Hotels.

Located next to the waters of Djurgårdsbrunnsviken near many of the embassies, Kallhagens Wardshus is in one of Stockholm's loveliest areas. From here you can easily walk to the center of town, or Gamla Stan, and you are next to the Naval Museum and other sights to see in Djurgården. Kallhagen was originally built by Lieutenant Anders Cytreaus in 1806. By 1810 he had opened an inn and a distillery here. The original building where the inn was located was called Roda Stugan (Red Room). Today the hotel is known as an intimate inn where one of the biggest attractions is the well-known restaurant, specializing in traditional Swedish cooking with an international flavor. The dining room is an attractive light and airy space with big windows and clean lines. The rooms are modern with simple furniture and wood floors.

Lady Hamilton
Gunnar and Majlis Bengtsson
Storkyrkobrinken 5
111 28 Stockholm
Telephone: 08 98 23 46 80; **FAX:** 08 411 11 48;
E-mail: info@lady-hamilton.se
Rates: Single, 1,210 to 1,570 kr.; Double, 1,420 to 1,940 kr. **Restaurant:** Breakfast. The hotel is a member of Countryside Hotels and Romantik Hotels and Restaurant.

Whether you are staying in the Gamla Stan (Old Town) a day or more than two weeks, the Lady Hamilton Hotel provides a charming, centrally located base. The Royal Palace is a next-door neighbor and the Central Train Station is only 1 kilometer away. In 1975 Majlis Bengtsson bought the three old houses that make up this hotel and immediately began restoration. Mrs. Bengtsson, together with her husband, Gunnar, already owned the Lord Nelson Hotel in the Old Town and decided to name this one after Lord Nelson's famous mistress. The street on which the hotel is located used to be the northern entrance to the center of town and was probably quite busy during its heyday. Although not documented, the building probably dates to the 1470s and the time of Sten Sture the Elder. What is documented, though, is a drawing from 1746 that shows a water well discovered in the building. That well is now in the room used as a sauna and bathers may use it.

The Bengtsson's large collections of naval artifacts and Swedish folk art are utilized in the decor of the hotel. A large ship's figurehead of a woman greets the guests in the lobby, and ship models and marine paintings are everywhere. There are 34 guest rooms, each with a different Swedish flower painted on the door, representing the 34 counties of the country. In a separate building are 4 apartments that can be rented for a minimum of two weeks. Each apartment has a fully equipped kitchen. Twice-weekly cleaning service, cable television, and breakfast in the hotel dining room are included. The modern kitchens and baths complement the antique charm of the other rooms. Old porcelain stoves, wooden beams, paintings, and other lovely objects enhance the charm of the rooms. Although modern furniture dominates, one often sees an antique grandfather clock or an old piece of Swedish folk art furniture next to something from this century.

Lord Nelson
Gunnar and Majlis Bengtsson
Vasterlånggatan 22
111 29 Stockholm
Telephone: 08 23 23 90; **FAX:** 08 10 10 89;
E-mail: hotel@lord-nelson.se
Rates: Single, 940 to 1,260 kr.; Double, 1,210 to 1,680 kr. **Restaurant:** Breakfast only, served in hotel dining room. The hotel is a member of Romantik Hotels and Restaurants.

As you approach the hotel from the street, there is no doubt that the owners have a strong interest in nautical objects. The first two floors have large picture windows displaying everything from figureheads to ships' wheels. There are even two cannon neatly pointed toward the street. Each floor of the hotel, named after the great English sea admiral Lord Nelson, has been given the name of a part of a ship, such as Poop Deck and Gun Deck. Each of the 31 guest rooms is named after one of the old model ships found scattered throughout the building. An impressive model is even suspended in mid-air in the stairwell. To further extend the sea motif, each guest room was refitted with a ship's floor during the 1995 renovation. Although each guest room has all the modern amenities, objects from the owners' private collection of antiques and folk art find their way into the decor. On each floor a grandfather clock, wound by hand each night by a hotel staff member, adds the calming sound of mellow ticking.

The hotel's location on the main street in the medieval Old Town, or Gamla Stan, is ideal for walking tours and close by many restaurants, museums, and shops. From near by, a boat leaves for the archipelago. Traffic is limited in this part of town, helping to create a more relaxed cultural environment. Close to the hotel are opportunities to watch the changing of the guard at the Royal Palace or to visit the cathedral.

Malardrottningen

Malardrottningen
Brigitte Eriksson, manager
Riddarholmen
111 28 Stockholm
Telephone: 8-24 36 00; **FAX:** 8-24 36 76
Rates: Single, 600 to 1,500 kr.; Double, 700 to 1,500 kr.; Children up to 7 years free; Extra bed, 150 kr. **Restaurants:** Breakfast buffet, lunch, and dinner are served in the ship's dining room. The Captain's Bar is in what was the wheelhouse. During the summer months, meals are also served on the foredeck.

If you are in Stockholm and want an experience that is totally unique, you may choose to stay on *Malardrottningen* (the Queen of Lake Malaren), a gorgeous ship anchored next to Riddarholmen Island in the city's Old Town, Gamla Stan. Imagine what it would be like to live aboard the yacht formerly owned by Woolworth heiress Barbara Hutton. When her father gave it to her on her nineteenth birthday, it was called the *M/S Vanadis*. Eventually Miss Hutton sold the yacht, which had been built in 1924, to Great Britain's Royal Navy for one pound sterling. During the 1950s it found its way to Stockholm under the name *Court Adeler*. For several years it was a passenger liner traveling between Sweden and Finland. Now it is a floating hotel with 59 cabins, each with a private bath, color television, telephones, and air conditioning. The rooms are the size of normal ships' cabins, but pleasantly furnished and outfitted to make the visitor comfortable. A sauna is available free of charge to guests. From the ship's windows and decks there is an excellent view of the Town Hall and Gamla Stan. The location could not be better, with a subway station 200 meters away, accessibility to the railway and bus stations, and parking next door.

Victory Hotel
Gunnar and Majlis Bengtsson
Lilla Nygatan 5
S-111 28 Stockholm
Telephone: 08 14 30 90; **FAX:** 08 20 21 77;
E-mail: info@victory-hotel.se
Rates: Single, 990 kr.; Double, 1,450 kr. **Restaurant:** Restaurant Leijontornet serves lunch and dinner and specializes in fish, fowl, and game. There is a wine cellar with 400 types of wine. The Loherummet Bistro serves breakfast and a more informal lunch and dinner, with Swedish specialties. The Leijonkulan (Lion's Den) serves drinks and lighter meals and features a window into the hotel's kitchen. The hotel is a member of Countryside Hotels.

Named after Lord Nelson's flagship, *HMS Victory*, this hotel took four years to restore and is the sister hotel to the Lord Nelson and Lady Hamilton hotels. The building was originally constructed in 1642 for Pastor Primarius Olav Laurelius and is built on part of Stockholm's defensive wall dating back to the fourteenth century. In fact, when you visit the hotel's restaurant, Leijontornet, you can see the preserved ruins of the medieval wall. The bistro, Loherummet, is named after the family who lived here in the late eighteenth century.

One of the most interesting historical notes about this building is the discovery in 1937 of 18,000 silver coins and 84 silver objects buried under the floorboards in the corner of what is now the bistro and breakfast room. This is the largest discovery of silver ever made in Sweden. The treasure is believed to have been left behind by the rich Lohe family, although no one knows why. Copies of some of these pieces are on display in the hotel. As with the Bengtssons' other two hotels, Victory also has a nautical theme. When you enter the lobby filled with antiques from the great sailing era, you also find an original letter from Lord Nelson to his mistress, Emma Lady Hamilton.

Each of the guest rooms has a portrait of a well-known ship, along with photographs of the captain after whom the room is named and his wife. The decor of the rooms is a delight. The guest will find modern furniture and fabrics combined with antiques and other nautical artifacts, such as ship models and marine paintings. The Captain Johansson suite, for example, has hand-painted beams, antique furniture, and a crystal chandelier. The private baths are all equipped with the most modern amenities.

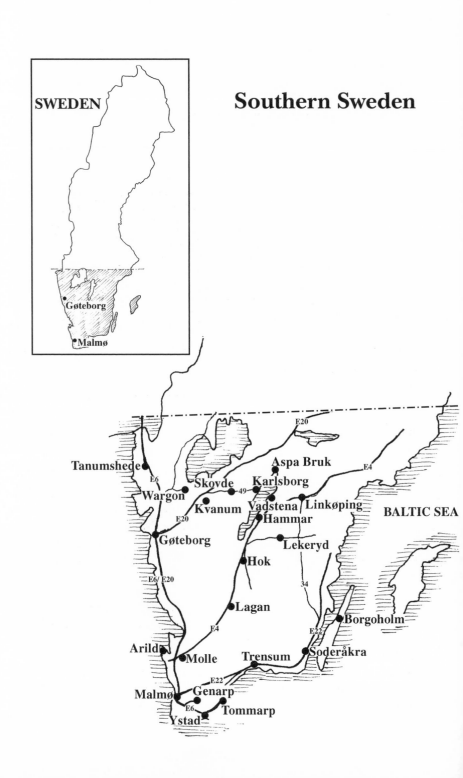

SWEDEN

Southern Sweden

Gøteborg

Malmø

Tanumshede

Aspa Bruk

E20

E4

Skovde

Karlsborg

E6

49

Wargon

Kvanum

Vadstena

Linkøping

E20

Hammar

BALTIC SEA

Gøteborg

Lekeryd

Hok

E6/ E20

34

Lagan

Borgoholm

E4

E22

Arild

Soderåkra

Molle

Trensum

E22

Malmø

Genarp

E6

Tommarp

Ystad

Southern Sweden

ARILD

Rusthallargården

Rusthallargården
Eva and Peter Malmgren
S-260 43 Arild
Telephone: 42 34 65 30; **FAX:** 42 34 67 93
Rates: Overnight rate per person, 400 to 650 kr.; Per person rate for a weekend stay, including dinner, 485 to 925 kr. per person; Family rooms, 950 to 1,200 kr.; Half board supplement, 295 kr. per person; single room supplement, 295 kr.; Special children's rates. **Restaurant:** Breakfast, lunch, and dinner are served in the hotel dining room. This hotel is a member of Countryside Hotels.

Overlooking the harbor on a little peninsula just north of Helsingborg, Rusthallargården's picturesque coastal location and accessibility to over 14 golf courses make it a lovely place to visit in Sweden's southwest region. The building was originally an armory, built in 1765 with large granite stones taken from an old watch tower at Krapperup Castle. At the beginning of the nineteenth century, P. Hogberg was given permission by the lord of Krapperup Castle to operate a restaurant

295

in the old house. Once again stones were taken from the old castle, this time to build the main staircase to the entrance. A distillery next to the manor house produced Swedish vodka. One of the innkeeper's granddaughters married well-known Danish artist Bernard Middelboe in 1880 and ran the restaurant until it was sold a few years later. Since 1948 the hotel has been in the hands of the same family.

The original granite stones from the castle still provide a welcoming, if not regal, look to the facade of the hotel. A cozy, beamed library with country furniture and books to the ceiling is as delightful as the bright dining room, with white-painted furniture, crystal chandelier, and white grandfather clock. Guest rooms are simple but very pleasant, with country fabrics and, as described by the hotel, "a provincial atmosphere." Most of the 56 rooms overlook the wonderful harbor and all have private bath, cable television, and telephone. The menu of the hotel reads like a poetic invitation to the mouth-watering dishes that earned the restaurant a place in a book entitled *Sweden's Best Tables*. Fresh fish from the harbor just a few feet away and the homemade aperitif from local elder flower juice are some of the specialties of the house.

ASPA BRUK

Aspa Herrgård

Aspa Herrgård

The Oholm family, owners; Ann-Britt Oholm, manager
696 93 Aspa Bruk
Telephone: 583-502 10; **FAX:** 583-501 50; **E-mail:** info@aspaherrgaard.se;
Web site: http://www.aspaherrgaard.se
Rates: Single, 990 to 1,290 kr.; Double, 1,480 to 2,090 kr. **Restaurant:**
Breakfast, lunch, and dinner are served in the dining room. The hotel
is a member of Countryside Hotels, Relais & Chateaux.

Aspa Herrgård is an elegant place. Although many manor houses
are wonderful places to stay, some are more informal or country-like
than others. This herregård has taken great pains to make every detail
perfect. From the red-and-gold-tasseled room keys lined up neatly in a
row, to the large white porcelain stove with its blue garlands and fluted
column, it is simply a visual experience to be enjoyed. A salon has
red brocade furniture with beautiful carpets and original works of
art. One of the dining rooms has book-lined walls while another has
crystal chandeliers and stucco-ornamented walls. The guest rooms are
tastefully decorated with Laura Ashley fabrics and wallpapers. Aspa
Herrgård was added in 1994 to the list of "Sweden's Best Hotels."
    Located between Stockholm and Gothenburg (Goteborg) next to
Vattern and near the Tivedens National Park, this estate and its natural
surroundings could not be more beautiful. Aspa Herrgård is from the
eighteenth century and holds an important place in Sweden's cultural
history. To preserve and celebrate this distinction, the Bellman Museum

298 SCANDINAVIAN HISTORIC INNS

has been established on the estate. The purpose of the museum is to collect the original music, instruments, and artifacts relating to the life of Sweden's most admired troubadour and songwriter, Carl Michael Bellman. The reason for this association with Aspa Herrgård is that Bellman's major patron was Baron Johan Diedrich Duwall, one of the owners of the estate. A significant object in the collection is a life-size wax portrait of King Carl Gustaf II. It is the only one in Sweden. For groups, the hotel will arrange cultural experiences relating to Bellman, such as a luncheon in one of the historic rooms with a guided tour of the museum.

BORGHOLM

Guntorps Herrgård

Guntorps Herrgård
Susanne and Ulf Olsson
Guntorpsgatan
387 36 Borgholm
Telephone: 485-13 000; **FAX:** 485-13 319
Rates: Single, 660 kr.; Double, 795 kr. **Restaurant:** Breakfast and dinner are served in the hotel dining room, which specializes in Swedish cuisine with a French touch.

Oland is an island on the Baltic Sea off the southeastern coast of Sweden. Steep cliffs line the coastline, and the interior is composed of forests, limestone outcrops, and farmland, all a paradise for nature lovers and bird watchers. It is an ancient place, with 16 prehistoric Iron Age forts. Two of the oldest churches, Gardslosa and Kalla, date from the Middle Ages. You will find Guntorps Herrgård in the island's largest community of Borgholm, which has a population of about 3,000. The atmosphere is relaxed and unhurried. A horsewoman and wealthy estate owner named Gunborg Sjogren originally owned Guntorps. She was a neighbor of Solliden, the estate owned by Queen Victoria of Sweden, and visited her there often when she was in residence. Herrgård eventually became a summer spot where city children could retreat for fresh air and a country experience. It later served as a restaurant school until Ulf Olsson bought it in 1985.

The estate has been carefully restored and now combines original architectural charm with modern conveniences. The hotel has become known for its excellent cuisine, thanks to chef Bjorn Lagnemar, trained in France and Sweden, and his skill in combining fresh game and vegetables from Oland with innovative recipes. An eighteenth-century bread recipe is still used in the restaurant. The hotel complex is made up of six main buildings and two separate wings, all with guest rooms with private bath and television. A heated outdoor swimming pool is available to guests.

Halltorps Gastgiveri

Halltorps Gastgiveri
Lars Olof and Margareta Forsberg, Josef and Christina Weichl
Halltorps Gastgiveri AB
S-387 92 Borgholm
Telephone: 485-85 000; **FAX:** 485-85 001
Rates: Single, 610 to 795 kr.; Double, 495 to 545 kr. per person; Suites, 660 to 760 kr. per person; Children up to 3 years of age free, children from 4 to 12 years 120 kr. extra; Half board and special weekend rates; Special golf, wine- and snaps-tasting, nature, and spa packages also available. **Restaurants:** Breakfast, lunch, and dinner are served in the hotel dining room. This hotel is a member of Romantik Hotels, Countryside Hotels, Chaine des Rotisseurs.

Located six miles from the town of Borgholm overlooking Kalmar Sound in southeastern Sweden, Halltorps Gastgiveri is an ideal spot for exploring the island of Oland. In May and June the whole island is in bloom, but the forests and fields surrounding the inn are beautiful all year round. Halltorps Gastgiveri is the oldest estate on Oland, dating from the eleventh century, and is documented as being one of the ancient Viking settlements. Because of the abundant oak forests, groves of hornbeams, and excellent hunting areas, it became a royal farm during the seventeenth century.

In 1723 Halltorp was given to Major Sven Åderman by the crown as thanks for his "invention to discharge swift shots with muskets" during the wars of King Karl XII. The manor house at Halltorp was built in 1760 during the time it was owned by Captain Edvard Liljehorn. In 1820 the estate was divided and ownership of Halltorp passed to Colonel and Chamberlain A. von Franchen and Baron M. Falkenberg. By mid-century it was owned by a member of the Swedish Parliament, and in 1918 was purchased by the municipality and turned into a home for elderly citizens. It became an inn in 1975 after an extensive restoration that involved building heavy girders to strengthen and consolidate the old manor house.

An annex with 25 new rooms along the Sound was built in 1991. A different craftsman from 25 Swedish provinces designed each room. You will find the names of the provinces on the doors of the guest rooms. Some of the designers created furniture in the style of their own areas of Sweden, and special attention was paid to the textiles used. For example, the unique blue light one sees in Oland, appreciated for many years by artists who have come there to paint, inspired the design of the textiles by Marianne Lundgren for some of the rooms. The inn has also become known for its excellent cuisine, always using fresh produce from the island, as well as fish caught nearby in the Baltic and lambs that were raised on the *alvaret*. Herbs from the inn's garden are used to flavor the food, as well as the snaps. All bread and pastries are made in the inn's kitchen. In this lovely natural location, there is much to do outside. On the grounds, one can play croquet on the lawn or take a sauna and then jump into the cold (16 degree C.) water from the inn's artesian well. The water at the beach is warm enough to swim in by July. A 27-hole golf course is about a half mile away. Various activities such as bird watching and fishing can be arranged by the inn.

GENARP

Hackeberga Wardshus

Hackeberga Wardshus
Sam Hellhager
Vardshusvagen
240 13 Genarp
Telephone: 040-48 05 41
Restaurant: Open Tuesday to Saturday, 11:30 A.M. to 2 P.M. and 6 P.M. to 11 P.M.; Sunday, 11:30 A.M. to 5 P.M.

I had the delicious pleasure of attending a birthday dinner at this wonderful old inn in the southern Swedish area of Skåne. Less than an hour's drive from Malmø and a half hour from the historic town of Lund, Hackeberga Wardshus is worth a visit even if you are staying in another town. The restaurant is located in the village of Genarp and is surrounded by the tranquil, pleasing countryside of this part of Sweden that was once ruled by Denmark. At the present time there is only a restaurant here, but there are plans to add overnight accommodations.

The building was constructed as a poorhouse in 1869. Local citizens provided the money for the building, and the nearby Hackeberga estate donated the land. A barrier was built between the estate and the poorhouse so the wealthy would not be disturbed. Documents from the period relate a life of hardship for those within the poorhouse walls. They were forced to beg for their food and clothing, and they lived in small, cramped quarters. The floors were bare clay. Rules for conduct and work were posted. The building became a nursing home in 1963. I thought of the house's past inhabitants as I enjoyed its contemporary warmth and luxury. Sam Hellhager, the inn's current owner and head chef, prepared for us a meal consisting of specialties from Skåne. As each course was served, he explained the history of the dish and how it was prepared using local ingredients.

Nearby is Flyinge Kungsgård, a large estate from the 1600s with a long tradition as an equestrian center. It is now well known as a school offering different types of horse-related training for advanced students. Tours are available between 9 A.M. and 4 P.M. daily. Hackeberga Castle, originally built by the Dane Holger Ulfstand in the fourteenth century, was rebuilt following a fire in the middle of the eighteenth century. It is now a restaurant and is open to the public.

GOTHENBURG

Gota Kanel

Gota Kanel
Britt Marie Brax
Gota Kanel Steamship Company
Box 272
S-401 24 Goteborg
Telephone: 31 80 63 15; **FAX:** 31 15 83 11;
Web site: http://www.gotacanal.se
Rates: Two-day cruise, 3,500 to 5,700 kr. per person; Four-day cruise,
5,900 to 9,700 kr. per person; Six-day cruise, 9,400 to 12,700 kr. per
person; Golf cruises, 7,150 to 9,895 kr. per person; Single cabins and
rates available. **Restaurant:** All meals on board are served in the dining
room or on deck. This hotel is a member of Romantik Hotels and
Restaurants, De Historiske Hotel.

What better way to explore Sweden and stay in a historic place than
aboard an antique steamer? These vessels are veritable moving "hotels
on water." The *Juno* was built in 1874, the first vessel built by this group
of shipowners. The *Wilhelm Tham* was launched in 1912. The original
steam engines of both were replaced by diesel engines in the 1950s.
The *M/S Diana* was built in 1931. The steamers were built especially
for the Gota Canal and are 31 meters long and 7 meters wide. The first
canal was finished in 1800. As early as 1715, plans were made to link
Gothenburg and Norrkoping. War and blockages to the canal inter-
rupted the work, and an even more modern canal with a better lock
system eventually became a reality in 1916. Everyone from kings and

nobility to peasants and priests has traveled this canal. By the middle of the nineteenth century, thousands of immigrants used this route as they traveled west to America. The vessels were built with as much deck space as possible for the poorer passengers who could not afford cabins. As more railroads were built, canal traffic steadily decreased. After World War I, bus transportation became the choice of most travelers.

During the four-day, three-night journey from Stockholm to Gothenburg, the boats glide through some of the loveliest scenery to be found in Sweden. Castles, ruins, small villages, and churches may be seen from the deck. It is a relaxing and comfortable way to travel, never faster than the five knots established at the turn of the century. The route winds through two large lakes, Lake Vanern and Lake Vattern, as well as through 65 locks. As the boats pass through the locks, many guests choose to use one of the on-board bicycles and pedal along the canal bank. When the boat docks, short tours may be arranged, so there are always plenty of places to explore.

There are about 30 cabins on each boat, although the shower rooms and toilets are down the hall. Meals are served on linen tablecloths with silver in a wood-paneled dining room. Many of the guests choose to dress formally for dinner. Coffee is served either in the lounge or on deck, where blankets are provided for the cool evenings. The restaurant becomes a bar after the evening meal.

Hotel Eggers
Gunilla and Jan Ramen, owners; Barbara Nordberg, manager
Drottningtorget, Goteborg
Telephone: 031-80 60 70; **FAX:** 031-15 42 43
Rates: Single, 595 kr. on weekends, 1,085 kr. on weekdays; Double, 840 kr. on weekends, 1,325 kr. on weekdays; Extra bed, 205 kr. **Restaurant:** The restaurant Eggers serves breakfast, lunch, and dinner. The bar also serves lunch. The hotel is a member of Countryside Hotels.

Hotel Eggers is one of the few hotels built during the early railroad boom that still remain. The second oldest hotel in Sweden, it opened in 1859, shortly after the completion of the railroad station in Gothenburg. The hotel accommodated many people leaving for the New World, as well as refugees fleeing the Russian Revolution. Even today many of its guests are Swedish-Americans returning home for a visit. The oldest part of the building dates to 1820, although the foundation of the hotel rests on the old city wall from the sixteenth century. In 1876 the new owner, only the second proprietor to receive a license to operate a restaurant, renamed it Hotel Christiania. One of his employees, a young man named Emil Eggers, later married the owner's daughter and in 1883 took over management of the hotel. After an extensive renovation program, Eggers wrote, "Through hard work . . . I finally reached the point . . . when I was able to inaugurate my new hotel. . . . In order to avoid confusion with other not so elegant hotels and to keep the hotel just for me I decided to name it Hotel Eggers." Hotel Eggers played a notable role in the evolution of

Swedish art. An artist named Anders Zorn, while occupying a room at the hotel, began an art revolution known as The Opposition against the conservative, iron-fisted rule of the Swedish Art Academy. Previously the Academy had enforced stringent guidelines as to what standards and styles of art were acceptable.

The elegant, four-story facade of the hotel faces the Queen's Place in the center of Gothenburg, next to the train and bus stations, the Opera, and the Maritime Museum. In the lobby, white columns decorated with gold stand on marble bases, and from the high stucco ceilings hang crystal chandeliers. The Eggers Restaurant has beautifully patterned rugs, stained-glass ceiling decorations, and dark wood paneling. The diner may choose to eat in one of several separate dining rooms that have only one table each. The guest rooms are cozy, old-world style, and all differ in their furnishings.

HAMMAR

Bastedalens Herrgård

Bastedalens Herrgård
Pia Stenstromer
S-696 94 Hammar
Telephone: 583 77 02 73; **FAX:** 583 77 00 87
Rates: Single, 350 to 450 kr.; Double, 500 to 600 kr. **Restaurant:**
Breakfast, lunch, and dinner are served in the dining room. Breakfast
is 50 kr. extra. There is a coffee shop.

It isn't often one encounters a Swedish manor with its own Chinese
Park. That is exactly what one finds at Bastedalen and what makes it a
most uncommon place. Located on the eastern shore of Vattern, south
of the town of Hammar, the estate was originally owned by Harge
Tegelbruk, a mid-nineteenth-century immigrant from Bohmen-
Mahren, a part of what is now the Czech Republic. The family owned
the property until 1958. The main house burned to the ground in
1933 and the present house was rebuilt in 1934. In 1959 it was bought
by Ebbe Johnson, editor-in-chief of a Swedish publication. He had had
a longstanding interest in the Far East as a result of a trip there during
his youth. He had managed to assemble a nice collection of Chinese
antiquities but also dreamed of building a Chinese garden. This
became a reality in 1960 when he converted an overgrown limestone
quarry into the Garden of the Harmonious Valley. His idea was to create
an area that appeared to have existed since ancient times. He
designed the garden with pavilions, ponds, and bridges according to
the ancient traditions of China.

Today it is possible to visit the gardens daily all year round, even though you may not be staying at the hotel. A small museum and gallery offer exhibitions and sales of Chinese objects. If you do choose to stay overnight at Bastedalens Herrgård, it is a pleasant place to be, with many activities. The hotel has a tennis court and can arrange fishing and boating trips on the lake. Thanks to the renovation efforts of present owner Pia Stenstromer of Stockholm, the manor house offers beautiful and comfortable surroundings for the guest.

HOK

Hooks Herrgård

Hooks Herrgård

Dan Tervaniemi and Benny Nygren, managers
560 13 Hok
Telephone: (0) 393 210 80; **FAX:** (0) 393 215 67
Rates: Single, 1,050 kr.; Double, 1,260 to 1,490 kr.; Suite, 2,050 kr.;
Extra bed, 495 kr.; Full board and special weekend rates available.
Restaurant: Breakfast, lunch, and dinner are served in the dining
room. There is a bar. Packed lunches for day trips may be ordered.
The hotel is a member of Countryside Hotels.

If your vacation aim is to combine the opportunity to play two 18-
hole golf courses and a 9-hole pitch and putt course with a stay at an
eighteenth-century manor house, then Hooks Herrgård is the place
for you. Its location on Lake Hook in the middle of the countryside
in Småland makes it a golfer's dream. A driving range is on the
grounds, and golf lessons are available, along with a pro shop and
clubhouse where the golfer can relax with a sauna or Jacuzzi after an
invigorating round. For those whose interests turn more toward tennis
and swimming, there are also courts and a heated saltwater pool. If
fishing is your sport, there are many pike, perch, and eel in the lake
right outside the manor house's door. The lake can be explored by
borrowing a canoe or rowboat from the hotel. There are 103 rooms,
many of which are in keeping with the traditional atmosphere of the
manor house.

The manor house is a lovely building with a red tile roof, flanked
by side buildings in the same style. Its history can be traced to the
fourteenth century when owner Herger Joarsson was listed on a
medieval document written in Latin. His property was thought to have
been composed of a grouping of modest wooden buildings that he
gave to a nearby monastery before his death. When Sweden became
a Protestant country after the Reformation, the property was no

longer a part of the monastery. The right to live there and reap the benefits of its large land holdings was granted by the Crown as thanks to those who had served the king's interests. By 1630 the estate had been acquired by Peder Gudmundsson, a powerful man in Småland. His family owned the property for the next 85 years. Peder's son began to raise sheep, supplying the entire Swedish army with wool socks.

In the early part of the eighteenth century, the wife of a general major, Brita Sofia Stromberg, was the owner. She had nine children, five of whom were killed fighting in the war of 1718 in Frederikshald. There were no male heirs to the estate, so her daughter, Anna Margareta, took charge and operated the property by herself. Apparently this was common during the period, when most of Sweden's young men were away fighting in the Hundred Year's War. Women managed everything from small peasant farms to large estates and apparently did so successfully.

KARLSBORG

Kanalhotellet

Kanalhotellet
Ann and Eric Axelsson
Storgatan 94
546 32 Karlsborg
Telephone: 505-121 30; **FAX:** 505-127 61
Rates: Single, 500 to 650 kr.; Double, 680 to 850 kr. **Restaurant:**
Breakfast, lunch, and dinner are served in the dining room.

In 1894 Anna and Johan Axelsson wrote to their employer, U.S.
President Grover Cleveland: "It has been our pleasure to serve in the
White House during your presidency. However, we wish to return to
Sweden to pursue our dream of owning and operating a hotel." When
they returned home, that is exactly what they did. Roads in Sweden
at the time were poor, but steamboats traveled along Lake Vattern and
the Gota Canal. In 1879 the railroad built a station in Karlsborg so that
its "boat train" could pick up passengers brought by the canal
steamboats. Kanalhotellet stands within a few feet of the Gota Canal
and has always been one of the stops meant to provide food and lodging
for travelers on the canal. In fact, the hotel's first contract with the
Gota Canal Company stipulated that the hotel must maintain a waiting

room for passengers who were going further. The waiting room is now the hotel's dining room. The present owners are the fourth generation of the family to run the hotel.

In addition to the canal, there is much to see in this area halfway between Gothenburg and Stockholm. Within walking distance is Lake Vattern, the second largest lake in Sweden. These waters are home to the Red Belly Salmon known as Vattern Roding, a specialty on the hotel's menu. Just north of Karlsborg you will find Tiveden National Park, Sweden's southernmost wilderness, where the Ice Age left huge formations of stone blocks and deep forest pools. Also close by is Karlsborg Fortress, a 90-year project begun in 1809 after the loss of Finland to Russia. It was to serve as a military assembly point and a place of protection for the royal family and the national gold reserve. Within the walls of the fortress is a small town with a church, houses, and stores.

KVANUM

Bjertorp Slott

Bjertorp Slott
Helen and Anders Junger
Bjertorp Slott
535 91 Kvanum
Telephone: 0512-203 90; **FAX:** 0512-200 77
Rates: Single, 595 to 945 kr.; Double, 890 to 1,145 kr.; Suites, 1,150 to 1,695 kr.; Extra children's bed free. **Restaurant:** Breakfast, lunch, and dinner; light meals and sandwiches served (also on the terrace) each day from 2 P.M.

Bjertorp Slott is Sweden's newest castle, built between 1911 and 1914. In 1856 Sven Henrik Littorin bought this property, which he worked as a large agricultural concern. His son, Knut Henrik, was sent to Gothenborg's Business College, and this education enabled him to get a job with Nobels Oil Company. He advanced quickly and in 1913 was sent to Moscow as the Swedish consul. There he made a fortune in oil and gas. He was a clever manager of his money and was able to buy Bjertorp from his father after deciding that this was the place for a home for his family. He went to a well-known architect, Ferdinand Boberg, designer of Stockholm's main post office and the NK House. He wanted the most impressive residence in West Gotland and told Boberg to spend as much money as was necessary to produce the desired result.

It was Littorin's wife who was responsible for increasing the house's size. It was transformed from a country home into a manor house on a grand scale. Only the best materials, such as Italian marble, French wallpaper, and mahogany paneling, were used. Littorin lived in the house until his death in 1939 and the family kept the residence until 1956. The state then purchased the estate, and it was turned into a school of home economics for young women. In 1980 it finally became a hotel.

Guests enter the estate through an impressive gate of rusticated stones. The house is situated in a park of beautiful proportions that is now the location of many outdoor activities of the hotel. The interior is of the Art Nouveau style and is filled with remarkable details. Italian stucco craftsmen were called in to do the dining room ceiling, which took several years to complete. There are also rooms with mahogany wood paneling, an old gymnastic hall for the children of the family, the original pool table, bas-relief panels of sculpture on the exterior of the building, and a room said to be an exact copy of the Czar's Room in the Kremlin. Much of the original furniture is still in use. These are but a few of the delights that await the guest at Bjertorps Slott.

The castle is known for its excellent cuisine, with a menu that changes with the seasons, following the availability of fresh ingredients. An impressive wine list is overseen by the owner. An 18-hole golf course and a golf school are part of the hotel's extensive offerings, along with horseback riding, billiards, fishing, and free bicycles. The hotel will also arrange various types of activities, from hot air ballooning to music festivals, for small or large groups.

LAGAN

Toftaholm Herrgård

Toftaholm Herrgård
Torbjorn Colfach and Anders Haggbom
Toftaholm
S-340 14 Lagan
Telephone: 370-440-55; **FAX:** 370-440 45
Rates: Single, 790 to 940 kr.; Double, 990 to 1,240 kr.; Suite, 1,490 kr.; Weekend packages with half and full board, 275 to 350 per person; Children up to 12 years, 150 kr. supplement. **Restaurant:** Breakfast, lunch, and dinner are available in the dining room. This hotel is a member of De Historiske Hotel, Romantik Hotels and Restaurants.

Evidence of Toftaholm's 600-year history, complete with ghosts, secret tunnels, and kings, abounds. Beginning with a rune stone on the property, there is evidence that this area was inhabited at least 1,000 years ago. In 1389 Jons Skotta Tofholm founded the herrgård, or estate. It was during the time of his grandson, in 1460, that it was secured as a fortress called Toftaborg, which was to protect the estate and the local population against attacks by the Danes. Later, under the guidance of the Stenbock family, it became the largest estate in Småland, reaching its zenith in the middle of the sixteenth century. One of the owners, Field Marshall Gustav Stenbock, became the father-in-law of King Gustav Vasa when the 56-year-old ruler married Stenbock's 16-year-old daughter. During one of the king's visits to his young lover, he was chased by a group of Danes and had to use a secret tunnel from the fortress to the north wing of the house to escape.

According to legend, while fleeing he lost the two rings he was bringing to Stenbock's daughter. The rings have never been found and the legend continues.

The bright yellow wooden building with green lawns sloping down to the lake is a delight to the eye. Forest and water can be seen from all the windows, and the common rooms are graceful, elegant, and perfectly decorated with a combination of traditional and country-style furnishings. The 45 guest rooms have an almost English-cottage appeal, with light, floral fabrics and pleasing decor. The hotel's tavern is from the seventeenth century. There is much to do here, including hiking and skiing on the many marked trails, fishing, swimming at the private beach, golfing at the two nearby 18-hole courses, and canoeing or rowboating on the lake. Toftaholm is 400 kilometers south of Stockholm and 210 kilometers north of Malmo.

LEKERYD

UFFE-

Sunds Herrgård

Sunds Herrgård
The Geiger and Wegele families
Sunds Hergård
S-560 28 Lekeryd
Telephone: 36-820 06; **FAX:** 36-821 40
Rates: Single, 595 kr.; Double, 475 kr. per person. **Restaurant:** There is a breakfast buffet, large smorgåsbord and cold and warm dishes a la carte for lunch, and three-course meals served for dinner. There is a bar. Outdoor grilling in the Grill House or on a small island in the lake can be arranged. The hotel's own organically raised livestock provide meat for the menu. The hotel is a member of Countryside Hotels.

The hotel was originally a working herrgård (estate) or large farm, dating from around 1850. It has been operating as an inn since 1930 and has been in the same families since the beginning of the nineteenth century. The hotel is actually a complex of buildings, including riding stables and a sauna, on the shore of a gorgeous lake. The main building is a cheerful yellow wooden structure looking out over the water. Located just east of Jonkoping and Huskvarna, the hotel is set amid beautiful natural surroundings. The wildlife in this area is abundant, and deer or wild boar hunting can be arranged by the hotel. Hiking and fishing trips are popular ways of exploring the surrounding woods. So are mushroom-picking expeditions. If you want to take a bicycle tour, the inn will pack a lunch to take with you. The inn has its own horses, so riding is one of the more popular activities. There are also tennis courts, a small pool, a workout room, and a playground for the children.

MALMØ

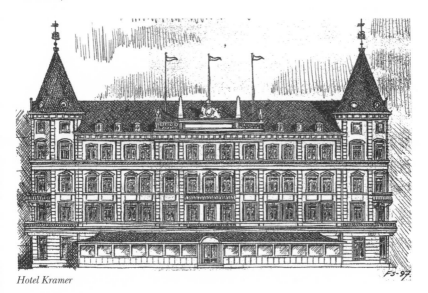

Hotel Kramer

Hotel Kramer
Stortorget 7, Box 107
S-201 21 Malmø
Telephone: 40-20 88 00; **FAX:** 40-12 69 41;
Web site: hotel.kramer@postbox.postnet.se; **International Toll Free
Reservation Number:** 46 08-411 40 40
Rates: Single, 590 to 690 kr.; Double, 690 to 790 kr. **Restaurant:** Lunch
and dinner are served in the dining room. There is a breakfast room
and tea veranda. The bar also serves light meals. Room service is
available. The hotel is a member of Provobis Hotels.

Hotel Kramer is one of those hotels that looks as though it has been
there forever. It is firmly planted in the middle of Malmø on the
Stortorget Square just a three-minute walk from the railroad station
and the hydrofoil boats that ferry passengers back and forth to nearby
Copenhagen. It is a classical building topped with flanking obelisks
and sculptures, balustrade, and a round tower. The four-story white
hotel was thoroughly renovated in 1995 and immediately received a
top rating by the Swedish newspaper *Dagens Industri*. Its polished marble
lobby, which has remained the same since it was built, has rounded
arches and crystal chandeliers that give an indication of the luxurious
standard of the hotel.

The guest rooms are of two types. The more common rooms are decorated in what the hotel calls "turn-of-the-century classic," with parquet floors, oriental carpets, light-colored fabrics, and dark wood furniture. They are light and airy with tall windows, many of which look out over the main square. The Club Rooms, as they are called, have what *Gourmet* magazine called "mahogany decor that has not been seen since the days of the Atlantic liners." The shiny wood molding, mirror frames, furniture, and closets are all in rich mahogany that certainly exudes a classy atmosphere of days gone by. All guest rooms have cable television, minibar, trouser press, and iron. More than half the rooms have computer connections for e-mail.

In 1846 a hotel was built on the spot where Hotel Kramer stands today. The present building that houses Hotel Kramer, however, was built in 1878 by Fritz Kramer and his wife, Anna, both of whom came from Germany. He had been working in Copenhagen as a waiter at the famous Hotel d'Angleterre (see the listing under Copenhagen) and his wife prepared the cold buffet. They married in Denmark and moved to a small farm outside of Malmø. That farm is now within the city of Malmo and the street has been named Kramersvagen in their honor. They decided to go into the hotel business. Anna had become an excellent cook, even though female chefs were not widely accepted in that age.

At first they rented a hotel. Later they bought an old hotel and tore it down to make way for the new French chateau-style hotel. A Danish architect, Carl-Ferdinand Rasmussen, was commissioned to create the design. Fritz Kramer died in 1893, and Anna and their eight children carried on the business. One of the sons, Hermann, became the manager, and the hotel remained in the Kramer family until 1938.

MOLLE

Molle Turisthotell

Molle Turisthotell
Lottie and Bjorn Samuelsson
Kullabergsvagen 32
S-260 42 Molle
Telephone: 42-34 70 84; **FAX:** 42-34 74 84;
E-Mail: molle.turisthotell@hoganas.mail.telia.com
Rates: Single, 600 to 750 kr.; Double, 650 to 800 kr.; Suite, 1,000 kr.
Restaurant: Breakfast, lunch, and dinner are served in the hotel dining room. There is a bar.

In this century Molle has become known as a mecca for artists and others interested in nature. Located close to Helsinborg, just over the short distance of water from Denmark, it was considered quite a fashionable seaside resort at the turn of the century. Built in 1872, the hotel attracted musicians, artists, and authors, as well as the likes of King Oscar II and Kaiser Wilhelm II. The white building, with its tower and terrace facing the sea, is charming. All of the 14 rooms, each decorated differently in a Victorian style, have private baths. Many of the rooms also have a balcony overlooking the water. The food served in the restaurant is classic Swedish, and *fisksoppa*, or fish soup, is one of the specialties. The dining room is a glassed-in area with plenty of sunshine and a delightful seaside view. The library is a cozy common room with bits of the hotel's history framed on the walls. During the summer jazz music is performed every Saturday.

SKOVDE

Knistad Herrgård

Knistad Herrgård
Berit and Dag Johansson
Knistad Herrgård
54192 Skovde
Telephone: 500-46 31 70; **FAX:** 500-46 30 75;
E-mail: knistad.se. hemsida: www.knistad.se
Rates: Single, 595 to 890 kr.; Double, 795 to 1,080 kr.; Suites, 1,350 kr.; Special weekend, golf, and fitness packages available. **Restaurant:** Breakfast, lunch, and dinner are served. In summer serving is outdoors. The Grill overlooks the golf course. This hotel is a member of Romantik Hotels and Restaurants, Countryside Hotels.

Knistad Herrgård is more than a historic hotel. It is a complete resort, with its own 18-hole golf course and all sorts of fitness and spa amenities. Within the setting of this yellow wooden building and its grounds you can play tennis, use the driving range and pro shop, exercise in the fitness center, enjoy walks in beautiful natural surroundings, or be pampered with a massage or skin treatment session. Nearby, the guest can also find horseback riding, hot air ballooning, and many other types of activities. Afterward, you can indulge in the herrgård's fine cooking that includes typical Swedish herrgård cuisine as well as gourmet food inspired in the four corners of the world. The chef and his kitchen staff pride themselves on the creative use of herbs from their own garden to flavor their own vinaigrette, oils, and snaps. Cakes and breads are also homemade. In the estate's old vaulted potato cellar, the contemporary visitor can participate in the hotel's wine-, beer-, and whiskey-tasting gatherings.

Six years ago, Knistad Herrgård went through a thorough restoration process that included careful consideration of the original style, even to the point of consulting with the National Museum and commissioning special copies of the original carpets from 1748 for the main building. Colors for the wooden paneling were studied carefully to determine what had been there in the eighteenth century. Another wing, now with 54 guest rooms, formerly served as the estate manager's residence and a meat storage area. The rooms now all have private baths, television, and telephones. The classical herrgård style with wooden floors and lovely fabrics gives the guest rooms a special appeal. The original estate can be traced to the fourteenth century. From 1646 it was owned by the Crown of Sweden. It was Barbro and her husband, Jacob Lind of Hageby, who gave the estate its present look. In 1799 Knistad was sold to a man named Gyllenberg, whose only son built a 20-meter-high tower out of stone blocks. He died when the tower collapsed on him.

SODERÅKRA

Stufvena Gastgifveri

Stufvena Gastgifveri
Inger and Sigvard Johansson
Pl 7488, 385 97 Soderåkra
Telephone: 0486-219 00; **FAX:** 0486-218 68
Rates: Single, 725 to 875 kr.; Double, 1,050 to 1,250 kr.; Special weekend
package with full board. **Restaurant:** Breakfast, lunch, and dinner are
served in the hotel dining rooms. There is a wine cellar. The hotel is
a member of Countryside Hotels.

Located 35 kilometers from Kalmar on the coast near Oland, this
area was inhabited more than 5,000 years ago. The property on which
the hotel is situated was originally part of a well-known estate named
Warnanas and was owned by a succession of famous Swedish families
from the tenth century on. One of the more notorious owners was
Bo Jonsson Grip, a financier who after the Black Death gained ownership of most of the county of Kalmar. At the beginning of the sixteenth
century, the estate was owned by King Gustav Vasa. He was not an
absentee owner, and his second wife, Margareta Leijonhuvud, often
stayed here. King Erik XIV was also a frequent guest. The first estate
burned down in 1564 and was rebuilt by King Johan III. In 1645
Queen Kristina gave the property to Chancellor Axel Oxenstierna as a
reward for his role in the signing of a peace treaty.

The main building as it stands today is from 1798. Two other
buildings, a cottage for farmhands and a brewery, are from the early
part of the nineteenth century, when the property was a working farm.
Careful restoration was carried out to preserve the main house. The
present dining rooms still have their original floors, doors, and tiled
stoves, and the kitchen retains its original iron stove. For those interested

in nature, there are 600-year-old oak trees to complement the medieval origin of the estate.

This area has many wildlife preserves and bird sanctuaries. From the hotel, there is a view of Svårto (Black Island), which is home to Scandinavia's largest colony of cormorants. Some of the low islands are breeding grounds for Canadian geese, and there are several colonies of seals. An 18-hole golf course is only 3 kilometers away, and a 36-hole course is 35 kilometers to the north. The beach is only a few meters from the hotel. The hotel is famous for its Swedish cuisine, often made with vegetables and herbs from the manor house's own garden. Wild game can be found on the menu. The wine cellar has more than 500 different kinds of wine, and guests can arrange for special wine-tasting sessions.

TANUMSHEDE

Tanums Gestgifveri

Tanums Gestgifveri
Regine and Steiner Oster
457 00 Tanumshede
Telephone: 0525 290 10; **FAX:** 0525 295 71
Rates: Single, 590 to 650 kr.; Double, 790 to 910 kr. **Restaurant:** Breakfast, lunch, and dinner are served in the dining room. The hotel is member of Countryside Hotels, Relais et Chateaux.

Tanumshede is in a beautiful coastal area not far from the Norwegian border. Evidence of its ancient history can be seen in the Iron Age grave fields and the more than 1,000-year-old rune stone at the local church. Equally fascinating are the ubiquitous rock paintings from 3,500 years ago scattered throughout this part of Sweden. These petroglyphs depict all manner of subject matter, from kissing couples to farmers plowing their fields. Before searching for some of the more than 10,000 examples of this art, it is best to begin with one of the rock carving museums, where it is possible to learn about the culture that produced them.

A great place to stay in this province is Tanums Gestgifveri, said to be one of the oldest inns in Sweden. The bright yellow wooden building is known to have been in operation as a road inn in 1663. Bjørn of Hee, the first innkeeper, built his inn on the highest point in town, next to the grave of a Viking king. This was an important Viking settlement from which expeditions westward originated in the early Middle Ages. A chief's grave is located behind the present butler's pantry. According to old documents, "Bjørn of Hee received of the Governor the right to become an innkeeper. The peasants were told to provide timber for a stable for travelers' horses. Earlier it had been the duty of the local priest to provide a place here for the upper class traveling through this area, a service for which he earned extra income. This part of Sweden was then part of Norway, and Norwegian law dictated this practice.

Recorded history reveals that two-course meals at the inn cost 22 ore, while a dram of distilled liquor cost 4 ore. A court record from 1706 shows that a few of the inn's guests drank too much and attacked several passersby. The assailants were fined and put into the pillory next to the church. By 1749 the area was Swedish. Swedish law stated that one floor of an inn should be reserved for nobility, one floor for "honest folk," and another for the "common folk." Each of today's guest rooms has its own style and furnishings. The old taproom is now used as a restaurant, where a seventeenth-century atmosphere has been recreated. Fresh fish and seafood are specialties of the restaurant, and it is famous for its fish stew.

TOMMARP

Karlaby Kro

Karlaby Kro
Sophia Danielsson, manager
272 93 Tommarp
Telephone: 0414-203 00; **Web site:** www.karlabykro.se
Rates: Single, 665 to 1,050 kr.; Double, 465 to 680 kr. per person; Half board available from 830 to 1,200 kr. per person; Weekend and gourmet special available. **Restaurant:** Breakfast, lunch, and dinner are served in the inn's three dining rooms. There is a bar. The hotel is a member of Countryside Hotels.

Thanks to a recent restoration, Karlaby Kro looks exactly as it did in 1898. Its whitewashed walls, thatched roof, and multi-paned windows bid a warm welcome to visitors. The building was originally a farm owned by the Andersson family. The area surrounding the inn is still farm land, the source of fresh ingredients for the gourmet meals prepared by the inn's chefs. Local farmers supply ducks, fresh lamb, and geese, as well as wild hare and deer. The inn bakes its own bread and makes it own ice cream. The 21 rooms are lovely. Spanish terracotta tiles are covered with oriental rugs, rich fabrics in beautiful coordinated patterns are used for the draperies, upholstery, and bedspreads, and the views from the windows are relaxing and refreshing. There are many opportunities for various types of activities at the inn, including cooking courses, wine- and whiskey-tasting, and riding Icelandic horses. The inn has a gorgeous glass-covered indoor pool that gives the sensation of swimming outdoors in the warmth of the heated pool. Also available are a sauna, fitness center, and solarium. Ten kilometers away is an 18-hole golf course by the sea.

TRENSUM

Guo Vardshus

Guo Vardshus
Horst Gottlieb
Guoviksvagen 16
374 94 Trensum
Telephone: 0454-603 00; **FAX:** 0454-601 00
Rates: Single, 525 kr.; Double, 590 kr. **Restaurant:** Breakfast, lunch,
and dinner are served in the dining room.

Guo Vardshus is in Sweden's beautiful Blekinge area, known for its
lovely nature and water views. Guo Vardshus is a neighbor to Eriksberg's
Nature Preserve, where walking is a pleasant way to enjoy the beauty of
the forests. Swimming, boating, and fishing are also available to guests,
although just sitting in the hotel's restaurant looking out over Guo Inlet
is a pleasure. The 24 rooms are housed in an attractive yellow building.
The high ceiling reception rooms are decorated in a classic, calming
style with lovely antique furniture, oriental rugs, and gorgeous fabrics.
   The history of the hotel begins with a Swede, Berndt Svensson, who
traveled to the nearby port of Karlshamn and stowed away aboard a
ship bound for America in the middle of the nineteenth century. He
got only as far as Liverpool, where he eventually started his own hotel
and became a rich man. He always missed his mother country, however,
and on one of his many trips back home bought a large piece of
property in Guo. He hired several of England's best-known architects
and asked them to design a hotel that looked like an English castle.

They did so, and in 1883 the present building, with its four corner towers and large tower in the middle, was completed.

With Svensson's many social connections in England, he quickly became known among the country's high society who came to his hotel. This success story, however, began to sour when local citizens questioned Svensson's right to the property. Fights over whether the property was common land erupted among groups of locals. By this time, Svensson had turned much of the land into a beautiful park, which actually benefited those living in the area by bringing in tourists who spent money. But trouble persisted, and in 1894 the hotel burned to the ground. There was speculation that the fire might have been started deliberately. In any event, the building and its contents had been heavily insured, and it was rebuilt within six months. But Svensson had other problems. Family members who had been working with him suddenly left the hotel, and that was the beginning of the end. The interiors of several rooms were not completed, and in 1906 the hotel was sold for a mere 45,000 kroner. There are rumors that a ghost roams the hotel and that it may be Svensson.

VADSTENA

Vadstena Klosterhotel

Vadstena Klosterhotel
Johan Milton
Klosterområdet, 592 00 Vadstena
Telephone: 143 115 30; **FAX:** 143-136 48
Rates: Single, 775 to 875 kr.; Double, 895 to 995 kr. **Restaurant:**
Breakfast, lunch, and dinner are served in the dining room. The hotel
is a member of Countryside Hotels.

Vadstena Klosterhotel (Cloister Hotel) was once a "double cloister,"
housing both monks and nuns of the Order of St. Birgitta. The hotel's
story began in 1250 when Birger Jarl built the Family Bjalbo's mansion.
Bjalbo was one of Sweden's most powerful men during the Middle
Ages, and his son Valdemar became king in 1258. The estate remained
the summer palace of the Swedish royalty for 100 years. At the
beginning of the fourteenth century, King Magnus Eriksson and
Queen Blanka assisted Birgitta Birgersdotter, later Saint Birgitta, in
establishing her own order of nuns. In 1384 the cloister was built at
Vadstena to house 60 nuns and 25 monks. The monks left in 1545
and the nuns stayed on until 1595. During the seventeenth century,
the buildings were used as a home for soldiers who had been wounded
in war. Today the cloister church, with its high vaulted ceilings, long
nave, and tall glass windows, is a perfect example of the Gothic style of
church architecture in Sweden. It is situated between the hotel and
the hotel restaurant and still functions as a church. Its spire rises high

above the village and can be seen from afar. Concerts are often given here and can be attended by hotel guests.

The guest rooms, many with lovely views of Lake Vattern, have been carefully renovated and contain furniture by Swedish designers Carls Malmsten and Bodafors. The hotel still retains the architectural atmosphere of the cloister. Breakfast is served in the *Kungasalen*, which still has the heavy arches and columns. The nuns' dormitory, a long, tunneled walkway with rooms on either side, is now used for small conference groups at the hotel. A special garden, Ortagården, has been dedicated to the memory of the monks who once tended their own garden here. It is now used to grow herbs for the kitchen. With its old houses and cobblestone streets, the town of Vadstena certainly calls to mind the Middle Ages. The oldest town hall in Sweden is here, as are a number of craftsmen, such as lace makers, silversmiths, and glass blowers.

WARGON

Ronnums Herrgård

Ronnums Herrgård
Flloren and Tengblad families
468 30 Wargon
Telephone: 521 22 32 70; **FAX:** 521 22 06 60;
E-mail: ronnums.herrgard@ronnum.se
Rates: Single, 700 to 950 kr.; Double, 900 to 1,110 kr.; Suites, 1,200 kr. **Open:** Closed during the period around Christmas and New Year's. **Restaurant:** Breakfast, lunch, and dinner are served in the dining room. The hotel is a member of Countryside Hotels, Relais & Chateaux.

During the Middle Ages, when this property was known as Randhem, it was owned by Torne Skytte and an earl named Erik, who was the son of Magnus Ladulås. They were powerful and well-known men in Sweden's history. In 1566, during the war between Sweden and Denmark, the buildings on the estate burned to the ground. Evidence of battles can be seen today in Ronnum Park, where cannon balls can still be found. At the beginning of the eighteenth century, a chamberlain of the king, Gabriel Oxenstierna, bought the estate. It passed into the hands of a lord, Ture Ollenberg, by the middle of the century, and was acquired by one of the owners of the East India Company by the end of the 1800s. The facade of the yellow wooden manor house with its white engaged columns resembles a pastel birthday cake, one layer upon the other.

Located on the shores of Lake Vanern, the eighteenth-century building has undergone restoration while retaining its essential architectural integrity. A separate building from the seventeenth century can also be used by guests for overnight accommodations. The guest rooms are pleasantly and simply decorated, and suites have their own sitting room and sauna. In the salon rooms of the manor house are porcelain stoves, ceiling paintings, crystal chandeliers, and fireplaces. The king's hunting parks, Halle and Hunneberg, are nearby. There are many places around the estate where one can enjoy a walk. Boat trips on the lake are also available.

YSTAD

Änglahuset
Ystads Saltsjöbad

Ystads Saltsjobad
Ann and Kent Nystrom
Saltsjobadsvagen 6
271 39 Ystad
Telephone: 0411-136 30; **FAX:** 0411-55-58 35
Rates: Single, 850 kr.; Double, 440 kr. per person; Family of two adults
and two children under the age of 12, 470 kr. per adult; Family room
with two bedrooms, 1,520 kr.; Special 5- and 7-night summer packages
available. **Restaurant:** Breakfast, lunch, and dinner are served in the
dining room. There is outdoor dining on the terrace next to the water.
A grill is located next to the pool. An intimate restaurant called
Apotheket offers a la carte dining. Dancing is available several nights
a week. There are two bars.

Ystads Saltsjobad is a seaside resort in every sense of the word, offering
guests the advantages of being next to the water and having a large
swimming pool area with a huge slide. The hotel was built in 1897 as
a place where members of high society could vacation at the beach.
It was built by a pharmacist and musician, Salomon Smith, a native of
Ystad. His wish was that the hotel should be only 15 meters from the
sea, although this original building was located further away, where
the hotel's restaurant now stands. At that time, the hotel had its own
railway station. Another building was added but both were destroyed
by fire. According to legend, a cavalryman staying at the hotel had to
be dragged out while trying to save the contents of the wine cellar
from the flames. A new hotel was built in 1927, and the building
now known as Krookska huset was opened two years later. A newer

addition, copied after the Hotel Riva del Sole in Italy with all balconies overlooking the sea, was constructed in 1960.

This hotel is very child-oriented, with lots of activities for the whole family. Ystad is a charming old town with over 300 half-timbered buildings and a cloister from the fifteenth century. Tosselilla, an amusement park, is only 25 kilometers away. Special water gymnastics classes are available in a pool kept heated during the summer months. Within two minutes of the hotel are tennis courts, jogging paths, and a golf course. The interior of the hotel is modern and inviting, with special rooms for disabled guests.

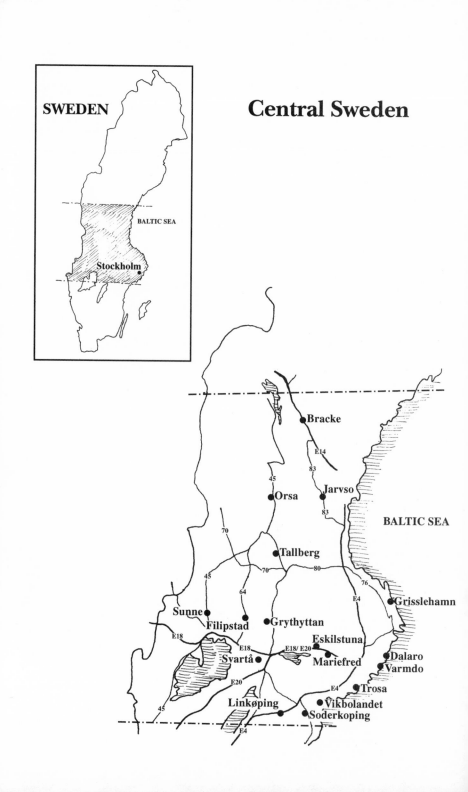

SWEDEN

BALTIC SEA

Stockholm

Central Sweden

Bracke

E14

83

45

Orsa

Jarvso

83

BALTIC SEA

70

Tallberg

70

80

76

45

64

E4

Grisslehamn

Sunne

Filipstad

Grythyttan

E18

E18

Eskilstuna

E18/ E20

Svartå

Mariefred

Dalaro

Varmdo

E20

E4

Trosa

Linkøping

Vikbolandet

45

Søderkoping

E4

Central Sweden

BRACKE

Bjorknasgårdens Pensionat

Bjorknasgårdens Pensionat
Gunnel and Lars Eliasson
Box 188, 840 60 Bracke
Telephone: 693-160 20; **FAX:** 693-160 80
Rates: Single, 535 kr.; Double, 480 kr. per person. **Restaurant:** Breakfast, lunch, and dinner in dining room. Drinks are available in the Spelflotten Pub. A member of Countryside Hotels.

Bjorknasgården is located between Sundsvall and Ostersund, next to the waters of Lake Revsundssjon. The closest town, Bracke, is 5 kilometers away. This building was first used to house soldiers. Then it became the home of the manager of a flourishing timber company that cut logs from nearby forests and floated them down the lake a century ago. This was also the site of one of the stops for the 1870 steamer *Alma*, still operating and ready for tours around the lake during the summer months.

The yellow building with white trim sits in a lovely parklike setting with a lawn sloping down to the lake. The original building has something of the old atmosphere in its guest rooms. The annex also has guest rooms. The simply decorated rooms with large windows look out over the lake and forest. The surrounding area offers much for the walker who would like to enjoy nature. Cross-country skiing is popular during the winter months. Fishing, canoeing, rowboating, and ice fishing are available on the lake. Indoor attractions include the sauna, a cozy pub, and inviting living rooms with fireplaces.

DALARO

Smådalaro Gård

Smådalaro Gård
Harriet Oholm
Smådalaro Gård
S-130 54 Dalaro
Telephone: 08-501 53200; **FAX:** 08-501 53383;
E-mail: info @ smadalarogard.se
Rates: Single, 850 kr.; Double, 1,200 kr. **Restaurant:** Breakfast, lunch, and dinner in hotel's dining room.

Located next to the water on Stockholm's archipelago, this manor-house-turned-hotel could not be in a more beautiful place. It is just a 45-minute drive from Stockholm, and yet it is in another world of forests and coastline. Captain Carl Peter Blom built the manor in 1810, although Danish King Valdemar mentions the area in a thirteenth-century document. Many well-known celebrities from Stockholm have visited the manor house through the years, including August Strindberg, who wrote his work *Hemso* here.

The manor house has a wonderful view of the water, just a few meters away. The hotel has the distinction of having one of the most visited saunas, a separate building that was built over the water. The sauna is wood heated, and it is possible to jump directly into the water after having experienced the sauna. Many visitors have had their first "winter swim" here. The hotel also has its own dock, from which guests can take one of the rowboats or sailboats. A tennis court and a 3-hole golf course are also a part of the complex, along with a billiards room, badminton court, and croquet lawn. The vaulted dining room has paintings on the walls and ceiling. During the summer months, guests can eat outdoors while the chef prepares their meal on the grill.

ESKILSTUNA

Sundbyholms Slott

Sundbyholms Slott
Patrik Andersson, manager
S-635 08 Eskilstuna
Telephone: 016-965 00; **FAX:** 016-965 78; **E-mail:** hotell.konferens @
sundbyholms-slott.se; **Internet:** http://www.sundbyholms-slott.se
Rates: Single, 690 to 1,000 kr.; Double, 980 to 1,400 kr. **Restaurant:**
Breakfast, lunch, and dinner served in the castle's dining room. A
member of Romantik Hotels and Restaurants, De Historiske Hotel.

During the Middle Ages, Sundbyholm Castle was the property of
the monastery of the Order of St. John, although after the Reformation
it was given over to the king. In 1597 Duke Karl, Karl IX, gave the
castle to his son, Reich Admiral Carl Carlsson Gyllenhielm, who
opened the first elementary school in Sweden on the grounds.
Throughout the eighteenth century, various leaseholders ran the castle, and Duke Karl, Karl XIII, became the new owner in 1779. It was
Baron Salomon Lofvenskold who, in 1819, built the manor house as
you see it today. The next occupant, Captain Gustav August Coyet,
increased the estate to 100 hectares and added parks, gardens, and
beautiful boulevards. Baroness Coyet helped the castle to acquire a
reputation as a center of hospitality in the 1890s when Prince Eugen
and a colony of painters lived at the castle. The latest renovation took
place in 1987.

The castle sits next to Lake Malaren and Europe's most northern
beech forest. A rune stone from 1,000 years ago on the far side of the
river Ramsundsån tells a tragic story about Sigurd. A large marina next
to the castle can be used by boats coming from Stockholm. Filled with

secret rooms, the castle today hosts courtly balls and Viking banquets, where guests can dress in appropriate costume and enjoy the food and entertainment of the era. The mini suites, located in a building behind the castle, offer views of the lake and are luxuriously modern. The Sundbyholm championship 18-hole golf course also has a 3-hole course for training and a driving range. A restaurant with a bar and a golf shop are also available.

FILIPSTAD

Hennickehammars Herrgård

Hennickehammars Herrgård
The Backman family
Box 52, 682 22 Filipstad
Telephone: 590 60 85 00; **FAX:** 590 60 85 05;
E-mail: hotel@hennickehammar.se; **Internet:** www.hennickehammar.se
Rates: Single, 645 to 815 kr.; Double, 425 to 535 kr.; Half and full
board, as well as special weekend packages available. **Restaurant:**
Breakfast, lunch, and dinner served in dining room. A member of
Countryside Hotels.

Hennickehammars Herrgård is located 300 kilometers from both
Stockholm (two and a half hours by train) and Goteborg, near the
small town of Filipstad in the middle of Sweden. This part of Sweden
has played an important role in the mining of iron since the beginning
of the sixteenth century. There were many mines in the mountains
and, in later times, the forests became crisscrossed with railroad tracks
used for transporting the iron ore. A major stream ran into the lake,
and a waterfall produced power to run the ironworks and smithy. It
was during the time of the Earl Carl (1550-1611) that Hennickehammars
was founded. The manor now used as the main building for the hotel
was built in 1722 and was lived in by a succession of managers who
oversaw the iron operation.
    One of its more famous inhabitants was Erik Janson, also known as
"the Hammer," perhaps because of his hard personality. He was an

important member of the business community who also held great power in the local area. He died in 1898, leaving twelve children, although none of them continued in the iron business or in managing the estate. One of the later owners, Julia Ekman, was an aunt of author Selma Lagerlof. This lovely old building is situated next to the water and houses 19 of the oldest guest rooms. The salons, now used for the dining rooms and reception areas, are in the old manor-house style. Some modern additions include sauna, swimming pool, and Jacuzzi, as well as modern baths and cable television for each guest room. As is customary in Scandinavia, a building in the forest houses the sauna, which the guests can enjoy before jumping directly into the chilly waters of the lake.

GRISSLEHAMN

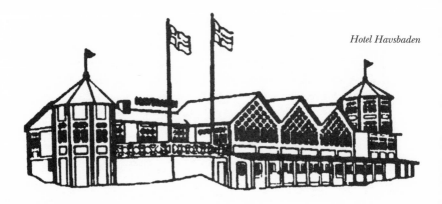

Hotel Havsbaden

Hotel Havsbaden
Box 3018, 760 45 Grisslehamn
Telephone: 175 309 30; **FAX:** 175 330 14
Rates: Single or Double, 430 kr. per person. **Restaurant:** Breakfast, lunch, and dinner served in dining room. There is a piano bar and live disco music for dancing. A member of Countryside Hotels.

Why would giants of the literary and artistic world such as playwright August Strindberg and painter Anders Zorn have sought out this turn-of-the-century hotel along the coast of Sweden? It must have been for the ideal beauty and quiet serenity of the quaint little fishing village of Grisslehamn and the rocky, windswept shores near the hotel. Only 80 minutes from Stockholm's airport via a bus that stops just outside, this hotel overlooks the archipelago that gives this place such beauty. In 1903 Hertha Kitzing came from Germany to establish a spa where one could "take the cure" with healthy food, fresh air, special baths, and doses of culture and nature thrown in. A special bass singer was even hired to sing to the various categories of guests who came here. The little fishing harbor seemed like the ideal spot for this type of resort, and Hertha was always on hand to welcome his guests.

A sign from that era was recently unearthed, presumably one that stood next to shallow waters, and states: "For women and others who cannot swim." Today you not only can swim along one of the sandy beaches, but also may relax in the hotel's pool or sauna. The guest rooms overlooking the islands offer some of the best views in Sweden, and all have private baths and tasteful decor. The suites have a bright, glassed-in Jacuzzi area that provides a view over a large balcony to the water. The cuisine served in the hotel is excellent, and the chefs sometime prepare food for cruises of the archipelago. Along the way, the boats stop in lovely locations where dinner is served and some type of cultural entertainment is provided. For those seeking an active stay, there is tennis, riding, jogging trails, fishing, and, in the winter, ice skating.

GRYTHYTTAN

Grythyttans Gastgivaregård

Grythyttans Gastgivaregård
Carl Jan GranqvistPrastgatan 2
S-712 81 Grythyttan
Telephone: (0) 591-141 24; **FAX:** (0) 591-147 00
Rates: Single, 750 to 1,010 kr.; Double, 1,010 to 1,520 kr.; Half and full board available with special rates up to seven days; Weekend packages available. **Restaurant:** Breakfast, lunch, and dinner served in dining room. There is a wine cellar. A member of Countryside Hotels.

Grythyttans Gastgiveregård must surely be one of the most spectacular hotels in Sweden, not only because of its size but also because of its beautiful setting, significant collection of art, emphasis on superb service and cuisine, and a lovingly cared for building whose history is treasured and even revered. If you are a devotee of historic preservation and want to see a prime example of what has been accomplished in this area in Sweden, then this is the hotel to visit. In the 1960s the hotel was in jeopardy of being lost forever when the city council gave an order for the building to be razed. During an auction of the hotel's contents, so many people showed up and put such a heavy strain on the building's tired structure that a huge beam, eaten away by worms, came crashing down. Luckily, no one was hurt, but the incident was thought to be the end of a more than three-century history of caring for guests on this site. But clearly it wasn't. Thanks to the leadership of owner Carl Jan Granqvist and others, such as the local heritage and needlework societies, Grythyttans Gastgivaregård was preserved and is now more beautiful than ever.

Queen Kristina in 1641 decreed that the military commander, Baron Carl Bonde, should build a road between Orebro and Grythyttan and that there should be a place for travelers to rest. The population of the town had to build the outside of the inn and the innkeeper was responsible for finishing the interior. Guests began to arrive the same year and the hotel was run continuously by the same family until the beginning of the twentieth century. Each room of the now-restored hotel is a delight to the eye. Such careful planning went into the restoration of each room that even the wallpaper was made from a design copied from other manor houses.

Museum-quality paintings, most of which are portraits of royalty and other important personages, hang in each room. In the reception area, for example, an old pharmacist's bench from 1870 is used as a desk. In the buffet dining room one finds German Renaissance-style corner cabinets that were once part of a suite created by King Karl XV for Ulriksdal Castle near Stockholm. The Karl Jan Drawing Room is decorated with original Biedermeier furniture. Two museum curators wrote a book about the extensive art and antique holdings of the hotel. The publication, available in both Swedish and English, takes the reader through each public room of the hotel and discusses the many marvelous objects now in the collection. Another book, a gorgeous coffee table-type cookbook and history of the hotel, takes the reader through the 12 months of culinary celebration at Grythyttan.

JARVSO

Jarvsobaden

Jarvsobaden
Gunborg Pehrsson, manager
Box 43, 820 40 Jarvso
Telephone: 651 404 00; **FAX:** 651 417 37;
E-mail: info@countrysidehotels.se
Rates: Single, 500 to 600 kr.; Double, 700 to 800 kr.; Annex building: Single, 425 to 500 kr.; Double, 600 to 680 kr. **Restaurant:** Breakfast, lunch, and dinner served in dining room. There is a bar. A member of Countryside Hotels.

Jarvsobaden began at the turn of the century as a health spa offering special curative treatments based on baths and massages. This continued until 1935 when it became a regular tourist hotel catering to the traveler. It has been run by the same family since its opening in 1905 and is now managed by the third and fourth generations of innkeepers. Jarvsobaden is located 340 kilometers from Stockholm in the middle of eastern Sweden, at the foot of Ojeberget Mountain. The red and white wooden buildings making up the hotel complex are surrounded by grassy lawns, and the effect is similar to that at the older mountain resorts in the southeastern United States. The setting for the hotel is the beautiful forest landscape of this part of Sweden, perfect for the hiker and skier.

The food served at Jarvsobadens Hotel is based on the traditional cuisine of Halsingland. When the abundant buffet table is set in the homey green and white dining room, the food seems to stretch on forever. It is difficult to choose from so many tempting dishes. Many of the vegetables and berries served are from the hotel's own garden. After dinner, coffee and cake are served in the salon, perhaps next to one of the fireplaces. If you prefer to exercise by walking through a unique environment, you may want to go to the Jarvzoo, an animal park whose entrance is near the hotel. A wooden nature walk 3 kilometers long takes the visitor through a beautiful natural setting of changing terrain where the animals live. It is an untraditional type of zoo where the animals thrive in their own habitat. There is a special section for children.

When you return to the hotel to relax, you will find comfortable guest rooms of the type one would expect to find in a country hotel. The furniture is white wood and the decor is bright and airy.

LINKOPING

Frimurarehotellet

Frimurarehotellet
St. Larsgatan 14, Box 1536
S-581 15 Linkoping
Telephone: 13 1291 80; **FAX:** 13 1395 44;
Internet: hotell.frimur@postbox.postnet.se. For international reservations at Provobis hotels: 46 08-4411 40 40
Rates: Single, 590 to 1,250 kr., Double, 690 to 1,450 kr. **Restaurant:** Breakfast, lunch, and dinner in hotel's dining room. There is an english-style pub, Albert's Hall, where lunch is served, and the Down Under Night Club. Dancing. A member of Provobis Hotels.

The word *Frimurare* in Swedish means Freemasons—the group that originally built this hotel. The building was completed in 1912, having been commissioned and paid for by Masons who wanted their own lodge in this area. The same architect who had done some work on the Cathedral in Lund was brought in to design this hotel in a style reminiscent of a medieval English castle. King Gustav V was invited to a gala opening celebration, which included the decoration of the hotel with colored electric lights, quite a spectacle when one considers that Lindkoping had only had electricity for ten years. A fire necessitated some rebuilding in 1942, at which time more guest rooms were added. A major restoration project was completed in 1990.

The gabled roof of this major downtown hotel dominates its location in the center of the city. The property provides easy access to shops, restaurants, the airport (3 kilometers away), and the train and bus stations (600 meters from the hotel). The classic lobby, in dark maroon tones, is supported by impressive marble columns with gold capitals and vaulting. The guest rooms, of which almost half are smoke free, range from small attic rooms to larger, more comfortable accommodations with high ceilings and windows the length of one side. This is a particularly nice place for women traveling alone, since there is a "women only" floor where furnishings and amenities have been planned with the female guest in mind. The hotel offers an impressive and healthy breakfast buffet.

MARIEFRED

*Gripsholm Vardshus
and Hotel*

Gripsholm Vardshus and Hotel
Peter Enberger, manager
S-647 23 Mariefred
Telephone: 159 130 20; **FAX:** 159 109 74;
E-mail: info@gripsholms-vardshus.se
Rates: Single, 1,180 kr.; Double, 1,550 kr.; a special package that includes a three-course dinner in addition to breakfast already included in the other rates: Single, 1,480 kr.; Double, 2,250 kr.
Restaurant: Breakfast, lunch, and dinner in hotel's dining room, where French and Swedish cuisine are featured. Skankrummet is the hotel's bar, where guests can also order salads, sandwiches, and other lighter meals. A member of Countryside Hotels.

Five hundred years ago, a Cathusian monastery called Pax Mariæ once stood on the same site as this hotel. In fact, the current wine cellar remains from the monastery. Perhaps this is why the town is called Mariefred, or Mary's Peace, a name that reflects the monastic history of this area. After the Reformation in the sixteenth century, King Gustavus Wasa, an ardent defender of Protestantism, demolished the monastery. The bricks were recyled for a castle financed by the king on the other side of the bay across from Gripsholm. A hospice was built here in 1609, establishing the present hotel and making it one of the very oldest hotels in Sweden. In 1987 considerable effort was put into a thorough renovation process that endeavored to maintain the original atmosphere and history of the building. Folk art from the province of Sodermanland and antiques were combined with up-to-date materials to produce a comfortable and elegant interior. Many of the rooms have unique porcelain fireplaces, and each of the 45 guest rooms is different. Some are quite lavish. In one of the suites, for example, one can enjoy a Jacuzzi bath while relaxing next to an eighteenth-century fireplace. All of the rooms have hand-painted stencil decorations on the walls as well as French blue-tiled bathrooms with heated floors. All also have cable television, minibars, and safes.

Gripsholm Vardshus is located 31 kilometers southwest of Stockholm and a 4-hour drive northeast of Gothenburg. You may also take the train and then transfer to an old-fashioned railroad that takes guests almost to the door of the hotel. A fun and picturesque way to arrive is by boat from Stockholm, a 3-hour trip from the harbor next to the city's town hall. While dining at the hotel you can enjoy the wonderful view across the bay to Gripsholm Castle. After a glass of wine in the medieval wine cellar, guests may enjoy the fresh ingredients from Sodermanland chosen by the chefs for the international cuisine produced by this exceptional kitchen. All breads and pastries served in the restaurant are baked at the hotel. For recreation, there is a billiards room and fitness center with sauna and solarium. If you wish to explore the deer park next to the castle, the hotel will lend you a bicycle. An 18-hole golf course is located 500 meters away. Clubs may be rented from the hotel.

ORSA

*Fryksås Hotell
and Gestgifveri*

Fryksås Hotell and Gestgifveri
Ulla and Elmar Schwarzenberger
Fryksås fabod
794 98 Orsa
Telephone: 250-460 20; **FAX:** 250-460 90
Rates: Single, 525 kr.; Double, 775 kr. **Restaurant:** Breakfast, lunch,
and dinner in hotel's dining room. There is a wine cellar. A member
of Countryside Hotels.

The assemblage of buildings that makes up this hotel is unique.
Located high in the mountains in a wilderness where bears, moose,
lynx, and other wildlife freely roam, these buildings were originally
the summer farms for a group of 40 families. In the summer, the
animals were brought up from the regular farms in the lower altitudes
to this mountain range to spend the warmer months. Here the grass
was better and the climate surprisingly mild. In clear weather you can
see up to 100 kilometers away. Beginning in the 1700s, the cows were
brought here and milked during the summer. Cheese was also made.
Each farm was comprised of a house for lodging, stables for the animals,
and other buildings for the storage of hay and feed.

In the 1800s, tourists began to discover the peaceful beauty of Orsa
and stayed in some of the farmhouses. In 1954 a restaurant was finally
built, and tourists were accommodated in a more professional manner.
Today Orsa has the largest collection of summer farm buildings in
Sweden. The Fryksås hotel dates from the sixteenth century and has

been carefully restored. Each room has its own bath and color television. The forest is perfect for hiking and is full of all types of wild berries, mushrooms, and even wild orchids. In winter there are ski slopes, cross-country tracks, dogsledding, and even rides on Icelandic horses. Various types of excursions can be arranged by the hotel. With the Orsa and Siljan lakes nearby, there are plenty of fresh fish for the hotel's kitchen as well as wild game.

SODERKOPING

Soderkopings Brunn

Soderkopings Brunn
Stig Ekblad
Box 44
614 21 Soderkoping
Telephone: 121-109 00; **FAX:** 121-139 41; **E-mail:** info@romantikhotel.se;
Internet: http://www.romantikhotels.com
Rates: Single, 600 to 975 kr.; Double, 850 to 1,175 kr. **Restaurant:**
Breakfast, lunch, and dinner served in dining room. During the
summer months, food service is available on the veranda. Weather
permitting, there is dancing and a bandstand outside. A member of
Romantik Hotels and Restaurants, De Historiske Hotel.

Soderkoping, a medieval town developed as a trading center over
1,000 years ago, is located on Sweden's famous Gota Canal. Here is
also found the St. Anna archipelago, with the ruins of Stegeborg Castle
guarding the approach by sea. The town has many old buildings,
including the thirteenth-century town church, St. Laurentii, where the
coronation of Queen Helvig took place in 1281. The hotel Soderkopings
Brunn is located on the Gota Canal, always a peaceful place to sit and
enjoy the passing of the boats. The hotel owns two boats, *M/F Lindon*
and *M/F St. Ragnhild*, both of which can be rented for special parties
and trips and offer full dining service.

During the Middle Ages, Ragnhild's Spring, which was said to have
produced 180,000 liters of clear, fresh water per day, was discovered in
Soderkopings. In 1719 Magnus Garbriel von Block made it known that

he had discovered in the water certain medicinal properties that made it extremely healthy. For this reason, King Gustav III gave a royal charter to Soderkopings Brunn in 1774, and it became known as a health spa where one could "take the waters." The health resort reached its heyday in the nineteenth century and the first few decades of the twentieth century after Dr. Johan Lagberg discovered that iron and other important minerals made the water so healthy. A restoration, mindful of the integrity of the old style, has been made of the old buildings from the spa. The 103 rooms are now all up to modern standards, with private baths, cable television, and telephones. There are also 4 rooms especially equipped for handicapped guests.

The grounds of the hotel have the look of an old-style resort, complete with a romantic church called Brunnkyrkan. Emphasis is placed on the preparation of food and its presentation. Try the hotel's famous waffles and punch. You can rent bicycles and canoes for a leisurely day trip, and an 18-hole golf course is only a few kilometers away.

SUNNE

Lansmansgården

Lansmansgården
Biorklund/Edberg family
S-686 93 Sunne
Telephone: 565 140 10; **FAX:** 565 71 18 05
Rates: Single, 550 kr.; Double, 730 kr. **Restaurant:** Breakfast, lunch, and dinner in the dining room. A member of Countryside Hotels.

The great Swedish writer Selma Lagerlof wrote in her *Gosta Berglings* saga: "On the eighteenth of the month of March Scharling celebrated his birthday . . . people came from east and west . . . to Lansmansgården. Everyone was welcome. Everyone found enough food and drink and plenty of room in the dancing salon." Apparently good hospitality was being offered here in the nineteenth century just as it is today. Built in the typical manor-house style of Varmland, the white wooden exterior and its blue-and-white-striped awnings and columned portico provide a welcoming feeling to those who stay here. The primarily white dining room with its corner fireplace looks exactly the way I would want mine to appear if I had a country home in Sweden. Cheerful wallpapers, homey objects, brass chandeliers, and white-painted country furniture convey just the right atmosphere. Documents show that this property was recorded as early as 1540 and established as an estate called Ulfsby in 1630. By 1649 Queen Christine had positioned military quarters here. The estate has been in the ownership of the same family since 1914.

SVARTÅ

Svartå Herrgård

Svartå Herrgård
The Frantzen family
693 93 Svartå
Telephone: 0585-500 03; **FAX:** 0585-503 03
Rates: Single, 600 to 900 kr.; Double, 500 to 800 kr.; Special weekend rates with board: Single, 950 kr. per person; Double, 950 to 1,250 kr. per person. **Restaurant:** Breakfast, lunch, and dinner served in hotel's dining room. A member of Romantik Hotels and Restaurants, De Historiske Hotel.

The mansion that is now the hotel, a beautiful example of the Gustavian style of architecture, was built by the Marshal of the Court, Carl Falker, from 1775 to 1782. It was part of a property on which a foundry, Svartå Bruk, was located. Most of the local population took part in the building of the three-story house, a structure of stones with a mansard roof. Two one-story wings, made of rough-cast and plastered timber, were from an earlier time. After Carl Falker died in 1795, his daughter, Christina Charlotta, and her husband, Baron Per Adolf Fock, Marshal of the Court of King Carl XIII, inherited the estate. Five hammer mills were added, and beautiful parks and gardens were built, even on the nearby islands just off the coast. Believe it or not, 13 young boys were employed just to keep moss off the trees. The property continued to prosper as a foundry, expanding until 1925 when it was sold to become a domestic science school.

In 1966 the Frantzen family acquired the property and opened it as a hotel. A separate half-timbered mansion, Villa Lugnsbo, underwent restoration in the 1970s and today houses 40 of the guestrooms. The rooms of the Svartå Herrgård are simply beautiful. Although only the tile stoves remain from the original house, the hotel is filled with pleasing antiques and paintings appropriate to its architectural style. In what is now the dining room and previously was the great parade room, a 1950 restoration project revealed blue paintings of mythological motifs on wall panels created by Fritiof Eriksson. The room is now a delight. In other rooms golden garlands of wood with ribbons grace the doors, and, in others, bunches of laurel wreaths and flower garlands are painted on the walls. The guest rooms are beautifully decorated with an abundant use of draperies on the high windows, lavishly upholstered chairs, oriental rugs, and old-style furniture.

TALLBERG

Åkerblads

Åkerblads
The Åkerblad family
S-793 70 Tallberg
Telephone: 0247 50800; **FAX:** 0247 50652
Rates: Single, 495 kr.; Double, 445 kr.; Mini suite, 595 kr.; Family room
for 2 adults and 2 children, 950 kr.; Half board and Special Weekend
rates available. **Restaurant:** Breakfast buffet, luncheon smorgåsbord,
and dinner served in hotel's dining room.

It isn't every hotel that can claim to have been owned by 21 generations of the same family! The Åkerblad family still continues this
remarkable tradition. Originally called Gatvgården, or Street Farm, it
is the oldest farm in this area and was registered in 1630, although
the family can trace it to 1539. Although it was once a large farm, it has
been divided into many smaller plots. The farm was so important in its
time that many family members sat in Parliament, including one who
lead a farmers' revolt. Another family member was responsible for a
rash of witch burning instigated by Parliament.

As you walk through the building today, you can still find wonderful
reminders of when it was a center of agricultural activity. In the pub
you can recall that it was once the birthing room for the women of the
family, and later a pig sty. Another room, Arsstugu, was a cold room
heated only during holy and feast days. Even then, only the head of
the family could give permission to enter. The room now used for
parties was once a thrashing room, and the large salon was the hay

barn where traditionally the great-grandfather spent the first night in the newly cut hay. The wine cellar, where vegetables were stored for the winter months, has the year 1410 inscribed in the roof. The hotel's sauna and solarium served as the grandfather's carpentry shop, and his stove, where the glue was kept liquid, is now in the bar. The small salon was the farm's blacksmith shop.

Beginning in 1910, the farm began to take in overnight guests, the first being a professor who stayed a year! The property continued as a working farm until 1943, although the inn part of the business continued to flourish. Located on a hillside above Siljan Lake in the village of Tallberg, between Leksand and Rattvik, the hotel appeals to families and has guest rooms of great charm. Laura Ashley fabrics are used on the four-poster beds. The white, small-paned windows in the rooms are combined with colorful wood panels on the walls and Swedish country-style furniture.

Hotel Klockargården

Hotel Klockargården
The Sandberg family (Inger, Klockar Per Anders, and Lars)
Siljansvagen 6
793 70 Tallberg
Telephone: 0247-502 60; **FAX:** 0247-502 16
Rates: Single, 525 kr., Budget, 325 kr.; Double, 425 to 525 kr. per person; Suites, 725 to 825 kr. per person; Half board and weekend rates available; Golf packages. **Restaurant:** Breakfast, lunch (also a smorgåsbord), and dinner served in hotel's dining room. A member of Countryside Hotels.

Although this hotel dates only from 1937 and the present buildings are from the 1950s, Hotel Klockargården is included in this book because it offers such an incredible presentation of the traditions and cultural history of Dalarna. Situated next to Siljan Lake, it is about 280 kilometers northwest of Stockholm. This is a hotel that offers the opportunity to participate in a well-planned program of activities in an ideal location. Each year a full listing of all that the hotel has to offer is published. To enjoy nature, a guest may choose to visit the hotel's own nature center, Nybodalen, where there is dining al fresco in the woods.

The cultural program brings folk dancers in regional costumes, musicians who play the music of Dalarna on traditional instruments, and craftsmen who demonstrate the making of those objects indigenous to this part of Sweden. During the summer months, special exhibitions of art and crafts are organized. In order to create the perfect atmosphere for these cultural events, the timber hotel has been filled with antiques and decorative arts from Dalarna. Special tapestries showing rural life in Dalarna were created by artist Stina Sunesson. Each guest room is different, although all are charming and created to blend in with the country surroundings. In a mini suite one might find a canopied bed, Swedish country-style furnishings, a Jacuzzi tub, and a private balcony. In a regular double room, there may be huge oak beds with a Victorian look or the clean lines of blond wood furniture. The courtyard and lawns surrounding the hotel are an excellent setting for the costumed dancers.

Special celebrations take place at Christmas and New Year's, and there are plenty of opportunities for sledding, skiing (both downhill and cross country), kick sledging, and riding Icelandic horses. The hotel also has a new area with sauna, Jacuzzi, Japanese bath, and solarium.

TROSA

Bowmans Hotel

Bowmans Hotel
The Gripwall/Olsson-Hedenstedt family
S-619 30 Trosa
Telephone: 0156-132 20; **FAX:** 0156-133 80; **E-mail:** bjorn@bomans.se
Rates: Single, 600 to 800 kr.; Double, 850 to 1,090 kr.; Special rooms,
1,200 to 1,400 kr.; Extra bed, 200 kr.; Half board, Weekend and golf
packages available. **Restaurant:** Breakfast, lunch, and dinner served in
the dining room.

Just 70 kilometers outside of Stockholm is the picturesque harbor
town of Trosa. With only 4,000 residents, the town and its small streets
of eighteenth-century wooden houses are quaint and relaxing.
Charming little shops line the streets, and a walk along the river is a
good way to spend an afternoon. Just 300 meters from the town's main
square, where a market has been held since 1580, is Bowmans Hotel.
Its gold and red facade, with the balcony stretching across the second
floor, faces the harbor and the river. In front of the hotel is the old fish
storehouse where the original inn once stood. It is now a cheerful
red wooden building with white trim. After owners Bjørn and Birgitta
decided they wanted to own a hotel in Trosa, they applied an imaginative
and artistic approach to the decoration and furnishing of the interior.
Birgitta went to New York to buy the interesting array of textiles used
throughout the hotel. From the trompe l'oeil cabinets and the funny
little wooden table made to look like a friendly Swedish pastor to the
antique nightgown hanging on the wall of a guest room, there is
always something beautiful and interesting to look at. Each of the 31

guest rooms is unique, with lovely borders on the walls matching the different fabric patterns. All have private baths and television with cable. In the dining room no two tables are set alike. Furniture and candleholders are often from earlier centuries. The owners love to go to auctions and purchase antiques for the hotel.

The kitchen serves traditional Swedish home cooking, including such dishes as meatballs with lingonberries and cream sauce and the Trosa herring with cucumber pickles indigenous to this region. The availability of fresh fish such as salmon and cod means that fish dishes are always an important part of the menu. Very imaginative dishes, such as a cold salad with smoked wild boar, are served in unique and novel ways. Two sommeliers are in charge of the wine cellar and are available for recommendations to diners. The hotel has been listed continuously since 1992 in "Sweden's Best Restaurants" and was rated in 1998 as one of the fifteen best country inns in Sweden. It has also been the recipient of the Swedish Gastronomic Academy diploma for its Trosa specialties and earned the Trosa Preservation Society prize in 1995. The hotel arranges special gastronomic and historical "happenings," as well as wine tasting and treasure hunts in Trosa.

Trosa Stadshotell

Trosa Stadshotell
Toni and Kerstin Betschart
Vastra Långgatan 19, Box 18
619 21 Trosa
Telephone: 0156-170 70; **FAX:** 0156-166 96;
E-mail: info@trosastadshotell.se; **Internet:** http://www.trosastadshotell.se
Rates: Single, 745 to 945 kr.; Double, 880 to 1,200 kr.; Suites, 1,500 kr.; Special weekend and golf packages available from 990 to 2,390 kr.

per person. **Restaurant:** Breakfast, lunch, and dinner in hotel's dining room. There is a pub, bistro, and outdoor serving area. A member of Romantik Hotels and Restaurants, De Historiske Hotel.

The history of Trosa goes back to 1250, although the small town was then located 7 kilometers from where it is now situated. It was primarily fishermen who lived here peacefully until 1719, when the Russians invaded this Baltic coast. They spared only the Trosa church, which the Russians needed as a stable for their horses. When the Russians left, the town began the process of rebuilding, and the foundation for Trosa Stadshotell was laid at that time. The city of Trosa bought the hotel in 1867. From the 1880s, it became known as a summer "bathing" resort for the upper class who wanted to get away from the city and enjoy the beautiful surroundings of the fjord. The tourists drank the famous "Trosa punch," produced locally and served in the hotel garden's "Punch Pavilion," which is still standing today.

Trosa is a 45-minute drive from Stockholm, with busses running from Liljeholmen and Sodertalje and trains to Vagnharad. A bus from Vagnharad can then be taken to Trosa. The town is in a lovely spot right on the Trosa River. Local sightseeing includes a medieval marketplace and Tureholms Castle. The hotel is a small collection of original and modern buildings joined together. The dining room is a light and airy eighteenth-century room with the typical white-painted country furniture with columns and beams to match. Depending upon which building is requested, the guest rooms are either comfortably country traditional or modern. The hotel offers such amenities as sauna, Jacuzzi, massage, and fitness center, as well as opportunities to take part in wine tasting, boat trips to the nature reserve, and Agatha Christie mystery stays.

VARMDO

Fågelbrohus
Harriet Oholm, manager
FågelbroHus AB
S-139 00 Varmdo
Telephone: 08-571 40100; **FAX:** 08-571 40171;
E-mail: info@fagelbrohus.se
Rates: Not available. **Restaurant:** Breakfast, lunch, and dinner in the hotel's dining room. A member of Countryside Hotels.

Although the current building was completed in 1991, this property has a long and interesting history. The hotel was built as an old Swedish manor house in the Carolinian style. The original house was burned by the Russians in 1719. The grounds, with 400 fruit trees, lake cottages, and acres of hops, are a fine location for a re-creation of the manor house that once stood on this site. Until the nineteenth century, sailors could not get through the Stromma Sound. A canal was completed in 1823 and a swing bridge, called Fågelbro (Bird Bridge), was built to allow the canal boats to go through. Several members of Swedish royalty came to visit here, including Prince Carl and Princess Ingeborg, Prince Wilhelm, and King Gustav V, who liked to fish and hunt in the area.

Like its sister hotel Smådalaro Gård, this hotel is close to Stockholm (a 30-minute drive). Because the old-style building is actually from the 1990s, it has all of the twentieth-century amenities that guests expect. The hotel is situated next to a golf course, and there are also tennis courts, several saunas, a gym, and billiards, as well as riding and jogging paths.

VIKBOLANDET

Mauritzbergs Slott
Liisa Lipsanen, owner; Tommy Rodin, manager
S-61031 Vikbolandet
Telephone: 125 50100; **FAX:** 125 50104;
Internet: http://www.mauritzberg.se
Rates: Rooms in the castle: Double, 2,100 kr.; Suites, 2,600 kr.; Rooms
in the wing: Single, 1,000 kr.; Double, 1,400 kr. **Restaurant:** Jagarsal
dining room in the castle serves breakfast, lunch, and dinner. Cafe
Kvarnen is a summer cafe where guests may choose to sit outdoors or
indoors. A member of Countryside Hotels.

Once named Bjorsatter, Mauritzberg Manor House is mentioned in
documents from the sixteenth century, and one wing dates from 1590.
It was owned at that time by Birger Nilsson Grip, who built several
other large estates in the area. His son Mauritz Birgersson, a Councillor
of the Realm, then owned the estate after his father's death. His
daughter, Ebba, renamed the manor house after her father, Mauritz.
Being a court tailor in the seventeenth century must have been lucrative,
because Ebba's son-in-law sold the estate to Queen Christina's tailor
after Ebba's death. The manor house met with disaster in 1719 when
the Russians burned it to the ground. It was rebuilt a few years later.
The manor has often been associated with stars of the literary world,
primarily because of author Birger Morner, who bought the estate in
1912. Here he wrote his novel *Bråvallahus*, based on the estate's
history. Another well-known author, Verner von Heidenstam, was
often a guest at the estate and wrote *The Carolingians* in what is now the
Heidenstam Room.

Today the literary tradition continues with a library that contains
more than 2,000 volumes from the seventeenth to the nineteenth
centuries. The manor house, set amidst several hundred acres of fields
and forests, is located next to the waters of Bråviken, 150 kilometers
south of Stockholm and 30 kilometers east of Norrkoping. If you are
coming from the north, it is best to take the Vagverket ferry, which
leaves every half hour, across Bråviken Bay. No expense was spared in
the house's renovation. The interior is impressive, indeed. In the
wooden-beamed dining room, guests sit next to a grand fireplace as
they gaze out over the waters of the bay. With only 5 guest rooms in the
main building and 12 in the wings, particular attention was given to
the decoration of each. They are elegant, tasteful, and in keeping with
the time period and atmosphere of the manor.

The stable has been converted into a gallery for exhibitions and concerts. On the grounds is also a seventeenth-century chapel where weddings and services are held. In addition to exploring the beautiful grounds, guests may also play billiards and tennis or fish and hunt. Rowboats are available for guests who want to go out into the bay. There are old-fashioned boats available to take guests on trips as well.

INDEX

NORWAY
CITIES AND TOWNS

INNS

(Cities and towns in parentheses)

SWEDEN
CITIES AND TOWNS

INNS

(Cities and towns in parentheses)

Halltorps Gastgiveri (Borgholm), 300-301
Hennickehammars Herrgård (Filipstad), 344-45
Hooks Herrgård (Hok), 310-11
Hotel Eggers (Gothenburg), 306-7
Hotel Havsbaden (Grisslehamn), 346-47
Hotel Kramer (Malmø), 319-20
Hotell Klockargården (Tallberg), 364-65

Jarvsobaden (Jarvso), 350-51

Kallhagens Wardhus (Stockholm), 288-89
Kanalhotellet (Karlsborg), 312-13
Karlaby Kro (Tommarp), 328
Knistad Herrgård (Skovde), 322-33

Lady Hamilton (Stockholm), 289-90
Lansmansgården (Sunne), 360
Lord Nelson (Stockholm), 290

Malardrottningen (Stockholm), 291
Mauritzbergs Slott (Vikbolandet), 370-71

Molle Turisthotell (Molle), 321

Ronnums Herrgård (Wargon), 333-34
Rusthallargården (Arild), 295-96

Smådalaro Gård (Dalaro), 341
Soderkopings Brunn (Soderkoping), 358-59
Stufvena Gastgifveri (Soderåkra), 324-25
Sundbyholms Slott (Eskilstuna), 342-43
Sunds Herrgård (Lekeryd), 318
Svartå Herrgård (Svartå), 361-62

Tanums Gestgifveri (Tanumshede), 326-27
Toftaholm Herrgård (Lagan), 316-17
Trosa Stadshotell (Trosa), 367-68

Vadstena Klosterhotel (Vadstena), 331-32
Victory Hotel (Stockholm), 292-93

Ystads Saltsjobad (Ystad), 335-36

Åkerblads (Tallberg), 363-64

TRAVEL NOTES

TRAVEL NOTES

TRAVEL NOTES

TRAVEL NOTES